through other eyes

A nursing novella about diversity

Also by Amy Glenn Vega

– *LIONS AND TIGERS AND NURSES*

– *BROKEN HEART*

– *THE RELUCTANT SANTA*

amy glenn Vega

through other eyes

A nursing novella about diversity

Pritchett&Hull

Published by
Pritchett & Hull Associates, Inc.
3440 Oakcliff Road, NE, Suite 110
Atlanta, GA 30340

Manufactured in the United States of America

For Addy Aurelia Martinez

Whose friendship was a tremendous influence over
the paths that I chose to walk in this life

ACKNOWLEDGMENTS

Thank you first and foremost to everyone at Pritchett and Hull for the amazing job that they do each time a Nursing Novella comes together. Ken Baumann, thank you for the terrific editing that you do, and for being a wonderful mentor in fiction writing. Michael Austin, I continue to be amazed by your artistic talent. Betty Westmoreland and Cecily Shull, thank you again for believing in me and in the idea of Nursing Novellas. Gary Owen and Jim Westbrock, thank you for all that you do to market and promote the series. All of you at P-H are a joy to work with, and I am grateful for each of you.

Thank you to my colleagues at Southern Regional AHEC in Fayetteville, NC, for reviewing this story and helping to shape it into a work that is both entertaining and educational. Andrea Novak, Russet Hambrick, Deborah Teasley, Claudia Biedelman, Karen Mantzouris and Harriet Lovick, thank you for being the guinea pigs each time a new novella is born!

Thank you to the Information Access Center at Southern Regional AHEC, and my librarian friend, Michael Wold, at OSF St. Mary Medical Center for helping me gain access to some of the many journal articles, books and other resource materials addressing diversity in health care. It is a wonderful thing to have librarians just a phone call or an e-mail away!

Thank you, Denise Guerrier at Duke University Medical Center, for sharing with me your many wisdoms gained from your work as a nurse and as a diversity facilitator. Thank you to the following individuals who assisted me with developing some of the characters and content about diversity for this story: Andrea Novak, Anupa Deshpande, and Yvonne Early. I appreciate you sharing your expertise and insights that helped to shape this story. Thank you also to Terry Hodges, Compliance Attorney with the North Carolina Department of Health and Human Services for his careful review of the discussion of law in the story.

I also thank Dr. Arthur Kleinman, Professor of Medical Anthropology and Social Medicine and Professor of Psychiatry at Harvard University, for taking the time to speak with me and for indulging some of my questions about culture and diversity in the real world of health care.

Thank you to Jeanne Ray Hardee at Richmond Community College in Hamlet, NC, for your review of this story, and for your support of the Nursing Novellas series. Richmond Community College is the first school (that I am aware of) to add Nursing Novellas to their curriculum. You can see what students and faculty have to say about the series at www.youtube.com/user/nursingnovellas. If there are other schools out there that are using Nursing Novellas in health professions training programs, I would love to hear from you!

Fran London, thank you for your friendship and for continuing to amaze and inspire me.

Karen Kelly McFarlane, Brandy Bryant and Patricia Emery, thank you for letting me use your names in this story! These three ladies won Nursing Novellas fan contests and each of them has a namesake character in this book.

Thank you to my family and friends for being Nursing Novellas cheerleaders and champions.

Nurses, thank you just for being who you are. You inspire me, and your adventures give life to these stories.

Thank you, God, for making human beings such diverse and interesting creatures. How boring life would be if we were all the same.

Dear Nurse,

I consider it a great privilege to present you with this third story in the Nursing Novellas series. The series started with *Lions and Tigers and Nurses*, a story about five nurses at Dogwood Regional Hospital, and how they tackled lateral violence on their med-surg unit. The second story, *Broken Heart*, followed the same characters as they each confronted major changes and losses at work and in their personal lives. I asked nurses who read those stories to tell me what interpersonal issues they wanted the nurses of Dogwood Regional Hospital to take on next. Overwhelmingly, the answer was diversity. People wanted to see how Haylie, Brad, Mel, Donna and Miriam would deal with patients and fellow nurses who were very different from themselves, and what insights their experiences could offer.

I began to research diversity in health care. As I read books and articles and talked to the experts, I found that there are a variety of different frameworks and concepts about diversity in health care, and I struggled with trying to choose the right one(s) to use for the educational content of this novella. In the end, I decided to do something different.

I talked to nurses to find out what their biggest challenges related to diversity were. What I found is that the most valuable and memorable lessons didn't necessarily fit into frameworks, models or guidelines. The stories and anecdotes that they shared from their real-world experiences were enlightening and fascinating. I drew the following conclusions about diversity:

- We must be self-aware of our own biases, because they can have a very powerful effect over the way that we treat others. We are entitled to our own opinions on any matter, but if our opinions could impact the way we treat others, we must put them aside – regardless of what they are – whenever we come to work.

- We should never assume that we know what the behavior of an individual or a group of people means. Stereotyping can lead to incorrect assumptions.

- We create the healthiest work environments and healing environments when we respect the differences and honor the preferences of others.

- When there is a misunderstanding that is rooted in diversity, we have the right, as well as the responsibility, to talk about it. The nurses who shared stories with me said that their greatest enlightenments came from asking questions and having respectful dialogues with others about the differences between them.

These four key ideas are the heart of this story, and almost all of the relationships in the story are impacted by them. I have included a suggested reading list at the end of the story with some of the published resources that I found to be helpful, and I hope that you'll take a look at them if you want to enhance your understanding of diversity. The one that spoke to me the most powerfully was the article, "The Problem of Cultural Competency and How To Fix It", by Peter Benson and Arthur Kleinman. The authors clarify that culture is not a fixed concept. It is ever-changing among individuals and groups, and it is thus impossible to reduce the understanding of culture down to a competency. When we do, the behavior that follows is a long list of do's and don'ts, and often includes harmful stereotyping.

Unlike many of the technical tasks in patient care, being mindful and respectful of diversity is an interpersonal skill. Communicating with a patient who doesn't speak English or planning meals for a patient who doesn't eat what is on the standard hospital menu is much harder than taking vitals or starting an I.V. will ever be. It can be equally challenging to work alongside the nurse whose first language is not English, or who doesn't eat the food that you prepare for the covered dish luncheon, or whose family and personal life are radically different from your own.

In the next few pages, you'll find the nurses of Med-Surg South bracing themselves for their next big adventure. A hurricane is headed toward Dogwood, North Carolina. As they make their preparations, a new nurse joins the team, and some patients with unique needs are admitted to the unit.

As usual, there are plenty of interesting things going on in the nurses' personal lives. I hope you'll be able to relate to some of the situations in which the nurses find themselves and that some of the wisdom they gain from those experiences will help you reflect on your own roles as a colleague and caregiver in this ever-changing world of ours.

Sincerely,

Amy Glenn Vega

"We may have come on different boats, but we're in the same ship now."

Martin Luther King, Jr.

The CNE for this educational activity expires 2 years from the date of publication. Renewal of CNE will be based on review of objectives, content and applicability to nursing practice.

EDUCATIONAL OBJECTIVES

Upon completion of this educational activity, the learner should be able to:

1) Discuss the importance of putting personal biases aside when working in a health care environment
2) Explain why it is important to avoid stereotyping and generalizing
3) Describe how respecting differences and honoring personal preferences supports healthy work and patient care environments
4) Identify one way to resolve misunderstandings rooted in diversity

Chapter 1
Monday
Haylie

"Vampires!" Haylie Evans said with genuine horror. She shuddered as she watched a blood bank technician insert a large gauge needle into the arm of a donor. Haylie's hands trembled as she pressed her pen down on the blood donor intake form. "Evil vampires. That's what they are. Who would want to make a career out of drawing blood? Gross!"

"Well you have to draw blood sometimes," her friend and fellow nurse, Jamie Rodriguez, reminded her. "So that would make you a vampire too."

"I am not. I'm a nurse. I get to do plenty of other stuff with patients, not just draw blood. And I only draw vials here and there, not big bags full of it. If I did nothing but draw bags of blood all day long, then I'd be a vampire."

Jamie signed her name to the bottom of the form with long, heavy strokes of the pen. "You big baby," she chided Haylie.

"I am not," Haylie whined.

"What's the matter? You don't like the sight of blood?"

"I have no problem seeing other people's blood," Haylie explained. "But mine, being sucked right out of me... well... that's another story."

"That's a problem easily remedied. Close your eyes and you won't see a thing."

"It's not just that. I don't like getting stuck with a needle either."

"Well yeah, that can hurt a bit, but it's not excruciating. Just take a deep breath, and relax, and the needle should slide right in. It's worse if you're all tense and scared. Kind of like the way you are right now."

Haylie signed her name at the bottom of the donor form. "I can't believe I'm doing this."

"Chill out, Haylie. You're giving a pint of blood, not signing over your firstborn child. It will be okay."

"I hope so," Haylie replied. Then she lowered her voice to a whisper. "Beware... vampire approaching."

A white-coated blood bank technician sat down between the two young women, collecting their forms, then reclining their chairs. "Who wants to go first?" She asked.

"I'll go first," Jamie volunteered.

The technician pulled on a pair of disposable gloves. Then she applied a tourniquet to Jamie's arm, found the vein, swabbed it with betadine and skillfully inserted the needle for the blood draw.

"See," Jamie said in a teasing tone. "Not so bad. You can do this."

The technician then turned to Haylie. "Are you afraid?" she asked.

"Not at all," Haylie insisted.

She raised an eyebrow. "You sure, sweetie? You're shaking like a leaf."

"Yes, I'm sure. I'm fine."

"It's her first time," Jamie laughed. "Go easy on her. She's a big baby."

"Thanks a lot," Haylie said, shooting her friend a dirty look.

"If the sight of blood makes you feel uneasy, just close your eyes," the technician suggested. "Take deep breaths. In through the nose, out through the mouth."

Haylie took the advice as the technician rolled up her sleeve, tied on the tourniquet, and palpated her vein. She felt the chill of the betadine swab as the technician rubbed it over her skin.

"Okay, big stick," she announced, just before sliding the needle into Haylie's arm.

Haylie jumped slightly, and took a few deep breaths.

"Doing okay?" The technician asked.

"Yep. Fine." Haylie nodded, her eyes still shut.

"Keep your eyes closed if it helps. You'll be done in no time." The technician removed the tourniquet. Then she pulled off her gloves and picked up their donor paperwork as she rose from her seat. Glancing over their completed forms, she gasped.

"No way," she said, looking at Haylie.

"What?" Haylie asked as she opened her eyes.

"You're B negative. That's great!"

"Oh," Haylie said with a sigh of relief. "I thought something was wrong for a second."

"Not at all. I was just so excited to see that we've got a type B negative donor right here under our own roof! That's a fairly rare type, you know. We don't have any B neg blood banked at the moment, in fact. So if you'd like to come back soon and give us another pint--"

"Let me just get through with giving you a pint for today, and I'll think about it."

"No worries, I understand. If and when you decide to come back and donate again, just know that you'll be a hero," the technician said with a smile. "There's never been an easier way to save a life." She left Jamie and Haylie to attend to other hospital employees that had arrived to give blood.

Haylie took a deep breath and closed her eyes again, retreating into darkness and quiet.

"How are you holding up?" Jamie asked her a few minutes later.

"I'm hanging in there and trying not to think about it. My arm burns a little bit from the needle, but as long as I'm not looking at the bag filling up with blood, I think I can do this."

"So are you going to come back and give another pint to the vampires?"

"Are you kidding? I can't believe I'm actually giving blood right now, so let me see if I can survive this before I go making plans for the future. Who knows how long it will take me to recover?" Haylie exhaled deeply. "I felt dizzy for a second there. Remind me why I'm doing this?"

"Because there may be a hurricane coming, and the blood bank is desperately short in supply. Your blood might just help save someone's life."

Haylie frowned. "Nope. I'm doing it because Dan is a jerk, and he's totally wrong about me."

Jamie sighed and rolled her eyes. "Come on, Haylie. Let it go. It's been more than two months."

"I can't let it go. Do you know what he said about me? He said we're different people. He said that he's adventuresome and he's a risk-taker, and I'm steady and predictable."

"And he's right. You are two very different people, and there's nothing wrong with that."

"Apparently he thought so. He dumped me."

Haylie's eyes welled with tears as she recalled the breakup with Dan, a fellow nurse at Dogwood Regional Medical Center. Dan and Haylie had attended the same nursing school and had graduated together, but didn't start dating until they bumped into each other one day in the hospital hallway. Haylie needed a date to her sister's wedding. She invited Dan to join her, and he asked her out on a date the following weekend. A romance between the kindred spirits quickly blossomed. They had been together for a little more than a year, and Haylie was blissfully happy. She was certain that he was too.

But then Dan decided that he had outgrown the small town of Dogwood, North Carolina, and was ready for a change of pace. He signed a contract with a traveling nurse agency. Haylie was blindsided when he broke the news to her.

Haylie, we need to talk, he had begun the conversation, in a very serious tone. *I'm leaving in six weeks for my first assignment in Phoenix, Arizona.*

We can still be friends.

Her knee-jerk reaction was to protest. *We can still be together. I could go with you,* she had offered.

But Dan didn't seem very interested in that option. *We'll be better off as friends. Even if I weren't moving... well... we're just too different,* he had told her. Then he began to list, in excruciating detail, all of their conflicting personal attributes. He did make a rather convincing case for their break-up.

I'm adventuresome, and a risk-taker, and you're steady and predictable...

The words still stung Haylie as much now as the day he'd said them to her, more than two months ago.

"Haylie," Jamie said, nudging her elbow and jarring her thoughts from the past back to the present. "Donating a pint of blood isn't going to change who you are, and it's not going to impress Dan or make him think any differently of you."

Haylie raised an eyebrow, taking offense at Jamie's comment. "Dan can think what he wants about me, but he's wrong, and I'm going to prove it. Not to him – to myself. I'm just as adventuresome as he is, and I'm all about taking risks and having new experiences, and even though I dread the thought of giving blood, I'm going to be brave and do it anyway."

"And you think if Dan's wrong about you, then he'll realize that he's wrong about ending your relationship, and he'll come back to you someday. Right?"

Haylie paused. "Right. I mean... no. Wrong. Like I said, I'm doing this for me, not him."

"You don't have anything to prove, Haylie. Not to Dan, not to yourself, not to anyone else. There's nothing wrong with being different. You're perfect the way you are, and someday you'll find a guy who--"

"Oh, don't do that," Haylie groaned. "Don't give me the 'you'll find another guy who loves you for who you are' speech. I've already heard it from my mom, and everyone on my unit, and even Dan himself."

"Well if enough people are saying the same thing, maybe you should take it to heart," Jamie said.

"Maybe there is some truth to what Dan – and everyone else says," Haylie admitted. "Maybe he does know me better than I know myself. But I miss him, Jamie. And yeah, you're right, donating blood isn't going to change his mind about anything. But at least it would give me an excuse to send him an email and say hello... and tell him that I did something out of the ordinary for once. Maybe it will help smooth the transition to 'just friends.' I seriously do miss him." Haylie's eyes blurred with tears. She looked away.

In an effort to lighten the mood, Jamie reached into her handbag for her mobile phone. "Well, maybe you should get proof," she said. "Let me take a picture for you to send him."

"Yeah. Hold on." Haylie smiled as she sat up to prep for the picture. She finger-combed her bangs away from her forehead and tucked them behind her ear, brushing away a tiny tear from the corner of her eye in the process. Then she donned a comical expression, with wide eyes and a gaping mouth.

Jamie laughed as she took the picture. "You look like you just saw a vampire."

"I did. They just call them blood bank techs around here."

"Well, maybe they won't seem so scary if you keep coming back to give blood more often."

Haylie groaned. "As if I'll have a choice with my B negative blood? The blood bank is going to haunt me, you know. They'll be hunting me down, day and night, until I surrender and let them drain me dry."

"So give them a few more. What have you got to lose? Other than a little blood?"

"Actually," Haylie said as her eyes blinked rapidly. "I sure hope I don't lose consciousness. I'm feeling a bit lightheaded. Am I almost done?"

"I think so. The bag is looking pretty full."

Knowing how uneasy the sight of her own blood would make her feel, Haylie knew that she shouldn't look. But she couldn't help it. She glanced down at the needle taped to the fold of her arm, and followed the tubing all the way to the bag of dark red blood that it had drawn from her vein. She leaned forward slightly, feeling her stomach twist into knots. A sensation of fuzzy warmth clouded around her head.

"Hey... someone, help!" cried Jamie. "My friend is going to faint!" was the last thing that Haylie heard.

Chapter 2
Tuesday
Brad

The evening had been wonderful. It had been nothing more than dinner and a movie, but somehow, it hadn't felt like just another date. Brad took Andrea's hand in his as they walked toward the front door of his apartment.

Being with Andrea was easy. She was a 'low-maintenance' girl, which made Brad the envy of his male friends. Never needy and far from clingy, Andrea was down to earth, comfortable in her own skin, and self-confident without being cocky. In a lot of ways, she was the polar opposite of Sue, his previous girlfriend. Sue was a 'perfect ten' when it came to looks, but plagued with insecurity, she hid her natural beauty under layers of makeup, elaborate hairstyles and the latest fashion trends. Sue's pretty face had caught Brad's eye, but it was her kind, albeit restless, heart that made him love her.

It was only four months ago that Sue packed her bags and moved to Croatia. It hadn't exactly been a breakup; not in Brad's mind, at least not at first. Sue had chosen to join her sister on a mission trip overseas at an orphanage. She explained to Brad that she desperately wanted to do something meaningful with her life, and overseas mission work seemed like the right fit.

Brad was simply stunned by the fact that Sue had waited until two days prior to her departure to break the news to him. Just after he had asked her to marry him, and she had turned him down. The rejection of his proposal was deeply shocking, but the following news that his live-in girlfriend was preparing to move overseas for at least a year was simply devastating.   It was shortly after Sue's departure that Brad met Andrea, a fellow nurse at Dogwood Regional Medical Center. He liked her instantly. She was smart, pretty, compassionate, and best of all, he knew exactly where he stood with her. There were no secrets, no games. She had made the first move in fact, letting Brad know that she was interested in him. Still, he had waited nearly a month to ask her out on a date. His mind was still very much on Sue at the time, and he knew that his heart needed some time to heal.

One day, when Brad saw Andrea chatting away her lunch break in the cafeteria with a young, single male resident, he decided that it was time to move on. Andrea was too much of a catch to stay unattached for very long, so Brad gave her a call that evening and invited her to join him and his newly adopted basset hound, Bella, for a day at the beach.

They had seen each other nearly every day after that. As of late, Andrea was spending more time at Brad's apartment than she was at her own home. When they'd first met, Andrea had just moved into her parents' home following a divorce. She talked about moving out and getting a place of her own. But as she and Brad grew closer, she put less effort into her search for a new home with every passing day. Brad suspected that it wouldn't be much longer before one of them brought up the topic of her moving in with him.

Maybe today is the day, Brad thought. *Tonight is the night.*

He was in love with Andrea, and had been for quite some time. He just hadn't told her yet. His reason for holding off seemed more foolish and selfish each time he thought about it.

Wait for the right moment, he had told himself again and again.

He had even thought a time or two about cutting to the chase, and just proposing to Andrea. Brad was surprised that the thought of marriage was already on his mind again. It was not an uncomfortable – nor unwelcome – thought. He wasn't getting any younger, he knew. And he didn't envy his single friends. In spite of their insistence that unattached living was great, Brad knew that they had their share of lonely moments. And they were dwindling in numbers.

Mel, his best female friend and colleague from Med-Surg South, had sworn off love after a painful divorce. But then she unexpectedly fell for Rodney, a man that she met on a blind date, and had been dating him for the past few months. Then Brad's best male friend, Sam, was the next holdout to bite the dust. Sam had touted himself as a confirmed bachelor for as long as Brad could remember, but all of that changed when Sam met the new bartender at his favorite pub, a petite, doe-eyed brunette named Laura. He told Brad that he was sure that Laura was 'the one' and that he was thinking about giving her a diamond ring for her upcoming birthday. *This is just what people do*, Brad had told himself many times. *They find someone to love, they get married, and they live happily ever after.*

This is what I'm supposed to do, too.

Brad could feel the pressure coming from every angle. Except from Andrea. And that made Brad love her even more.

In spite of occasional lingering thoughts about Sue, Brad knew that Andrea was the one that he wanted to marry. And he felt certain that the next time he asked the question, the answer would be yes. Andrea was the one. He didn't have a ring yet, but he knew that it wouldn't matter to her. He knew she wouldn't mind waiting for one.

So what are you waiting for? Was the thought that suddenly popped into Brad's mind. *Why not just skip past the regular milestones... the 'I love you' and the 'let's move in together' and everything else... why not just pop the REAL question?*

Andrea... will you marry me?

He smiled confidently. He couldn't believe the decision had been that easy. Brad Jackson had never been more certain about anything in his entire life. There was no point in wasting any more time. They were just a few feet away from his doorstep when he reached for Andrea. He wrapped his hand around her wrist, pulling her to a stop.

"Brad, what's wrong?" She turned to him with a look of concern on her face.

"Andrea, will you--"

"Brad?" A third voice interrupted.

His heart skipped a beat.

A female figure stepped into their path. He hadn't left the front door light on, but the voice and the outline of the woman against the dusky sky were all that he needed to discern her identity.

"Sue," he replied, in barely a whisper.

He felt Andrea's skin grow ice cold, right before she pulled her hand out of his grasp.

"What are you doing here?" He asked his former girlfriend.

"I came back. It wasn't right for me," Sue replied. She took a step forward, suddenly illuminated in the glow cast from the streetlight. She looked at Brad, then at Andrea, and then at Brad again. She was confused.

"You could have given me some warning," he said coldly.

"Didn't you get my emails?"

"No. I stopped checking my personal email account because you were the only one who ever sent messages to it. Why didn't you call?"

"I did try calling a couple of times but when you didn't answer, I hung up."

"The answering machine is right where you left it."

"I know that too, Brad, but I wanted to talk to you, not a machine."

"Maybe … I should leave," Andrea said, taking a step back.

"No, don't," Brad insisted, shifting his attention to Andrea. "Don't leave."

But Andrea had already spun around and was walking toward her car.

"Wait! Andrea!" Brad ran to catch up with her. He reached for her, but she brushed him away and climbed into the driver's seat.

"I shouldn't be here right now," she said. It was obvious by the tremble in her voice that she was fighting the urge to cry.

"Please don't leave," he begged. "Andrea, this doesn't change anything between you and me. I'm not going back to Sue. We're done. I'll go tell her to leave right now. Just get out of the car and come in the apartment with me."

Andrea stared at him. "You can't make her leave," she insisted. "Her name is still on the lease. It's her place too." She put the key in the ignition and started the car.

"Please don't go. I know you're upset, and trust me, I'm just as shocked and surprised as you are. Just don't leave," Brad begged once more.

Andrea shook her head, no longer able to fight the tears. They began to spill from her eyes. "I should have known, Brad."

"You should have known what?"

"I get it. I'm the rebound girl. I knew I shouldn't have jumped into a relationship with you so soon after your fiancée left…"

"She was NEVER my fiancée!" Brad nearly yelled. "I told you, I asked, but she said no!"

Andrea looked up at him, brushing tears away from her eyes. "But you at least loved her enough to ask. You and I have been together for three months, Brad. You've never even told me that you love me."

Her words felt like a punch in the gut. Brad took a step back. He was speechless.

"Sue is waiting for you," Andrea said. "You should go." She pulled the car door shut and drove away.

Stunned into silence, Brad opened the door to the apartment. Sue followed him in. Bella greeted them at the door, jumped up on Sue, sniffed at her and barked.

"When did you get a dog?" Sue asked. Then to Bella, she pleaded for mercy. "Down, doggie, down." She gently pushed the hound's paws off of her legs.

Brad made a beeline for the bedroom that they had once shared, and closed the door.

Sue knocked once. When he didn't immediately answer, she knocked again. "Brad? Can we talk?" She waited a moment. "Please?"

"Not now," he shot back. "There are blankets and pillows for the sofabed in the hallway closet. Same as where you left them."

"Brad? Please, just let me explain."

He turned on the television to drown out the sound of Sue's voice. A perfectly coiffed news anchor appeared on the screen and announced mid-sentence "and that's the evening news. Stay tuned as we bring you updates on Hurricane Fortuna, currently a Category 3 storm gaining strength in the Atlantic, with a projected path targeting the Carolinas."

As Brad sank down onto the bed, a random thought entered his mind.

How do they choose names for hurricanes?

Fortuna – meaning Fortune – was a misleading name, he thought. Fortune was rarely associated with the devastation that a hurricane had the power to cause.

He began to run down the hurricane preparedness checklist in his mind. He had plenty of bottled water – check. Canned food – check. Batteries, flashlights, and a portable radio – check. Loved ones in a high, dry, and safe place – Bella, check. Andrea.... what about Andrea? What were her plans?

And what were Sue's?

"Be careful on the roads," the co-anchor on the news said. "We're already getting some strong wind and rain in Dogwood, which is going to pick up significantly as the hurricane heads this way. Log onto our website to get your hurricane preparedness checklist and more hurricane safety tips. Make sure you're stocked up on hurricane supplies and if you don't need to be on the road over the next several days, it's best to stay indoors right now."

Great, Brad thought as he rose from his bed.

As far as he was concerned, the real storm had just hit.

Chapter 3
Wednesday
Donna

"Sit up straight, honey," Donna nagged her twenty-four year old son, Darius.

"I don't think I could sit up much straighter if I tried, Mama." He reached up to his collar and adjusted his tie.

Side by side, they sat in silence for a long moment. "You look nice," Donna finally said. "Very nice. Your father – God rest his soul – would be very proud of you."

"Thank you, Mama. You know, you don't have to wait here with me. You can go on to work. I can take the bus home when I get done."

"Oh, I don't mind waiting," Donna said a little too quickly. She wrung her hands nervously. "I'll be on pins and needles until this is over."

"I'll do just fine. I promise. I've been praying. If it's God's will for me to get this job, then I will. If not, then it only means that the Lord has something even better in store for me."

Across the room, a set of glass double doors opened. "Darius LeShay?" A cheery young woman announced, reading his name from a clipboard.

Darius rose from his seat and nodded cordially.

"This way," she instructed. "Mr. Williamson will be interviewing you today."

Darius and the young woman disappeared behind the double

doors, and Donna's heart pounded as they closed. She drew in a deep breath through her mouth, and let it out through her nostrils. She closed her eyes and sent up a silent prayer of hope.

Dearest Lord, if it is in thy will, please, PLEASE let my boy Darius get this job. Let this be his fresh start to a new life, dear Lord. I ask this in Jesus' name. Amen.

When she opened her eyes, she focused them on the sign just ahead of her on the opposite wall. INVENTORY CONTROL, it said, in bold, black letters.

The word CONTROL seemed so much bolder, so much bigger. Donna almost felt as if the sign was mocking her, reminding her just how little control she really had.

When Darius had circled the advertisement for 'Warehouse Manager, Inventory Control' in the employment section of the newspaper and had given it to Donna to read, she responded with a quick series of questions, delivered rapid-fire style.

"What kind of inventory is kept in this warehouse? What's the salary like? What hours would you work? Where is the warehouse located, and how would you get to and from work?"

The one question that she hadn't asked, however, was the one still lingering in her mind, even now, after he had been called in for an interview. *How will your criminal record affect your chances of getting this job?*

Donna sighed deeply again as a wave of painful memories washed over her. It had been nearly fifteen years since her husband Phillip had died, leaving her to raise their children - Darius, Sean, and Jeanette - by herself. Darius had been the oldest, and most impacted by the loss.

He had struggled throughout his school years with dyslexia, and his father had always been the one who was the most patient and understanding of his son's special needs. When Phillip suffered a heart attack at a relatively young age, the entire family was blindsided by the loss of him. But Darius had lost not just a father, but a mentor, a role model, and a best friend. It wasn't long before Darius found a new crowd of friends, mentors and role models on the streets who had introduced him to a life of crime.

He dropped out of school in the tenth grade, and was arrested for the first time shortly thereafter. However, it was his second felony offense at the age of twenty-one – possession of a controlled substance, with intent to sell – that landed him in a medium-security prison for three years.

Donna smiled, recalling how the prison sentence had seemed like the end of the world at the time. How wrong she had been. Looking back, she realized that prison was the salvation that Darius had needed. Darius had found the Lord behind bars, and while his mother had been skeptical of his transformation at first, she realized with each passing day that Darius had indeed undergone a transformation – from a common drug-dealing thug to a man who was godly, compassionate and caring.

She had come to realize that potential employers weren't quite as forgiving and understanding.

Donna clasped her hands together and steepled her fingers, tucking them under her chin. *I'll just pray the entire time,* she told herself. *I'll keep a one-woman prayer vigil going in the lobby of this warehouse... Inventory Control nothing... it's the Lord who is in control and if I give up my heart to prayer and ask for my son to get this job, it will happen.*

If it is in God's will, it will happen.

It WILL happen.

Donna closed her eyes and prayed for what seemed like hours, but in actuality, was more like fifteen minutes. She looked up and returned her hands to her lap when she heard her son's voice. The double doors opened, and he stepped through them alone. Donna instantly felt that something was wrong. Still, she smiled and did her best to hide her doubts.

"How did it go?" She asked.

Darius frowned and looked down at the floor. Then he forced a smile and met his mother's eyes with his own. "It was going very well up until we got to the part about... you know..."

Donna clutched at her chest as if she could feel her heart breaking inside it. "What did they say? What did you say?"

He exhaled loudly. "Well, we talked a little bit about my charges and my prison time. Then he mumbled something about character being an important attribute for a leader in the workplace, and how past behavior is the best indicator of future performance... and a few other things that I can't exactly recall, but it was all a very sugar-coated way of telling me that I'm not going to get the job."

"Oh son, I'm sorry." Fighting the urge to cry, Donna rose to her feet and wrapped her arms around him. "I'm so sorry, Darius. I prayed so hard."

"It's okay," he said. "I kind of understand, Mama. I did some pretty rotten things and they don't want to hire that kind of person."

"The kind of person that you used to be," she said. "The person that are you aren't anymore."

"Right. But they don't know that."

They made their way to the exit door. "There were plenty of other jobs in the newspaper," he said brightly. "Maybe somebody else will be willing to give me a chance."

"I wish you could go to nursing school," Donna sighed loudly. "If you had 'R.N.' behind your name, then I promise you, you'd have absolutely no problem whatsoever finding a job. Speaking of, it's time for me to get to work now. Would you mind dropping me off?"

"Not at all," Darius said. "And if I can keep the car for the rest of the day, I can get out and do some more job hunting."

They made their way to Donna's car. Darius took the driver's seat and pulled out onto the highway.

"Something will turn up eventually," Donna said.

"I think so," he nodded. "I had the strangest feeling about this place, though, Mama. I thought this was going to be the one."

She shrugged. "The Lord works in mysterious ways, son. You never know. But it's wise to be looking elsewhere."

A strong gust of wind pushed against the car, and Darius struggled to stay in the lane.

"Just be careful driving around. The hurricane is still out in the Atlantic, but those outer bands of wind and rain are definitely hitting us here in the Carolinas. The roads aren't very safe right now."

Darius nodded. "I'll be extra careful. What about you, Mama? When the hurricane hits us, what are you going to do about getting around?"

"We'll wait a few more days to see what direction the hurricane is going to take. If it keeps coming toward us, I'll call a staff meeting so we'll look at the schedule to work out coverage. It may involve me and some of the rest of us staying overnight at the hospital if we won't be able to get to and from work safely. The roads won't be safe and public transit will be out of service."

Darius grinned. "Listen to you – taking charge and keeping everyone safe." He patted her on the shoulder. "My mom – the fearless leader of Med-Surg South."

"That's my job."

"You know, you're always telling me and Jeanette and Sean that you're proud of us. But you know what Mama?"

"Hmm?"

"We're proud of you too. Really proud."

Chapter 4
Thursday
Mel

"Take the epidural," Imelda Tagaro said. "Trust me on this." She took a sip of coffee, still trying to wake up and ready herself for her twelve-hour shift. She stared at her daughter, who was seated across the dining room table from her.

"No way!" Jenny, her daughter insisted. "I have a pretty high tolerance for pain, and I don't want the baby to come into the world all drugged up and freaked out."

"It's not going to freak the baby out, but you'll be freaking out if you don't take it. Believe me, honey, you don't know what pain is until you try to push a seven or eight pound baby out of your body."

Jenny arched an eyebrow as she flipped through the pages of the book from her prepared childbirth class at Dogwood Regional Medical Center. "I'm not worried, Mom. I think the other stuff that they taught me will work. The breathing, the imagery and meditation. I really think I can get through it with just that. Besides, you're going to be my labor coach, and since you're a nurse, I figure I'm in great hands. We can handle this, Mom."

Mel smiled. When she had delivered her two babies – Jenny first, who was born twenty years ago, and Michael five years later; it was her husband at the time, Bruce, who had served as her labor coach. Although they had divorced a little more than a year ago, and the process had been immensely painful for Mel, the hurt and sadness were finally wearing away. She was pleasantly surprised at her new ability to look back on her former life with her ex-husband and find that once again, she could smile at the happy memories that they had shared.

Mel's smile quickly faded to a frown as she stared back at Jenny, who was two weeks out from her due date. The pregnancy had been unplanned and had taken everyone by surprise, including Jenny's boyfriend and father of the baby, Jeremy. When Jenny decided to take some time off from school to return home and have the baby, Jeremy had apparently decided to take some time off as well. The first few times that Jenny had tried to call him on his mobile phone, the calls went straight to voice mail. She left a couple of messages, and began to worry when he didn't return them after several days. When she tried weeks later to call again, his phone line had been disconnected. Jenny then tried calling Jeremy's dormitory weeks later, only to learn that Jeremy was no longer a resident there. She sent countless emails but received no response.

"Jenny," Mel began. "Have you tried making contact with Jeremy again?"

At the mention of his name, Jenny's eyes began to mist with tears. "What's the point?" She asked. "He's missing in action. He obviously doesn't want anything to do with me, nor the baby. I can take a hint."

Mel shook her head. "It's not fair for you to go through this alone, Jen."

"No it isn't," she agreed. "But I can't change the way he feels. And I have no desire to hunt him down and fight him to take responsibility for his own baby. You can't force someone to care if they don't want to."

Mel took another long swig of coffee. "Honey... I hate to ask you this, but is there more to the story that you're not telling me?"

Jenny looked offended. "Of course not. Why would you say that?"

Shrugging, Mel gazed into the bottom of her empty coffee mug. "It's just very bizarre that he has completely removed himself from the picture, Jen. I've just been wondering if maybe the two of you have talked at all since both of you left school. I'm wondering if you had a fight of some kind... or if he's not the--"

"Mom!" Jenny interrupted, "How could you think that?"

"You didn't let me finish."

"You were going to suggest that he's not the father," she said. Tears began to flow down her cheeks. "I've been honest with you about everything. Everything. Of course he's the father, and no, we haven't talked since we both left school, much less had any kind of fight, and yes, Mom, I've tried my hardest to track him down and find him. But I can't. And all I can assume it means is that he wants nothing to do with me. He knows I'm pregnant with his child, and he chose to disappear, and that's all there is to the story. From my side of the story, anyway. There's plenty that he would need to explain, but I've put everything on the table that I have to share. I don't know how to make it any clearer than that." She reached for a paper towel and blotted her eyes.

"I'm sorry, honey," Mel said quickly. "Now don't go getting upset..."

"Because it isn't good for the baby," she finished her mother's sentence. "I know, I know. Everyone is so quick to tell me what's right for the baby, like how I shouldn't get upset because the baby will feel it, and how the baby needs to have a father and it's not fair that I'm bringing it into the world without a daddy." She cupped her hands over her face and broke into sobs.

"Jenny, I'm sorry," Mel said. "Honey, don't cry. I didn't mean to upset you." She stood and crossed the room to where her daughter sat, kneeling and wrapping her arms around her. "Baby, I'm sorry. I'm so sorry."

Jenny turned and hugged her mother tightly. "I know you didn't mean it, Mom, it's just that I'm scared about doing this alone. And I'm hurt, and I'm confused. I don't know why Jeremy would abandon me – I mean, us - like this. I love him so much, and at the same time, I hate him, and I'm so mad at him I can barely see straight."

Mel squeezed her even more tightly. "It's going to be okay, Jen. You come from a long line of very strong women. You're going to be a great mom, with or without Jeremy. And regardless of what happens, you're never, ever going to be alone. You've got me and I'll always be here for you."

"I know," Jenny said tearfully. "I love you, Mom. I'm so thankful that you're here for me now."

"Always, honey."

Jenny laughed softly. "Look at me. I'm twenty years old. I'm supposed to be an adult now, and I still cry on my mama's shoulder."

"And when that baby comes along, you'll take one look and you'll understand why. You're my flesh and blood, Jenny. You lived inside of me for nine months and just because you came out and grew up and went off into the world on your own, it doesn't mean that you don't belong to me anymore. You'll always be part of me, and whatever you're feeling – whether it's good or bad – I'm always going to feel it too. It doesn't matter how old you are, or how grown up you are. That's how I'll feel about you, all the days of your life. And right now, I'm hurting for you, and with you, and all that any mother wants is for her children to be happy. So please, honey, don't cry. Don't be upset. Everything is going to be okay and I need for you to believe that."

Jenny continued to weep for several minutes while Mel held her tightly. Finally, she regained her composure. "I love you, Mom," she said softly. "And yes, I believe that everything is going to be okay."

"Of course it will." Mel glanced down at her watch. "Except for when I come in to work late today. Donna is going to read me the riot act if I don't get going!" She stood up and grabbed for her purse and keys.

Jenny met her at the door and handed her an umbrella. "The weather is getting nasty. Be careful, Mom."

"I will," Mel said. "And you, miss Mommy-to-be, go get off of your feet and relax. I know you're not due for another couple of weeks, but don't you dare do anything that might make you go into labor."

"I guess high-impact aerobics are out of the question?"

"Very funny."

"Can I at least have Mexican food for lunch? Spicy enchiladas? Extra jalapeños?"

Mel hugged her. "You do what you want, my dear. Just keep in mind that if you go into labor in the middle of a hurricane and can't get to the hospital, you'll have to deliver the baby all by yourself here at home."

"Hmm. I see your point. I think it's time for me to go lay down and keep reading my prepared childbirth handbook."

Mel stepped through the doorway to leave, then turned around.

"Hey Jen?"

"Yeah?"

"I love you."

She smiled. "Love you too, Mom."

Chapter 5
Friday
Miriam

Miriam Simpson stared down at the massive pile of paperwork on her dining room table. Then she sighed loudly as she bounced her four month-old grandson, Timothy on her knee.

"So what do you think, honey? Should Gram-Gram retire so she can have more time to spend with you? Would you like that?"

Timothy tossed his head backward, staring at her upside down. "Dah," he said.

"I take it that means yes," Miriam said. "Could you please learn how to write really quickly so you can help me fill out all of the paperwork then?"

"Mmm. Dah."

"You're the best," Miriam said, planting a kiss on his forehead.

Just then, her mobile phone rang loudly on the table next to the pile of papers. She held the phone up to the level of her eyes, squinted, and turned her head slightly sideways as she glanced at the display. She recognized the phone number as that of her employer – Dogwood Regional Hospital.

She groaned as she pressed the 'Talk' button, just in time to keep the call from going to voice mail. "Hello?"

"Hi Miriam." There was no need for the caller to identify herself. Miriam had worked with Donna, the nurse manager on Med-Surg South, for nearly ten years. Not only was she readily able to recognize Donna's voice over the phone – she also knew the exact reason for the call.

"So much for a day off, eh?" Miriam grunted.

"Well hello to you too," Donna replied. "How is Timothy doing?"

"No need for the nice-nice talk. I know why you're calling. I can't today, Donna."

There was a brief moment of silence on the other end of the line, followed by a woeful sigh. "Come on, Miriam. You know how short staffed we are these days. I really, really need you, otherwise, I wouldn't be calling."

"What's going on?"

"Mel called in. Jenny is starting to have some pretty strong contractions, so she's taking her to the doctor this morning to see if she's going into labor."

"Oh my," Miriam softened. "It's a bit early, isn't it?"

"Yes. Jenny's due date is about two weeks out. Hopefully it's just false labor. I don't have to tell you how common it is with first pregnancies."

Miriam sighed. "You know I'd do anything for Mel. But Donna, I so needed this day off to spend with my little Timothy. What about the Indian nurse?"

"She starts Monday, and she's still got a couple of days of orientation. In the meantime, I've got every bed full on this unit and I need help. I'm begging you, Miriam, please."

"Can't you get someone from the float pool?"

"I tried. Everyone's having babies, heart attacks and car accidents right now, so all of the floaters are in Emergency and L & D."

Sighing dramatically, Miriam stood from the table, hoisting her grandson onto her hip. "Okay, okay. I've got to call my daughter-in-law first, and get Timothy back to her. It was supposed to be a Grandma day for me, you know. I had the little guy all to myself."

Donna whined. "I know, and I'm sorry. Trust me, my bags are already packed for the guilt trip."

Miriam laughed. "I wouldn't be so willing to be a good sport, had I not been a nurse manager myself in the past, and had I not been able to understand the tough position you're in. But I've been there and done that, Donna. I know what you're up against."

"I wish I could just plant seeds and grow some more nurses. This gets tougher and tougher to deal with as time goes on."

"I know," Miriam commiserated. "And I'm happy to help while I can, but one of these days, I am going to retire. You know that, don't you, Donna?"

"You keep saying that, but it hasn't happened just yet. So I'll remain in denial until you make it official."

Groaning playfully, Miriam made her way toward her bedroom, balancing Timothy on one arm while she used the other to nudge through her closet for a clean set of scrubs. "I'll see you shortly, Donna."

"Thank you so much, Miriam. I don't know what I'd do without you."

"Well, that day will come eventually, and you'll make do when it does. In the meantime, let me get off of the phone so I can send Timothy back to his mom and get to work."

"Okay. See you soon."

Miriam hit the 'end' key on her mobile phone and handed it to her grandson. He held it in his chubby hands, thoroughly fascinated with the new toy he had been given. "You take the next call, okay, Timmy-Poo? Whoever they are, and whatever they want, you tell them to NO WAY."

Just then, as if on cue, the phone rang. Miriam hit the speakerphone button, and listened as a voice on the other end of the line invited her to subscribe to the Dogwood Daily Times Newspaper for the low price of some random figure she couldn't quite make out, a special limited-time offer that included home delivery, and the first two weeks of service for free.

Miriam sighed deeply as she tugged her scrubs off of the hanger.

"Can we go ahead and sign you up for this fantastic offer?" The friendly voice on the other end of the line asked.

"Dah," said Timothy, as he moved the phone to his mouth, lubricating the keypad with baby drool.

"No," Miriam said emphatically, taking the phone away from him.

"Are you sure you want to pass up this special off--"

Miriam held the 'End' button again, silencing the salesperson's pleading monologue.

"What's wrong with these silly newspaper folks?" Miriam asked her grandson. "Don't they know – 'Dah' means NO?"

Only seconds later, the phone rang again.

"What is with these people?" Miriam asked. She pressed the 'Talk' button. "Listen," she spat into the phone. "I don't want to subscribe to the newspaper. How many times do I have to tell you folks that? The print is so small I can barely see--"

"Excuse me?" A confused female voice on the other end of the line asked. "I'm calling for Miriam Simpson. Is this the right number?"

"Oh... oh, I'm sorry," Miriam said with embarrassment. "I thought you were trying to sell me a newspaper subscription. Yes, this is Miriam Simpson."

"Ms. Simpson, this is Shelly from Dr. Salvo's office. I'm calling because we're trying to reschedule some appointments this week. I've got you scheduled to come in on Tuesday, but we will likely have to close the practice that day because of the hurricane. Can we move your appointment to the following Tuesday instead? Same time?"

Miriam frowned. "I suppose so," she said. "What if the hurricane changes direction? Will Dr. Salvo still be able to see me on Tuesday?"

"I don't know yet, Ms. Simpson. Right now we're just trying to be prepared in case the hurricane does hit. Even if it doesn't hit us directly, we are already getting so much strong wind and rain that we'll likely need to close down the practice later this week."

"I understand," Miriam said. "I just don't want to take too long, you know. It's unnerving to have to wait so long to find out what's going on."

"I understand, Ms. Simpson, and I'm sorry. If anything changes and Dr. Salvo will be able to keep your original appointment, we'll call you as soon as possible to let you know."

"Okay, thank you," Miriam said.

"You have a good day, Ms. Simpson."

Miriam sat down on the bed, hugging Timothy close to her. Then she drew back and stared at him for a very long time.

"You're a handsome little thing," Miriam smiled.

Timothy cocked his head and reached for his grandmother's face, tugging on her lower lip. She took his tiny hand into her own and kissed his palm. She continued to stare at her grandson for what seemed like an eternity.

"I just want to remember this moment forever, Tiny Tim. Just the way you look right now, at this very moment. You're the most gorgeous grandbaby in the world, you know that?"

He grinned. "Dah."

"Oh cut it out. We both know you're just being modest."

Chapter 6
Saturday
Patreeka

Prateeka Patel smiled as she stepped off of the airplane and onto the jet bridge.

My very first step into the United States, she thought with pride.

Reaching into her carry-on bag, she found her mobile phone and dialed her husband of two weeks.

"Hello?" He answered.

"Samir, I have arrived."

On the other end of the line, he paused. Then he laughed. "You are using English with your own husband?"

Prateeka laughed in return. "What is it they say? 'When in Rome, do as the Romans do?' Is that correct?"

Her English was impeccable, and the North Americans with whom she had spoken before delighted in her British accent. *Your English is perfect!* They would say. *But how is it that you're from India, but you sound like you're from England?* She would smile politely and explain that British English was taught in Indian schools, and that she – like many of her peers – had been learning and speaking the language in school since they were young children. Which meant that she, too, was a native speaker of English, in addition to Marathi, the most widely spoken language in the city.

Twenty-six year old Samir, also from Mumbai, was finishing

medical school in the United States. His family had known Prateeka's family for many generations, and their parents had decided nearly a decade ago that Prateeka and Samir would marry.

Prateeka, at the age of twenty-three, had just finished nursing school and had been dreaming for many years of living in the United States. She wanted to get married and start having children as soon as possible, as did Samir. Their families could not have asked for a more perfect match.

"We are not in Rome, Prateeka. And you are not in Mumbai anymore," Samir told her with a laugh.

"And we are not in Kansas anymore, are we, Toto? But from the way the wind was blowing the plane around before we landed, I was wondering if there was a tornado out there. I was looking out the window to see if I could spot any witches on brooms."

Again, her husband laughed heartily. "You have been watching American television, I see?"

"Every day since our wedding."

"I hope you do not think that that everything will be like what you see on television."

Prateeka paused as she stepped into the terminal, glancing overhead to find the baggage claim sign, and walked in the direction that it pointed. "Oh, I'm sure it's not all like what is on television. But the medical drama shows are very exciting. If they are realistic at all, then I cannot wait to start work."

"And when do you start?"

She smiled. "Monday."

"Monday?" Samir sounded alarmed. "Don't you need some time to unpack and rest? The flight is so long from India."

"Not to worry. I got plenty of sleep on the plane, and I packed very little. The rest of my bags will be shipped to me later in the week."

"Prateeka," he scolded, "It takes some time to adjust to life in the United States. Things are different. The American way of life is different. The Americans themselves are different. And hospitals are--"

"Different," she interjected. "Yes, I know. You have told me many times. And if you will hurry up and finish medical school in Maryland, then you can come join me in North Carolina and we can adjust together."

"Seven more months, Prat. You know I can't hurry the time along."

"So I will wait for you here."

"Unless you wish to join me here."

"Samir, we've been through this many times. I know what medical school is like! You will not have time for me and I know no one else in Maryland. I would be alone. But you want to do your residency here, and since I have acquaintances who are already working here in Dogwood, I will have their company while I wait for you. Priya and Anupa have already prepared a room for me in their apartment. And I can begin looking for a house for us."

"I remember, this is what we agreed upon," he said. And then added hopefully, "But if you change your mind..."

"I will do no such thing," she laughed. "I will wait for you here."

He paused. "I'll come to see you soon, Prat. I have a break in three weeks, so I will come to visit you in Dogwood."

"And I look forward to seeing you then."

"Good. Where are you now?"

"In the airport, walking toward baggage claim."

"How are you getting to the apartment in Dogwood?"

"I rented a car."

Her husband hesitated again before speaking. "Drive very carefully, Prateeka. Have you studied the road signs and--"

"Yes, yes," she interrupted. "I will be fine, I promise."

"But you did not drive in Mumbai, did you?"

"I will be fine, Samir," she said firmly. "You have nothing to worry about. Except for the bill for this international phone call. I have to go get a local phone soon. In the meantime, let's keep our calls short so we do not spend all of the money from the wedding gifts on the phone bill."

He laughed once more. "We wouldn't want that. Be safe, Prateeka. Call me again when you are settled into the apartment, and you have more time to talk."

"I will."

"It won't be long before we can be together. Not even a year before I finish school."

"I know. I am patient. Goodbye for now, Samir."

"Goodbye."

Chapter 7
Monday Morning

"A little to the right," Haylie said.

"It doesn't have to be perfect," Brad said.

"Yeah, I think it's fine as is," Mel insisted.

"No, I'm with Haylie," Miriam interjected. I think you need to shift it to the right a bit more. A welcome sign makes a first impression! We don't want the new nurse to think we're a bunch of slackers who can't get a piece of paper perfectly centered on the wall."

Haylie groaned. "Quit mocking me, Miriam."

"You know I'm only kidding," she said, patting Haylie on the shoulder.

"Well make up your minds," Donna said as she held the sign to the wall. "My arms are going numb."

"Okay, okay," Haylie relented. "It's fine as is."

Brad tore two pieces of tape from the dispenser at the nurse's station and pressed them to the corners of the welcome banner. "There," he said. "All done."

Donna took a step back, admiring the sign that she created on her computer and printed out earlier that morning. "Welcome Prateeka," she said aloud.

"What time does she get here?" Haylie asked.

"She's in orientation this morning, but she'll come up to the unit to meet us at lunch."

"I hope she skipped breakfast," Miriam said. "Between the five of us, we've brought enough food for a welcome party to feed a small army."

"And it smells so good, I may just have to sneak some of your Swedish meatballs from the crock pot before she gets here," Brad said to Miriam.

"Oh, help yourself, there's plenty," Miriam said.

"Don't forget my cheese dip in the other crock pot," Haylie said proudly. "With a plate of nachos, it's pure deliciousness!"

"Well, you all are making me feel woefully inadequate with my veggie tray," Mel said with a sigh.

"No worries. I'm sure she'll be appreciative of everything that we brought," Donna said with a nod.

"I'm just so excited that we'll have someone new here," Haylie said with an excited giggle. "You know what that means? I won't be the 'new nurse' anymore."

Donna smiled. "There are some advantages to that. You'll be a wonderful mentor to her, knowing what it feels like to have been in her shoes just recently. I'm sure you and Prateeka will have a lot to talk about. She's about the same age as you, Haylie."

Haylie's eyes lit up with excitement. "That's cool," she said. "Better watch out, or we young bloods will be taking over the unit."

"Young bloods always end up taking over nursing units," Donna said. "Who knows, Haylie? You stay here long enough, and you could very well be the nurse manager here someday."

"Oh, I don't know about that, Donna," Haylie said. "You run a tight ship. I don't know if I could ever fill your shoes."

"Well, somebody will have to someday," she said. "I won't be around forever. There was a time when I was the new nurse on the unit, and I thought the same exact thing about myself. And look at me now!"

"Yes, look at you now, holding a platter of melting éclairs," Miriam chimed in. "Put them in the freezer until Prateeka arrives, or else they'll be nothing but mush in a few minutes."

"Good point." Donna crossed the room to the refrigerator and stored her covered dish in the freezer. Then she spun around. "By the way, while I've got you all here in the same room, we do need to pull together for a moment and talk about our covering the unit through the hurricane plan. Refresh my memory... which of you are scheduled to work Wednesday and Thursday?

"Everyone except me, I think," said Mel. "I'm supposed to be off on Wednesday."

"I believe you're right," Donna said. "Most of you are supposed to be here, or else on call. If you're on call, plan on coming in. The hurricane is supposed to make landfall late Wednesday night or early Thursday morning. Right now it's only a Category 3, but they're projecting that it will be a Category 4 when it hits the coast. It will lose a little bit of strength when it comes inland toward us, but it's still going to be a very strong storm. One way or the other, we'll likely see trees and power lines down in the roads, which could make it hard to get to and from the hospital. For those of you who are coming in on Wednesday or Thursday, which sounds like all of you except for Mel, my advice is for you to pack a bag and plan on an overnight stay."

"Where are we going to sleep?" Brad asked.

"The Engineering Department is setting up cots in the auditorium and conference rooms."

Brad groaned. "Sounds comfy."

"Well, it's not the Holiday Inn, but it works in a pinch," Miriam said. "Donna and Mel and I have camped out here before. We had another bad hurricane a few years ago. We survived the night on cots so I'm sure you will too, Brad and Haylie."

Grinning, Haylie shook her head. "I'm not sleeping on a cot, and neither are the rest of you."

All eyes focused on her.

"I live in Dogwood Park Apartments now, remember?" She pointed over her shoulder. "Right behind the hospital. It's literally a five minute walk from Med-Surg South to my front door. I've got a guest room with a bed and a futon, and a pull-out sofa bed in the living room. If you all can brave a short walk in the bad weather, then you can be my guests for the evening. Not as ideal as getting to go home, but way better than sleeping on a cot in the conference room downstairs."

Brad let out of a sigh of relief. "Sounds like a plan. Getting away from home for a little while doesn't sound like such a bad thing right now, actually."

"Huh?" asked Haylie. "Why? What's going on at home?"

Brad shook his head. "Never mind," he said. "No big deal."

"Well, I'll certainly take you up on the offer as well," Donna nodded.

"Count me in too," Miriam said. "What about our new Indian nurse, Prateeka?"

"Sure. We'll make room for her too if she wants to join us. I can't wait to meet her." Haylie looked up at the sign on the wall, remembering her own welcome to Med-Surg South the previous year.

"Well that was the easiest disaster preparedness planning I've done in my entire nursing career," Donna said. "Thank you, Haylie. Time to get the day started."

***

"So how was it last night?" Miriam asked at the change of shift report.

"Oh, it wasn't a bad night, just a long one. I'm glad it's quitting time," said Karen McFarlane, one of the nurses who had just finished third shift. She stretched her arms out and yawned. "I can't wait to get home and crash. And I've got the next three nights off, thankfully. The school systems are letting out at noon today and will be closed for the rest of the week. No way could I leave my kids at home alone in a hurricane."

"I'll be right here, probably stuck until the darn hurricane passes. I'm exhausted at the very thought of it. Anyway, let's talk shop and then you go home and get enough rest for the both of us, will you?"

"Will do," Karen said. "I guess that's what happens when you're as good as you are, Miriam. No one ever lets you off the hook."

"Hmmm, you think?" Miriam rolled her eyes and shook her head. "One of these days, I am going to retire."

"Well, we've got you fair and square until then. Anyway, back to our patients - here goes. I think you had a few of these patients yesterday. Mr. Potter, Ms. George, and Ms. Colby. They all had a good, restful night. I gave Ms. Colby her morning meds, and Mr. George is going for a C.T. scan sometime today. We do have one new patient that got admitted after you left yesterday. Ms. Daphne Wylie. She had gallstones and her gallbladder removed. She's a thirty-one year old blind lady and--"

"Hold up," Miriam said. "Before we go any farther, let's back up to the part about her being a 'blind lady.' There's a better way to say that."

Karen looked confused. "What are you talking about?"

"I'm talking about the fact that you labeled her as 'blind' before anything else. She's not a blind lady, she's a lady who is blind. Or a lady with a visual impairment. If you call her a 'blind lady,' then you're using her blindness to define her. We're trying to move away from doing that, because people are more than just a diagnosis or an impairment. They're people first and foremost, so we need to use the right words. And we call that--"

"Person first language," Karen said, smacking her forehead. "I remember from nursing school. We talked about 'people with diabetes' and 'people living with AIDS,' but I didn't make the connection with people who have disabilities."

Miriam nodded. "Be careful about using a word like 'disability.' That's a pretty strong word, and sometimes it can be offensive."

"Got it," Karen said with a quick nod, and then smiled. "You're going to like her, you know. She's a riot."

Karen then reviewed Daphne's chart with Miriam, and briefly discussed the charts of the other patients before clocking out.

After reviewing her newly assumed patients' records, Miriam rounded the corner of the nurse's desk and made her way down the hall to room 5. From the doorway she caught a glimpse of Daphne. The patient was a pretty young woman with her dark hair trimmed into a pixie cut. She was lying on her back and appeared to be staring up at the ceiling.

"Good morning, Ms. Wiley," Miriam said as she entered her patient's room.

"Ms. Wiley is my mom," replied her patient. "Call me Daphne.

I'm too young for that Ms. Wiley stuff. You're Miriam, right?" She sat up. Her eyes redirected toward the sound of Miriam's voice.

"You got it," she said.

"I recognized your voice. I heard you talking to Karen down the hallway."

Miriam was taken aback. "You did?"

"Yeah. I heard my name so I tuned in."

"Wow. You've got an impressive sense of hearing."

Out of habit, Miriam crossed the room and wrote her name on the dry erase board mounted on the far wall. Daphne laughed softly. Miriam turned to look at her and saw that Daphne had turned to face her.

"Thanks for doing that," Daphne said.

"Doing what?" Miriam asked.

"Writing your name on the board."

"Oh," Miriam was taken aback. *Why did I do that? She wondered. The patient is blind, she obviously can't read it.*

"I can't read it, as you know, but my friends and family who come to visit can," she said. "I want to make sure they know your name just in case I get loopy on medication and forget. So if I've got someone here visiting, I can send one of them out to chase you down if I need anything. Gotta make sure we know exactly who to pester today."

Miriam laughed. "You're not being a pest. That's what we're here for."

Daphne smiled. "So I guess you got the news – you got the blind lady today. Congratulations. And by the way, it's okay to call me a 'blind lady' or a 'blind patient' or whatever else you can think of to put behind 'blind.' I've been called much worse."

Miriam wrinkled her brow in confusion. "So you heard that whole part of our conversation too?"

"Yeah. Lots of us blind folks are perfectly happy being called blind. Not people who are blind, not visually impaired, just plain blind."

"Oh," Miriam was taken aback. "They do? May I ask why?"

"Sure. Ask away."

Miriam chuckled. "Okay then, why?"

"Well, our blindness makes us pretty distinct from everyone else, doesn't it? It's an important part of who we are. We're different and that's fine with us."

"Okay then." Miriam nodded. "Now I feel like an idiot for correcting Karen this morning. She was right, and I was wrong."

"Shame shame, nurse Miriam," Daphne mocked. But lucky for you, I'm an easygoing kind of gal. I'm going to let this one slide. But go politically correct on me again, and there's going to be trouble. Where did you get the wacky idea that blind people shouldn't be called blind, anyway?"

Miriam laughed as she pushed a button to inflate Daphne's blood pressure cuff. "I went to nursing school more than thirty years ago, back when we called people by their diagnoses, not their names. But things are always changing. I went to a continuing education class a few years ago about person-first language and I've been trying to be conscientious about it since then."

"I get the intent of person-first language," Daphne said with a quick nod. "And when it comes to diseases and stuff, then yeah, I think it makes sense to say that someone is a person living with AIDS instead of an AIDS patient or something like that."

"Right. It's all about using language to show that the person living with AIDS is a still a person just like everyone else."

"Yep. It just doesn't work with someone like me. I'm not like everyone else."

"Why do you say that?"

"Well, you wouldn't feel comfortable giving me your keys and letting me take your car out for a spin, would you?"

Miriam stifled a laugh. "Well, no."

"You wouldn't walk me through an art museum and ask for my opinion of all the paintings on the wall, would you?"

"No."

"Of course not. Because I can't see. I'm blind. It's not a disease, nor a disability. It's just who I am. I'm not ashamed or bothered by it, and there's no need to come up with a fancy way to talk about me just for the sake of political correctness. I can't speak for every single blind person in the world but as far as I'm concerned, I'm blind – so just call me blind. It's really and truly okay."

"I understand. That makes perfect sense," Miriam said.

"Cool. Now that we're past all that blind-lady business, could you get me a sip of water please? I'm really thirsty. Not a patient who is thirsty, or a patient living with thirst, but a thirsty patient. "

Miriam stifled a laugh and reached for the water pitcher and poured a glass of ice water into a plastic cup. She held the straw to Daphne's mouth while she sipped.

"Ahhh," she sighed with relief. "Water never tasted quite so good. I just hope it's not the fancy stuff. You know, that bottled spring water flown in from the Swiss Alps. I'm pretty sure my insurance only covers tap water."

Giggling, Miriam placed the cup on Daphne's bedside tray. "Not many people come out of surgery in as good a mood as you're in. Those who can pull it off usually heal a lot faster. You're quite a comedian."

"That's exactly what I am," Daphne beamed. "So now that you got your free preview, I expect you to come to one of my shows once I get out of here."

"Seriously? You're a career comedian?" Miriam settled into the chair next to Daphne's bed, newly intrigued.

"Pretty much. I write, act and direct theatrical productions, and I do a little performing here and there. Comedy is my genre of choice, as you may have guessed. As far as my 'day job,' I'm the Executive Director of the Dogwood Performing Arts Center. Heard of it?"

"The good old DPAC. I sure have. We used to go to shows all the time. That is… when my husband was still alive. I haven't been since he died."

"I'm very sorry to hear about your husband," Daphne said, uncharacteristically serious for a moment.

"Oh, thank you," Miriam said. "I miss him a lot. It's been a big adjustment."

"Whenever you're ready to see another show, come on back," Daphne said. "Bring a friend or two. Call me in advance and I'll get you the best seats in the house."

"I may just have to do that," Miriam said.

"Although being in a show is even more fun than coming to see one. We're holding auditions soon for our next play. So if you like being in the spotlight, we might be able to make you a star. We're in desperate need of good actors."

"I've never been in a play before."

"No better time to start than now."

"What will the show be about?"

"It's an original play – written by yours truly," Daphne smiled. "Titled 'Love is Blind.' It's about an attractive, successful young blind woman named Claire who meets a guy through an Internet dating site. When they get together, the chemistry is amazing and they quickly fall in love. But when she introduces him to her friends and family, they flip out because they don't think that he's very good looking. Which doesn't matter a bit to her, obviously. But her folks try to convince her that she's too good for him. She's torn between following her heart and trying to live up to others' expectations for her."

Miriam smiled. "That sounds like a great story. A comedy?"

Daphne shrugged. "Sort of. It's part drama, part comedy. A dramedy."

"And you think I could be a character in the play?" Miriam laughed. "I don't know about that. I've never had any formal training."

"Some people have natural abilities. With a little bit of coaching in the fundamentals, I think you'd be great on stage."

Leaning forward in her chair, Miriam watched Daphne as she spoke. "You do? Really?"

"Yeah. I heard you talk to the nurse from night shift. Other than the person-first fiasco, you really know your stuff, nurse Miriam. And you care. You're passionate. You talk, and people listen. You could bring that to the stage."

"So… you really did hear everything we said. Wow." Miriam knew that Daphne wouldn't be able to see the surprise on her face, but she made no effort to hide it in her voice. "We were talking at the nurse's station. That's all the way down the hall from your room. It's a long haul."

"True, but my door was open, and there were very few other distractions. I could hear the entire conversation just fine."

Miriam was in genuine awe. "You must have superhero ears. I certainly don't. I know I couldn't hear a conversation all the way from here. Not well enough to follow an entire conversation, anyway."

Daphne grinned. "That's because you're not blind. Poor you."

Miriam laughed again.

"It's a simple equation, really. We've got a total of five senses, and sight is only one of them. I've still got four other senses, and that leaves me with plenty of other ways to get information about what's going on around me. In fact, I have to depend a bit more heavily on my other four senses than a sighted person does. So because of that, I'm naturally more attentive to things that I hear."

"Makes perfect sense," Miriam said. "Although I am highly dependent on my sight, so if you don't mind, I do need to take a look at your surgical incision."

"No problem," Daphne said, carefully lifting up her gown to expose the site.

"Wow. Poor baby, they had to open you up instead of doing a lap procedure." Miriam paused for a moment. "Hmmm…. okay, thanks. You can cover back up now. What's your pain on a scale of one to ten?" Miriam asked.

"I'm about a four right now. It's not horrible. Only if I move or take a deep breath does it really hurt. As long as I stay still and relax, it's not so bad."

"Good to know. Just let me know if that changes."

"I will. How about hooking me up with some antibiotics?" Miriam literally took a step back. "What?"

"Antibiotics. Ya know, that stuff that kills the funky bugs and germs. You're a nurse, Miriam. I figured you'd know this kind of stuff."

"Wisecracker," Miriam laughed. "I will call your doctor to ask for antibiotics, but I'm curious as to why.

"Because my incision is starting to look infected, right? Ask me a tough question next time."

Miriam was astounded. "Did someone else tell you that?"

"Nope."

"So how did you know?"

"Well, it feels a bit warm to me, even through my gown. I was resting my arm across my belly earlier, and I could feel heat from the area around the incision, so I knew then it was getting infected. Plus, I heard it. You lowered the tone of your voice after you saw it. That told me something was off kilter. Just because I'm blind doesn't mean I can't see. I see through other eyes."

For a moment, Miriam was speechless. "I guess you do," she finally said. "But you're right, we do need to get some antibiotics going. Let me go put in a call to your doc and I'll be back shortly."

Daphne smiled. "Sounds like a plan. And don't forget, we've got to set up your audition for 'Love is Blind' once I'm out of here and back at work, and this darn hurricane passes. Bet you thought you could get out of it by changing the subject and making this all about me, did ya? Well, you should know better, nurse Miriam. Bring your calendar the next time you come in here, and let's talk dates."

"Oh… let me think about it."

"What's there to think about? You and your late hubby loved the theatre, didn't you? Come back and be a part of the show. It would make him proud to see you up there on stage. Besides, I've already got a part for you in mind. You'd be great in the role of Claire's mother."

"Is her mother one of those people that tries to talk her into breaking things off with the homely boyfriend?"

"At first, yes. But then the mother comes around. It's a lovely transformation. You'd be perfect for the part."

Miriam smiled. "I'll think about it. But first things first – let me go get those antibiotics lined up for you."

"You do that. And I'll see you later."

Miriam laughed. "I guess you will, won't you?"

"Count on it."

***

Mel groaned. After three days off, she was struggling to direct her attention away from the impending arrival of her first grandchild, and refocus on work.

She scanned through her patients' charts after report, paying special attention to the one belonging to Mr. Loren Allimore. He was sixty-six years old, with a badly scarred body from which a countless number of bullets and shrapnel had been removed during his two-year tour of duty in the Vietnam war. He was missing the index finger from his right hand. Mel, who had cared for a number of war veterans while working at the V.A. hospital, remembered some of her patients telling her stories of having their fingers amputated as a torture tactic in prisoner of war camps. She shuddered, wondering if Loren Allimore had lost his missing digit through the same horrific means.

There was no question, however, about how the most recent loss of part of his anatomy had occurred. He'd had his prostate removed the day before after a diagnosis of cancer had been made. It had spread to his lymph nodes, and imaging revealed lesions on his liver. He would be starting chemo as quickly as possible after recovering from surgery. Mel had cared for countless patients who had suffered even more traumatic experiences in their lives, and had been given diagnoses that were even less hopeful than Mr. Allimore's. Still, for a reason she couldn't quite discern, her heart was aching for him.

Perhaps it was because of the story that had been shared with her at report by Cassie, the nurse who had cared for him through the night. Mr. Allimore had awoken around midnight, whimpering as if in terrible pain, but lacking the strength to cry out more loudly. His roommate, hearing Mr. Allimore's distress, pressed the call button for help on his behalf. Cassie arrived to find that Mr. Allimore's blanket and gown were lying on the floor, and his sheets drenched with sweat. He had torn out his I.V. from all of the tossing and turning in his bed, and a steady flow of blood was dripping from his arm. It took Cassie and a fellow nurse to calm him down, start a new I.V., put a new gown on him, and make a quick call to the doctor, which resulted in orders for a stronger sedative. Several moments later, Mr. Allimore had finally returned to sleep, but the way that he whimpered and trembled throughout the rest of the night made Cassie wonder just how restful it really was.

Approaching his bedside, Mel watched him sleep. At last, he seemed to be enjoying a sedative-induced rest, free from the stressful thrashing and crying out that had plagued him during the night.

He looked so much older than sixty-six, Mel thought to herself. His face seemed rugged and weary, as if each wrinkle and crease in his skin were scars from wounds he had sustained in combat.

Mel looked down at his right hand and shuddered when she saw the gap where his index finger had once been. Her heart wrenched. This man had known a great deal of pain in his life, she knew. All she wanted to do in that moment was take it away. Without knowing what else to do, she rested her own hand on his disfigured one, and held it there for a long moment.

***

When Brad stepped into the room to introduce himself to his patient, he found her sleeping soundly on her side, facing away from him. She had just been admitted to the unit from the Emergency Room, shortly after the change of shift. The nurse who had transported her to the unit handed Brad the chart and rattled off a quick report, but his mind had been so focused on his Sue and Andrea that he hadn't paid close attention. He took a minute to scan through the patient's chart.

Lee Matthews, age 26, had been diagnosed with bilateral post-op infection from a breast surgery that she had undergone in a hospital in Florida just the week before.

Brad wrinkled his brow with confusion. Donna almost always assigned patients with diagnoses involving the genitals or breasts to a caregiver of the same gender.

I'm the only male nurse on the unit right now, and Donna gives me a female patient who is post-op from a breast surgery? Why not one of the female nurses?

He looked over her lab report and the doctor's notes from the E.D. He couldn't find any mention of the type of breast surgery the patient had undergone. When he was done reading, he glanced up at Lee again. Although she was sleeping on her side, he could tell that she was a very small person. Maybe five feet tall. Her weight was recorded as one hundred and two pounds. Her slender shoulder and her arm that rested on her side were indicative of a petite frame hidden under the covers. It appeared that she had very little body fat and most likely hadn't needed a therapeutic breast reduction. And because of her young age, Brad guessed that she hadn't undergone tissue biopsies; at least not in both breasts at once. That left one likely possibility – breast augmentation surgery.

The out of state hospital raised a red flag in his mind. Brad had seen this kind of thing before. Young women who didn't have much money but who dreamed of having perfect bodies would travel great distances out of state – sometimes even out of the country – to go under the knife at the hands of inexperienced or unqualified surgeons who performed cosmetic procedures. The surgeons would cut corners wherever they could in order to cut direct costs. Many of them operated on a cash-only basis. Their practices were unethical at best; illegal at worst. They advertised their services in celebrity and fashion magazines, and through spam emails. The idea of buying beauty at a fraction of the regular price was alluring, Brad knew, but he wondered how many women took the time to read the fine print and ask the important questions about the safety of the surgeries. Ironically, many of those young women developed post-op complications and ended up with costly hospitalizations that they had hoped to avoid in the first place. Glancing at the I.V. pumping antibiotics into Lee's arm, Brad guessed that Lee Matthews was the latest victim of a cheap cosmetic surgery gone bad.

Looking at the masses of long, shiny blonde hair cascading down the patient's back, he guessed that she was a very pretty young woman. Just as pretty as all the other patients he'd seen in this same situation before; women who were beautiful just as they were but who were convinced that they needed surgery to be perfect.

He shook his head sadly, and found himself thinking of Sue. To Brad, she had always been stunning. But when Sue looked in the mirror, she didn't see the same person that he did. She wouldn't set foot outside of the house without first spending hours on her meticulous grooming routine. Even for a simple trip to the mailbox, there were self-imposed requirements that Sue had to have in place: makeup, a glamorous hairstyle, fashionable clothes, and almost always a push-up bra underneath it all. Sue had brought up the topic of a breast augmentation a few times during the three years that they had been together. She truly thought that she needed it, and at one point, had gone to a consult with a surgeon. But Brad talked her out of it. He told her about all of the risks and potential complications of surgery. He told her that he loved her just the way she was. No surgery could ever make her more beautiful in his eyes.

And even after she had returned home unannounced from Croatia; even as angry and confused as he was about the entire situation; and even though he was still giving her the cold shoulder and making her sleep on the sofa, she was still beautiful to him.

Lee took Brad's thoughts away from Sue when she mumbled something in her sleep and stretched out her arm. She shifted slightly, and rolled onto her back.

When Brad saw her face, he could almost feel his jaw drop. Lee Matthews was more than just beautiful. She was angelic. Her skin was porcelain and flawless. Her nose was small and rounded. Her lips were a perfect cupid's bow. Although her eyes were closed, he had a feeling that they were her most beautiful and memorable feature.

For a moment, all he could do was stare.

He felt his heart begin to pound.

Lee not only reminded him of Sue. She looked like Sue.

***

"Everyone, this is Prateeka Patel," Donna announced cheerily. She had invited Med-Surg South's latest addition to the staff to come and meet her new colleagues at work. Donna had gathered all five of the nurses working first shift to say hello, and each of them introduced themselves to her one by one.

Prateeka gave a friendly wave. "Hello, everyone," she said. Then she looked up and smiled as she read the welcome sign that Donna had posted earlier that day. "Oh, how sweet!" she said, her eyes sparkling with excitement.

"That's not all we have for you," Donna said. "I hope you're hungry!" She led Prateeka to the break room, where the nurses had assembled a buffet from the foods that they had prepared. Paper plates, cups, napkins, and plasticware waited at the corner of the table closest to the door.

"Oh," Prateeka said, looking out across the display of steaming crock pots and covered dishes. "This is so very nice of you," she said. "There is so much food here! I'm still quite full from the huge breakfast they gave us in orientation this morning."

"Hope you can make room for more," Miriam said.

"Guest of honor goes first," Haylie said, handing her a plate. "Make sure you get some of my cheese dip. It's the best!"

Prateeka nodded politely. "Thank you. What a warm welcome!" She picked up a paper plate, and the rest of the nurses filed in line behind her. Each of the nurses prepared a plate of their own and took a seat. The table was full, so each of the nurses grabbed a seat and balanced their plates on their laps.

"You're right, Haylie," Brad said, in between nacho chips. "You make the best cheese dip I've ever tasted."

"And I'm loving the Swedish meatballs, Miriam," said Donna, covering her mouth as she chewed and spoke at the same time.

"So Prateeka," Miriam said, "won't you tell us a bit about you?"

At the mention of her name, she looked up from her plate and smiled. "What a tremendous question! What would you like to know?"

"How long have you been a nurse?" Haylie asked.

"I graduated nursing school six months ago," she said. "I worked in a hospital in Mumbai for a short while, and then I met my husband, Samir. He was at home visiting family, and we were introduced to each other."

"Wow," Mel said. "So you guys didn't date for very long. When did you get married?"

"Two weeks ago," Prateeka said. "We had a beautiful wedding. And we actually didn't date at all. You have heard of arranged marriages, yes?"

Haylie winced. "Do people still do that?"

"Yes, they do," Prateeka said. "It's very common in India. We see marriage not as an individual decision, but a family decision. Our families have known each other for many years. They thought that we would be a good match for each other, so they introduced us. Of course, Samir and I had both been meeting other people to consider for marriage through our families. But in the end, we chose each other."

"So your parents didn't make the decision for you?" Haylie asked.

"Not exactly," Prateeka laughed. "I got to make the decision too. We decided as a family."

"So tell us about the lucky guy," Brad said.

"He is a medical student," Prateeka replied. "He graduates in seven months, and he is hoping to find a residency here in Dogwood."

"What specialty?" Donna asked.

"Internal Medicine," Prateeka said with a nod. "His father is also a physician, and that is his specialty as well."

"So you guys just got married, but you aren't living together?" Haylie asked. She looked confused.

"Not yet.   He will move to Dogwood when he finishes medical school."

"I can't imagine getting married and then having to go your separate ways," Haylie said with a frown. "Did you even have a honeymoon?"

Prateeka laughed. "No," she said. "We didn't have time. For Samir it would be impossible to take time away from medical school right now, and I was anxious to move to the United States and begin my nursing career. And we both wanted to save our money to buy a house, so no honeymoon."

"How did you end up here in Dogwood?" Mel asked.

"I know a couple of other nurses who live here in the area," Prateeka said. "We went to nursing school together in India, and they have been working here at Dogwood for the past year. Perhaps you know them? Anupa works on Med-Surg North, and Priya works on the Neuro unit. They really like it here."

"The names sound familiar," said Brad. "How about you, Prateeka? Do you like Dogwood so far?"

"Yes, I do," Prateeka smiled. "Everyone has been very nice."

"Nice and nosy, right?" Miriam asked. All of the nurses laughed.

They continued their friendly interrogation of Prateeka for the next twenty minutes. Finally, she raised her wrist to the level of her eyes looked at her watch. "Oh dear," she said. "It's almost time for me to get back to orientation." She rose to her feet.

"Hey, what's that on your hands?" Haylie asked, rising to her feet as well. She took a step closer to Prateeka, bending slightly at the waist to lean in for a closer look.

Prateeka raised one of her hands up for all of her new colleagues to see. They were covered with intricate designs of a reddish-brown color. "It's mendhi," she said. "From my wedding. It's a tradition in India for the bride to have her hands and feet painted with henna. It stains the skin, but fades away after a few weeks."

"It's beautiful," Donna said, as she stood up and reached for Prateeka's wrist, drawing her hand closer for a better view.

Haylie raised an eyebrow at Donna.

"Absolutely gorgeous," Mel agreed, stepping closer to look.

"Thank you," Prateeka beamed. "And thank you very much for the food. I look forward to seeing you tomorrow."

"I'll take your plate for you," Haylie offered as Prateeka stepped past her, moving toward the door.

"Thank you, Haylie," she said, and smiled as she left the break room.

The five nurses waited until Prateeka was out of earshot and began to compare notes.

"She seems sweet," Mel said.

"She's very pretty," Miriam remarked. "She's got the most beautiful skin and eyes, don't you think? And her hair is so dark and shiny. She's a lovely young lady."

"She sure is," Donna said. "And her English is perfect. What a beautiful accent she has."

Haylie looked around the room at her colleagues. "Why does she talk with a British accent?" She asked. "I mean, she's from India, right? So why does she speak like she's from England? It sounds kind of snooty to me."

Donna shrugged. "Maybe that's how she learned to speak," she said.

"I liked that stuff on her hands," said Mel. "What did she call it? Henda? Hendi?"

"Mendhi," Haylie corrected her. "The ink is made

from henna. I noticed that right off the bat and I thought it was strange that she'd show up to work with that on her hands. And I was surprised that all of you complimented her on it."

"Why?" Donna asked.

Haylie was perturbed. "Because when I first came to work here, one of my patients saw my tattoo on my lower back and had a fit over it. You told me to buy bigger scrubs so I could cover it up, Donna. Remember?"

Donna nodded. "Of course I remember. Seems just like yesterday that you were our newbie here on Med-Surg South. But Haylie, that's different from what Prateeka has on her hands. You can't compare the two."

Haylie sucked air through her teeth and rolled her eyes with discontent. "Why not? They're both body art, aren't they? Everyone just told Prateeka how gorgeous hers was, yet I was told to cover mine up so I wouldn't offend anybody."

"Prateeka said hers will fade away in a few weeks," Mel said. "So it won't be around forever."

"And with your tattoo, Haylie, all that you had to do was keep it covered up," Miriam said. "Nobody's picking on you, it's just organizational policy."

"Exactly," Brad said. Then he lifted up one of the sleeves of the white thermal shirt he was wearing under his scrubs, revealing a tattoo of a dragon wrapped around his upper arm. "I got this when I was in the Navy, but when I came to work here, Donna told me the same thing, that I'd have to keep it covered. So that's why I always wear long-sleeved shirts under my scrubs, whether it's hot or cold, rain or shine."

"And Prateeka will be wearing gloves most of the time that she'll be taking care of her patients, so hers will be covered up too," Mel interjected. "That is, until it fades."

Haylie crossed her arms over her chest. "I feel like you guys are all ganging up on me," she said.

"We're not ganging up on you," Donna said.

"Well you sure were kissing Prateeka's butt. We barely even know her, and already, everyone here just acts like she's the greatest thing since sliced bread. Everything about her is just so charming and wonderful."

"Haylie," Donna said firmly, "is there a problem?"

"No," she said with a slight shrug. "It's just that I didn't get that warm of a welcome when I came to work here."

"Oh come on. We made you a welcome sign just like Prateeka's," Mel said.

"Yeah, but no covered dish party for me. And by the way, if you had served me food, I would have at least been polite enough to eat it." She held up Prateeka's plate in one hand. A half of a carrot and a piece of raw broccoli remained. "Check this out," she said.

"What?" Mel asked with a laugh. "Are you mad because she didn't clean her plate? Looks like she's going to be a real troublemaker."

Haylie shot Mel a dirty look. "Didn't you notice? All she did was pick up a few things from the veggie tray. She didn't try the cheese dip, or the Swedish meatballs, or Donna's eclairs. How rude is that? I mean, we all spent money to buy that food, and we spent our own time and energy preparing it, but apparently she thinks she's too good to eat what we put together."

"Chill out, Haylie," Brad said. "Maybe she just wasn't hungry. She did say that she ate a big breakfast in orientation."

"Whatever," Haylie said. "I think it was just a huge slap in our faces for us to make all of this food and the guest of honor didn't even want to taste any of it. You all can think what you want, but I'm insulted."

Donna cleared her throat. "Try not to take it personally, Haylie. Prateeka starts work here tomorrow, and I'm expecting that you'll be as polite, helpful, and kind to her as you wanted people to treat you on your very first day on the job as a nurse. You remember what your first day was like, don't you?"

Haylie groaned. "Do I ever."

"So put yourself in Prateeka's shoes tomorrow morning when she comes to work, and make yourself remember what you felt like when you were the brand new nurse, just getting started on Med-Surg South. She's going to need a lot of mentoring and coaching, just like you did when you first started your career. Actually, she'll need even more than you did, because she just moved to a new country and she has a lot of adjustments to make. So be patient and understanding with her, Haylie. Try to see the world through her eyes."

Chapter 8
Monday Afternoon

Haylie looked down at Prateeka's plate again, then turned and tossed it into the trash can behind her. "I just wish that everyone had been that warm and fuzzy when I came to work here," she mumbled to herself.

"Viola! Antibiotics are officially on board now," Miriam said, after administering Ampicillin through Daphne's I.V. line.

Daphne laughed. "Viola!" She repeated. "That's what I'm talking about, Miriam. That little dramatic flair of yours. It's perfect. You're a natural born actor."

"If you say so. Where's your pain right now on a scale of one to ten?"

"Hmmm…. it's four or five-ish. Tolerable."

"Good. Let me know if it goes higher than a four or five, or becomes intolerable."

"I most certainly will. And you let me know when you want to set up that audition."

Miriam laughed as she checked Daphne's vitals. "Well, I have been thinking about it. I'll audition for your play if you can do something for me."

"What's that?"

"I'm not quite sure yet. I need your help, but I don't know what it would involve." Miriam sighed loudly as she planted herself in the bedside chair again.

"This sounds sinister. You're not going to ask me to rob a bank with you or something like that, are you? Listen, Miriam, I don't think you want me driving the getaway car."

"No, it's nothing like that, Daphne."

"I'm kidding of course. Why so serious all of a sudden?"

Miriam took a deep breath and exhaled slowly. "I need somebody to talk to. I haven't shared this with anyone else yet, but I'm having problems with my eyesight. I'm scared I'm going--"

"Blind?" Daphne interrupted her.

"Pretty much."

Quickly shifting back to a more serious tone of voice, Daphne continued. "Well how timely that you'd meet such a cool blind person like me. Not a person living with blindness, not a person who is blind—"

"A blind person. I get it." Miriam said. "Trust me, you've indoctrinated me."

"I'm not trying to pick on you," Daphne said. "It's just that some wacky nurse came into my room and told me yesterday that having a sense of humor can help me heal up faster, know what I mean?"

"Yes, I remember," Miriam said.

"Well, I certainly don't mean to make light of your situation. You sound scared. Tell me what's going on."

"It's been happening for a while now, and is getting worse. Sometimes things look fuzzy. Sometimes I see these little black spots. It's getting harder to read things, both close up and far away."

"I take it you've been to see an eye doctor?"

"Six months ago. I've got a family history of macular degeneration. He gave me a prescription for eye drops and put me on vitamins for eye health. He said to follow up if things weren't getting any better. Needless to say, they're not getting better, so I made an appointment to go back to see him tomorrow. But thanks to Hurricane Fortuna, his office canceled the appointment."

"Stupid hurricane," Daphne said. "I can't believe the doctor would cancel your appointment for such a frivolous reason."

Miriam smiled. "They rescheduled me for next week. It's going to be the longest wait of my life."

"Well, that's aggravating."

"It sure is. I'm on pins and needles. Of course I can't do anything about it right now, but I also can't think about anything else right now. I haven't said one word about it to my co-workers, nor my family. I don't want anyone to start worrying about me, not right now anyway. I don't know what I'm up against and what can be done about it, so I don't want people flipping out about it prematurely."

"That's understandable. I'm very honored that you felt like you could talk to me about it."

"I don't usually open up like this at work. We're here to take care of our patients and listen to them, not the other way around. But I'm really glad I met you, Daphne. You give me hope."

She smiled. "I do? Why is that?"

"The thought of blindness scares me to death. But I look at someone like you, and suddenly it doesn't seem so scary. You're successful and smart and you've accomplished more in your young life than most people with perfect vision accomplish in their lifetimes. You've got something that a lot of people in this world would call a disability, and yet you haven't let it hold you back from doing anything. In fact, it's part of what makes you so special. You've got this unique perspective in life, and you're using it to create and inspire… and help others."

For once, Daphne was at a loss for words. "Really?" She finally said, after a long pause, and smiled. "You think I'm helping others?"

"You've helped me tremendously already. Like I told you, you give me hope."

"Awww… thanks Miriam. I'm touched that you would say that."

"You said that you see the world through other eyes. But what I'd really like to do is see the world through yours. Like what you're going through right now. What's it like to be in the hospital after surgery, without being able to see everything going on around you? What does it sound like and smell like and feel like for you? I mean, I may be in that very position someday myself, so I want to know. I want to be able to see this entire experience the way that you do. Does that make sense?"

Laughing, Daphne nodded. "It makes perfect sense. If that's all you need from me, then I think I can help you out."

"You can?" Miriam leaned in expectantly.

"When I teach acting classes, I assign characters to my students. The students' job, prior to a performance, is to do character research and character building. The character could be, for instance, a disgruntled cab driver. So the best thing that the student could do is call a taxi and ride around with a real-life cab driver to observe his world. See all the sights, hear all the sounds and smell all the smells of life behind the wheel of a cab. Find out what it is that's got him so disgruntled. Is it the traffic? Is it people who don't tip? The student has to figure it out and discover who that character really is. So we can do the same thing with you, Miriam. You want to know what it's like to be a patient in the hospital without sight? Well, there's an empty bed right next to mine. Put on a blindfold and spend some time recuperating with me. I'll be your cab driver into the world of blind living. What do you say?"

Miriam pondered the proposal. "Well, that's a bit unconventional... but it sounds interesting."

"So let's do it."

"I would, except I've got all these other darned patients to take care of," she joked.

"How about tomorrow?"

"I've got the day off," Miriam admitted.

"So let's do it then."

"Wow... I don't know, Daphne. Let me think about it."

"What's there to think about? I'm offering you the chance to be blind for a day. You just said a moment ago that you wanted to see the world through my eyes, so here's your chance."

Miriam smiled. "Well... okay, why not. But I do need to run it by my manager, Donna, of course."

"Tell her it's a professional development activity. Personalized sensitivity training or something like that."

"That's one way to spin it," Miriam said. "You know, we actually have participated in trainings like that before. We went to a class that simulated what it's like to be a resident in a nursing home. The facilitators put restraints on us, made us eat baby food, and yelled at us really loud, like we couldn't hear them. It wasn't very pleasant, and definitely made us all think twice about the way that patients in long term care are treated."

"Oh that stinks. I wouldn't be that brutal to you."

"I'm sure you wouldn't. But maybe a professional development activity is exactly what it would be, so it's entirely possible we could make it happen."

"So talk to your boss, get her blessing and let's do it. And if it goes well and you pass as a blind patient, then maybe we'll consider that your audition for the part of Claire's mother. What do you think, Miriam?"

"Deal," Miriam said. "I've actually got a meeting with her this afternoon so I'll bring it up then."

"Excellent. I have no doubt that you'll do just fine as a blind patient... and that you'll be the hottest star on Dogwood's red carpet. Your name will be in lights – whether you can see it or not!"

***

Lee Matthews had slept through the morning. When she finally awakened, Brad was standing over her, checking her vitals.

As he had guessed, she had beautiful eyes. They were so blue they made Brad think of the ocean. He felt his stomach flip flop and his knees grow weak.

"Hello there," Brad said. "My name is Brad. I'm taking care of you today."

"Hi," Lee replied groggily. She rubbed her eyes. "What time is it?"

"A little after one o'clock." Brad found himself consciously slowing down as he went through the motions of taking her blood pressure and temperature, a routine which he repeated several times a day and could normally accomplish in under a minute on any given patient.

"I can't believe I've been sleeping all this time. I guess I needed it." Lee yawned and stretched out her arms.

"So how are you feeling today? What's your pain on a scale of one to ten?" Brad asked.

"Better. The pain is definitely easing up. It's only about a 3 right now. Do you need to take a look?"

Brad could feel his face reddening with a deep blush. "Not unless your pain isn't under control or if you're having any other problems. The doctor will be in this morning to look at your incisions, and see how they're healing up." Flustered, Brad blinked and looked away. He was certain that she could sense his embarrassment.

What's wrong with me? He wondered. *I'm a nurse, she's my patient, so why am I feeling this awkward?*

"Am I going to get lunch or something soon?" Lee asked, breaking his train of thought. "I'm starving. I didn't eat much at all yesterday."

"Yes. Dietary should be delivering a tray to you shortly."

"Great," she said. "I'm so hungry, even hospital food sounds good right now. No offense," she said.

"None taken," he laughed. "I don't do the cooking around here. Which is probably a good thing. If I were in charge, everyone would get Hungry Man TV dinners. I can't cook worth a hoot."

Lee laughed, and a chill went up Brad's spine. The sweet, goofy, high-pitched trill of her voice reminded him again of Sue. Who was still at home in the apartment, still sleeping on the sofa at night. He was still too angry to speak to her.

And Andrea was still refusing to speak to him. He had called her every day since Sue had returned. He left voice mails each time, but they were not returned.

"Believe it or not, I love Hungry Man TV dinners," Lee said.

"Are you for real?" Brad laughed.

"The meatloaf is my favorite."

"No way! Mine too."

And Andrea's too, he thought to himself, and his stomach went sour for a moment. He was suddenly struck by a memory from their second date. Instead of going out, they had chosen to watch the Yankees vs. Red Sox game over dinner at Brad's apartment. Andrea burned her thumb while pulling two meatloaf TV dinners out of the oven. She jokingly asked Brad to kiss her thumb well, so he did. Then she smiled at him. My turn, she said, and kissed him on the lips. It was their first kiss. He wondered if he would ever get to kiss her again, and it overwhelmed him with sadness and confusion.

"Well you know what they say. Great minds think alike," Lee said with another Sue-like laugh. Then she glanced up briefly at the TV, distracted by a commercial for Reese's peanut butter cups on the screen. "Actually, that sounds pretty darn good right now," she pointed at the glistening, brown liquid chocolate gushing like a waterfall down the TV screen. "I'll be the happiest woman alive once I get out of here. First stop, candy counter," she said.

"Sometimes chocolate is the best medicine," Brad said and forced a smile. He was thankful that Lee was so friendly and in such good spirits, and that she had helped pull his thoughts away from his troubled love life. "Lunch should be here soon, though. Is there anything else I can do for you right now?"

"No, I think I'm okay," Lee said. "Thanks." She smiled at Brad once more as he turned and walked out of her room.

At the nurse's station, Brad checked Lee's medical record. Normal diet, it said. No restrictions. He looked at his watch. He had a break coming up in a couple of hours.

And the hospital gift shop, he knew, had Reese's cups.

***

Donna pulled her office door closed as Miriam settled into the seat facing her desk.

Miriam feigned a nervous look. "What's going on, boss lady? Am I in big trouble or something? Closing the door always makes me break a sweat."

Donna laughed heartily. "No, Miriam. You know you've got nothing to worry about. I'm just trying to minimize distractions, that's all. You only get a performance review once a year, so I want this time to be all yours in case you've got questions or things you want to discuss."

"Nothing major right now. Just hit me with my scores."

Donna grinned. "I can always count on you to cut straight to the chase."

"I'm a no nonsense kind of gal."

"I know. Anyway," Donna said, reaching into a file folder, "here's an official copy of your performance review, with my notes. Go ahead and read over it, and let me know if there's anything you'd like to talk about."

Miriam donned her reading glasses, which were dangling on a chain around her neck. She held the pages of her performance appraisal at eye level, squinting to read them.

"Can you read it okay?" Donna asked, taking note of Miriam's efforts.

"Just barely. I think we should send you to one of those handwriting classes though. Where did you learn how to write, Donna? Chicken Scratch Elementary School?"

"Oh, it's not that bad. Just read."

After Miriam finished reading, she stood up, took a bow, and handed the paper back to Donna.

"As Dogwood Regional Medical Center's Nurse of the Year, I'd like to thank my manager, Donna..."

Donna doubled in laughter. "Sit down, you clown."

Miriam passed the written performance appraisal back to Donna. "What I mean, of course, is thank you. I couldn't be happier with the scoring and comments."

"And it's all very well deserved," Donna said with sincerity. "You've given Med-Surg South many years of excellent service, and you continue to go above and beyond the call of duty. I particularly appreciate how flexible you've been with your scheduling lately, and for being willing to come in some of the days that you were supposed to be off. You've been a good sport about the whole thing."

Miriam blushed slightly. "I'm glad I can be of help. But whenever I retire, you're going to have to start picking on the youngsters for a change."

Donna groaned. "I know, I know. Trust me, you don't have to remind me. Just give me plenty of heads up once you make the decision."

"Oh, I will," Miriam said. "Be looking for the news to come soon."

Donna's eyes grew wide. "How soon, exactly?"

Shrugging, Miriam sensed Donna's nervousness and looked away. "I don't know. Within the next couple of years, I suppose. I guess I'll know when the time is right."

"I'm seriously going to miss you, you know. When the time comes, that is."

Miriam nodded. "Yeah. I'll miss you too. But I'm not ready just yet. So until I give you the news that I am, let's just forge ahead. Business as usual."

Donna nodded. "Business as usual," she repeated. "And with that said, I do need some help with one part of your performance appraisal before I turn it in to HR."

Miriam made eye contact with Donna again. "Which part?" She asked, curiously.

"The professional growth and development. I'm truly at a loss for what to put down in that section. You've been in nursing for more than thirty years, and almost half of them have been spent right here on Med-Surg South. You've been precepting, you've participated in a ton of hospital-wide committees and task forces, and quality projects, you've done research, and you're up to date on all of your continuing ed. So I'm asking you, Miriam, what else would you like to learn or accomplish during your career that you've not had the chance to do just yet?"

Miriam wrinkled her brow. "Good question. Actually, I had an opportunity present itself just today."

"Okay," Donna said, poised with her pen and ready to complete the last section of Miriam's performance evaluation. "Shoot."

"I want to be blind."

Donna looked up. "What?"

"Well, not literally. What I mean is, one of my patients – Daphne Wylie – she's blind. And I'm very impressed with her. If you could spend five minutes around her, Donna, you'd begin to wonder how blindness was ever considered a disability. She's simply amazing, and I want to see everything the way she does. Well, not see, literally… but you know what I mean."

Donna planted her elbows on her desk and rested her chin in her hands. "Okay, you've got my attention."

"And I've got an idea. Actually, it was her idea..."

Chapter 9
Monday Evening

Brad peeked into Lee's room on the way to clock out. "Hey," he smiled at her. "How are you feeling?"

Lee looked away from the television and focused on Brad. "I'm okay. I'm not hurting up here," she said, pointing to her chest, "but when I used the bathroom earlier, it hurt. Like stinging, when I urinated."

Brad frowned. "Ouch. It sounds like you may have a urinary tract infection coming on. Those can be really painful."

Lee nodded and looked nervous. "Why would I get that?"

"Well, you've got a bacterial infection in your surgical wounds, so it may be that the bacteria has spread elsewhere in your body, and a secondary infection has developed in your urinary tract." He frowned slightly, and shut his mouth to hold back the questions that were on his tongue.

What were you thinking? Why did you go all the way out of state to have a cheap cosmetic surgery? Why would you risk your health and your life for a stupid boob job? Can't you see how beautiful you already are?

She frowned in return, mirroring his concern. "So all of these antibiotics that I'm taking... won't they kill the bacteria that spreads too?"

Brad shrugged. "It depends. It could be a different type of infection, or it's possible that it's not even an infection at all. It may just be an irritation. But I will let your next nurse know. My shift is over, and I've got to go give report to the nurse who will be taking care of you tonight."

"Okay," Lee said with a nod. "Will you be back tomorrow?"

Brad nodded. "I sure will."

"Cool," she said with a slight grin. "Drive home safely tonight."

"I will."

Lee glanced at the TV. "I've been watching the news, and they're saying that the hurricane is headed straight for us. They're projecting that it will make landfall sometime Wednesday night or early Thursday morning. And I can hear the wind out there, too. It's getting stronger. At times it sounds like it's going to blow the window right in."

"Oh, don't worry, I seriously doubt that would happen," Brad said. "You're safe and sound."

"I know I'm in good hands while I'm here," Lee said, and flashed a smile that made Brad go weak in the knees. "My doctor said I may be able to get discharged as early as tomorrow. I'm just wondering how the heck I'm going to get home if there's a hurricane spinning over Dogwood."

"It will be okay," Brad assured her. "The hospital is setting up a temporary shelter for employees, family members and patients who are waiting to be admitted or else have been discharged and are stuck here while it's unsafe to drive. We have a conference center on the first floor of the hospital. All of the tables, chairs and audiovisual equipment were moved out of there to make room for cots."

She exhaled a sigh of relief. "Good. I sure wouldn't want to risk my life or anyone else's driving home in bad weather."

Brad wrinkled his brow. "Don't you have someone who can come pick you up?"

Lee shook her head from side to side. "I just moved to Dogwood a few weeks ago. I haven't made a lot of friends in the area yet."

"What about family?" He asked.

Frowning slightly, Lee shook her head again. "Nope. Not a soul. All of my family live in Kentucky."

He leaned against the door frame. "So what brought you to North Carolina? If you don't mind me asking?"

"It's fine," Lee said. "I guess I just needed a change. We vacationed in Dogwood when I was a kid, and I've always had fond memories of being here. It was a great escape back when I was young, so I thought it would be a great place to escape to as a grown-up, too."

Brad nodded. "So how's life in Dogwood so far?"

Lee rolled her eyes and shook her head. "Ugh. That's a loaded question. These first few weeks have been pretty rough. For starters, the moving van delivered my stuff to the wrong address, and it took days for them to re-route it to the right place. Which screwed up my shot at getting a job. I had an interview lined up, but didn't have the right clothes to wear to it, and I couldn't afford to go out and buy a new outfit after having blown so much money on the move."

"That really stinks."

"Yeah it does. Well, the moving van finally made it, and I got some more interviews lined up. But then I went down to Florida last week for my surgery. The timing was terrible, but I had scheduled it a long time ago and if I had tried to reschedule, it would have meant another long wait. Anyway, the surgery went smoothly. Everything seemed to be going fine after I was discharged, and I was feeling great. But then I got back home to Dogwood, and what do you know, this infection hit me. So I went to an Urgent Care center thinking I would just get some antibiotics and go home, but they sent me to the Emergency Room. Next thing I know, here I am."

"And don't forget the hurricane headed this way. As if everything else that has happened to you wasn't enough already." Brad said. He shook his head sympathetically. "I'm sorry to hear that things got off to such a rough start. Hopefully they'll get better for you, Lee."

"It's okay," she said, and her face brightened with a smile. "In spite of all the chaos, everyone in Dogwood has been so nice to me. People haven't always been so kind in other places where I've lived. It's not something I take for granted."

You've got to be kidding, Brad fought the urge to say aloud. *As pretty and personable as you are, why in the world wouldn't people be nice to you? Men would be knocking each other out just to hold the door for you, and women would be lining up to be your friend.* "Well, I'm glad you've found a home here," he said instead, "and that you feel welcome."

"Thanks, Brad," Lee replied.

His stomach flip-flopped when she said his name. "I hope you have a good evening, Lee. I've got to head home." He reached into his pocket and pulled out a package of Reese's cups, then stepped into her room and placed it on her bedside tray. "Here's your feel-better remedy for the evening. Enjoy."

Her jaw dropped and her eyes grew wide. "Reese's!" She gasped. "Oh wow... thank you so much!"

"You're welcome," he said. "Good night, Lee."

"Heck yeah, it's going to be a good night! I've got chocolate!" She was already reaching for the candy. "You're my hero, Brad!"

He smiled as he stepped out of her room.

Chapter 10
Tuesday Morning

When Haylie arrived at work, she was surprised to find that Prateeka was already there, waiting at the nurse's desk in a fresh new set of scrubs, with a stethoscope draped around her neck. Her employee name badge shined, and Haylie cringed when she saw just how flattering her photo was. Prateeka's hair looked neat and perfect. Her eyes were bright, and her smile was perfectly framed with freshly glossed lips.

Haylie glanced down at her own for just a moment, silently cursing herself for having neglected to put more effort into her appearance on her first day at work. Little had she known at the time that her choice to skip on makeup that morning and her bad hair day would be captured on film and put on display for years to come as her Dogwood Regional Hospital employee name badge photo.

Haylie frowned slightly at the beautiful, smiling face of the Indian nurse, forever preserved on her name badge. Then she looked up at the real Prateeka, who was every bit as beautiful as her photo, and smiling with first-day-on-the-job enthusiasm.

"Good morning Haylie," Prateeka said.

"Hey. Good morning." Haylie nodded slightly.

As if Prateeka had been reading her mind, her eyes diverted to Haylie's name badge on her chest. She read the wording, then looked at the picture.

"I like your photo," she said.

I hate you, Haylie thought, and pinched her lips together to avoid saying the words out loud. "Are you serious?" She asked instead. "This is a horrible picture of me."

"I don't think so. I like it," Prateeka said. "Your hair looks very nice when it is pulled back that way. You look very professional. Very mature. And you have such pretty eyes."

Now you're just kissing up, Haylie thought. *A little late for that!* "Uh… thanks," she said. "So, Donna said that she wanted me to do part of your unit orientation with you. Just a quick tour around the unit."

"Oh, thank you," Prateeka said. "I'm so excited about working here. How long have you been working on the unit, Haylie?"

"A year and a half," she said proudly.

"Oh, so you are new, like me!" Prateeka smiled.

Haylie wrinkled her brow and frowned. "I'm not that new," she said. "A year and a half is a pretty long time."

"Yes, it must feel like forever," Prateeka said. "But you are young like me. You're the newest nurse on the unit, yes?"

"No. You are."

Prateeka laughed. "I meant other than me."

"Well… yes."

"Then I am in good company. We'll learn our way together and help each other, yes?"

Thoroughly irritated, Haylie glared at her. "I don't need that much help. I know what I'm doing."

Prateeka relented and gave a friendly smile. "Then I will do the learning, and you can help me when I need it."

"Right," Haylie said. "Who is your preceptor, anyway?"

"It is Mel. Did she precept you as well?"

Haylie's face melted into an expression of disdain. "No. I had Miriam."

"She seems very nice."

"She wasn't at the time. I asked for Mel, but Donna said no."

"Everything must have turned out alright. You and Miriam seem friendly now. All of you, actually, seem to make a good team."

"We are," Haylie said. "We're like a family on this unit."

"And now I get to be part of your family," Prateeka beamed.

Yes, apparently you do, Haylie thought. Her gut wrenched, but she didn't speak. *Just like that, Prateeka, welcome to the team. You walk onto this unit and everyone automatically likes you. Then you get a preceptor that actually treats you kindly, and nobody picks on the funky ink on your hands or makes fun of you because you're inexperienced. You got the welcome that I should have had. And now you have the nerve to compare me to you? You call me young and new, just like we're walking onto this unit together fresh out of nursing school? Well, I have news for you. I've been here a good long while, and I've paid my dues. I've suffered through some rough treatment on this unit, and it took some work for me to be accepted. Why did I have to go through all that, but you don't? It's not fair.*

***

It was time to check Mr. Allimore's vitals, and Mel didn't want to wake him.

Tiptoeing to the side of his bed, she pressed the button to inflate his BP cuff. It beeped softly, and Mr. Allimore turned his head from side to side a bit, mumbling in his sleep. He shifted his arm as the cuff began to tighten around it. Then he startled awake.

"Sorry to wake you," Mel said softly. "I'll be done in just a second."

Upon seeing her, his eyes grew wide. He gasped and shrank back against his pillow. Then, without warning, he let out a bloodcurdling scream. Mr. Allimore drew back his fist and punched Mel in the face, knocking her to the floor.

***

Miriam peered into Daphne's room, relieved to find that the second bed remained empty. Believing that Daphne was asleep, and not wanting to wake her, Miriam stepped softly to the empty bed.

"Good morning, roomie," Daphne said, after Miriam had taken three steps.

"I thought you were sleeping," said Miriam. "Sorry to wake you."

"You didn't wake me. I was just resting."

"I was trying to be super quiet."

"Yeah, I know. But I can smell you."

Miriam stopped and faced Daphne. "So what do I smell like?"

"Well," Daphne began, turning slightly in her bed so that she faced Miriam, "Like baby shampoo. I smelled it on you the other day. It was very faint, but it was there. Like maybe you had been holding a baby, and it had rested its head on your shoulder, leaving some of the fragrance on your clothes."

"Once again, you nailed it. I have a four month-old grandson named Timothy. I stopped by to see him this morning before I came in to the hospital."

"So can you smell it?" Daphne asked.

"What?"

"The baby shampoo."

"No," Miriam said.

"Close your eyes," instructed Daphne. "And take a few deep breaths through your nose."

Miriam stood still and closed her eyes. As Daphne had suggested, she took three deep breaths, and a few more for good measure."

"Can you smell it?"

"A little," Miriam said.

"Cool," Daphne said. "You better go ahead and get in bed," Daphne said. "You shouldn't be on your feet with that cranial rectosis."

"Cranial what?"

"Rectosis. That's your diagnosis. It's the medical term for being a butthead."

Miriam laughed. "Why do I have to be a butthead?"

"Because I'm the teacher. I assign the characters. You're the student. Get in bed, patient with cranial rectosis."

Miriam climbed into the empty bed and positioned two gauze pads over her eyes. With a noisy *riiiiiip*, Miriam stripped a piece of tape from the roll she kept in her pocket. Daphne giggled. Miriam taped the gauze to her right eye, then pulled another piece of tape with an even louder *riiiiiip* than the previous one. Daphne doubled over in her bed with laughter.

"Ow, ow," she said between giggles. "It's hard to crack up like this after surgery. Hurts the gut."

"So quit laughing at me," Miriam said. "I thought you liked this idea, anyway."

"Actually, I think you're a moron," Daphne joked. "I just agreed to go along with it so we could get Brad to be our nurse for the day. Did I mention how gorgeous his voice sounds?"

"You guys talking about me in here?" Brad asked, stepping into the room.

"Yep," Daphne said. "Miriam said she couldn't stand the sight of you anymore, so that's why she had to patch up her eyes and get admitted to the hospital for a day."

Brad laughed. "You're funny," he said to Daphne, then looked at Miriam. "And you look ridiculous."

"That's just the look I was going for," Miriam said, as she reached up and touched the gauze taped over her eyes.

"You can't see anything, can you?" He waved his hand in front of her face.

"Not a thing. Just pitch black."

"Good," Brad said. "I have a feeling I'm going to enjoy being your nurse today. So is there anything I can do for you?"

"Nope. Just leave me alone to suffer with my cranial rectosis." Miriam said with a groan. "Don't ask about my diagnosis."

In the bed next to her, Daphne laughed.

"Okay," Brad said curiously. "But at least tell me, what's the treatment for cranial rectosis?"

"It's very simple," Miriam replied. "Get out of here and leave me alone."

"I can do that," he said. "Is there anything you need before I leave, Daphne?"

"Not a thing," she replied.

Brad took his cue and left the room.

"Brad is hot." Daphne blurted out, after he was out of earshot.

"How do you-"

"Sexy voice," Daphne said. "Let me guess... he's about six feet tall, lean, really handsome... am I right?"

Miriam hesitated for a moment. "Are you SURE you're blind? I don't get it. How do you..."

"I can tell a person's height by where their voice is coming from. Super easy. Short person, voice comes from below. Tall person, voice comes from above. It doesn't take long to be able to match up sound to height fairly accurately, and I've had all my life to test it out. I can pretty much always guess a person's height within an inch or two. And I can tell that Brad's lean because his footsteps are light, and he doesn't move a lot of air around the room when he walks by. And as far as him being handsome, I have no idea what he looks like, but his voice sure sounds gorgeous. Which for me is much more important criteria than a gorgeous face."

"Well, he is a looker," Miriam said.

"Is he single?"

"Honestly, I'm not sure at the moment. You could always ask him."

"No point. It would just be wishful thinking for me. I've got a guy of my own already."

"You little stinker," Miriam said. "What's your boyfriend like?"

"Oh, he's a sweetheart," gushed Daphne. "His name is Dale and he's a big computer geek. He does computer programming, website development and hosting. He's the webmaster for the Dogwood Performing Arts Center, as well as four other organizations."

"Is that how you met him? Through work?"

"No, actually I met him online and we became friends. When I found out how smooth he is with computers, I hired him to develop and maintain a website for the D.P.A.C. He gave me a great discount."

"I bet. Let me guess… did your mother give you a hard time when she first met Dale? Did she think you were too good for him?"

"Hmmmm," Daphne replied. "Now what would give you that idea?"

"I think 'Love Is Blind' was inspired by real-life experiences. Am I right?"

"You'll just have to meet Dale and find out for yourself," she said. "You should be seeing plenty of him during play rehearsals."

"Sneaky."

"That's my middle name. Daphne Sneaky Wylie. Anyway, let's get started, shall we? Welcome to the world of the sightless. I'm your tour guide, Daphne. Keep your hands and feet inside your hospital bed at all times. If, at any time, I can be of assistance, just give a shout out and let me know."

Miriam giggled. "The first time I try to get out of this bed, it's going to be a catastrophe, I'm sure. I imagine I'll be shouting about something or other before the day is done."

"Well shout away," said Daphne.

"Are you sure you're feeling up to this?" Miriam asked. "After all, you did just have surgery. You're supposed to be recuperating."

"Oh trust me, I'm up to it," Daphne said without missing a beat. "And I'm doing this for me more than I am for you."

"Right, I know. You're looking for someone to be in your play."

"More than just that, Miriam. It's boring to be stuck in a hospital bed all day long! I'm too hyper to lay here and relax. I need company. And silly you, I suckered you into thinking that I was doing you a favor!"

"Well then, I suppose this is a mutually beneficial experience," Miriam said.

"Suuure, if it will make you feel better about being conned into giving up a day off to come back into work to be a pretend patient, just go ahead and think so," said Daphne.

Miriam laughed.

"First, let me just make sure you understand something. Putting patches over your eyes for a day isn't really going to show you what it's like to be blind, any more than putting a bra on Brad would help him truly understand what it's like to be a woman. There's way more territory than we could ever cover in one day in this little hospital room, so think of this is as just a glimpse… a scratch of the surface. You know what I mean?"

"Oddly enough, I think I do," said Miriam. "A glimpse is good enough for now."

"How about a glimpse of Brad in a bra?"

"No thanks."

"Got ya. Any questions so far?"

"Yes I do. When did you go blind?"

"Actually, I was born this way."

"You've been blind all your life. What's it like? I mean… never mind. I guess that's a stupid question, isn't it?"

"There are no stupid questions, Miriam. Only stupid people who ask them."

Miriam tried not to laugh.

"But I'm a good sport," said Daphne, "So I'll try and give you an answer anyway. What's it like to be blind? Well… the concept of seeing is about as foreign as it can get to me. I'm aware of how uncomfortable it makes the rest of the world that I'm blind, but as far as I'm concerned, life is good. I feel very 'normal.' I own a home, I've got Dale, I've got a job, I've got a guide dog named Jasper – he's my baby, that is until I get married and have babies of my own someday. Life is good. I have no complaints and I don't ever feel like I'm missing out on anything. Okay, my turn to ask you a question now. What's it like so far? Not being able to see?"

"So far, it's just really, really dark," Miriam said.

"Well how about some TV?" Daphne asked. She reached for her remote control and turned on the television.

Miriam laughed. "Okay," she said. "Enlighten me. How do you watch TV without seeing it?"

"There's this magical thing called 'sound,' you know," said Daphne.

"Oh, I've heard of that," Miriam responded.

"Yep. It's good stuff. Hey, it sounds like an episode of 'Friends' is coming up. Do you like that show?"

"Not particularly," Miriam said, "but if you're a fan, I'll watch. I mean, listen."

"Fair enough," Daphne said.

For the next fifteen minutes, they enjoyed the episode together.

Then Brad entered the room and went to Miriam's bedside.

"I need for you to sign a couple of forms," he said. "For your treatment of cranial rectosis." He placed a clipboard into her lap, and a pen into her hands.

"Hold up," Miriam said. "I can't read these."

"So what are you going to do about it?" Daphne asked.

"I don't know. What should I do?"

"Well, you've got a couple of options," Daphne said. "You can either ask for Braille versions, and use your hands to spend the next couple of hours reading it, or, you can do like the rest of the world. Ask your nurse for a simple explanation of what you're signing and get a copy to take home with you."

"I think I like the second option better," Miriam said. "Brad, what exactly is this you want me to sign?"

"Just a couple of consent forms," he said. "Donna wanted me to simulate a patient care experience for you, so before I can do anything, I need your signature on these."

"Okay," Miriam said. "So explain to me in a nutshell, what I'm consenting to."

"Well," Brad began, "the first form gives us permission to treat you. The second form asks for you to allow Dogwood Regional Hospital to use and disclose, where appropriate, your health information."

"Minding all HIPAA regulations, correct?" Miriam asked.

"Of course," Brad said.

"And if I wanted a printed version of this to take home with me, so that I'd have a record of what I had signed, you'd be able to provide me with one, correct?"

"Yes. I can provide one to you in English, that a family member or friend could read to you, or I could get you one in Braille."

"Well since I can't read Braille, I'll just take the English copy."

"Sounds good. Can you sign please?"

"Okay," Miriam agreed. She took the pen from Brad's hand. "Where do I sign? I need some help."

With the pen in her hand, he guided the tip to the signature space on the consent forms. "Right here," he instructed. "Sign away."

Miriam signed the form. "Now if there are any other consent forms dealing specifically with cranial rectosis, you'll be bringing those to me, won't you?" Miriam asked.

"Of course," he said. "This is just the beginning."

Miriam laughed heartily. "I'm sure it is."

After Brad had left, Daphne raised the television volume, and she and Miriam finished listening to the episode of 'Friends.'

"This is weird," Miriam said.

"Why?" Daphne asked.

"Because I'm hearing the show, without seeing what's going on. My imagination has to fill in the blanks."

"And why is that such a horrible thing?" Daphne asked.

"It's not," Miriam replied. "It's just different from what I'm used to."

"Well, this experience is all about doing things differently, right?" Daphne asked.

"Yeah," said Miriam. "It is."

"So tell me one thing, Miriam. In your mind's eye, who's the cutest – Joey, Chandler or Ross?"

***

Mel lowered the ice pack from her eye and stared into the mirror. Her upper eyelid was fat and red, and a halo of purple and blue was forming around the base of her lower lid.

Donna shook her head sympathetically. "It looks painful," she said with a sigh. "Just keep the ice on it." Then she sank down into a chair at the table in the break room with her clipboard in front of her. The strokes of her ink pen made scratchy sounds as she filled out the triplicate form in front of her. "Documentation Form: Assault on Employee," Donna read in an authoritative voice. "I've never had to fill one of these out before. This is a first for me as a manager."

Mel let out an angry grunt. "Well let me go back into Mr. Allimore's room one more time and after he strangles me with a stethoscope or impales me with a tongue depressor, you'll get plenty of practice."

"Mel," Donna scolded, "You don't have to be sarcastic about this. I told you I'm going to reassign Brad to be his nurse. You're officially relieved of caring for Mr. Allimore."

"Thank God," Mel said under her breath. She stared at her reflection in the mirror. "I just want to know why," she thought aloud. "Why would he hit me? I never did anything to him."

Haylie walked into the break room and caught a view of Mel's black eye in the mirror. "Whoa, what happened to you?"

Mel arched the eyebrow over her non-wounded eye. "I asked Donna for a raise, and she punched me."

Donna sat up abruptly in her seat. "I did no such thing," she insisted.

"I'm kidding, of course," Mel explained.

"I figured," said Haylie. "But seriously, what really happened?"

"It was actually a patient who punched me. Mr. Allimore."

Haylie's eyes grew wide. "No way! A patient did that? I can hardly believe it."

"Believe it. Here's the proof," Mel growled.

"Wow. Better keep your distance next time you go back in his room."

"She won't be going back into his room," Donna interjected. "I've reassigned Brad as his nurse."

"Why did Mr. Allimore hit Mel?" Haylie asked. "I hope he doesn't hit Brad too."

Donna looked up from the clipboard. "Mr. Allimore is going through a lot right now," she explained. "He has prostate cancer that has spread to his lymph nodes and liver. He's a Vietnam War veteran, and his family has shared that he still suffers from post-traumatic stress disorder. They say that he has bad dreams, and flashbacks. I'm guessing that the combination of him being in pain, and being disoriented after waking up in unfamiliar surroundings, and..."

"And looking at a face like mine, that just sent him over the edge," Mel interjected. "He looks at me and he doesn't see a Filipina nurse. He only sees yellow skin, black hair, Asian eyes, and suddenly, thinks he's back in Vietnam. And I'm the enemy."

"We don't know that for sure," Donna said.

"But it's the most likely explanation," Mel retorted.

"Whoa," Haylie said. "That's some heavy stuff."

"Yes it is," Donna agreed. "That's why I think that Brad will probably be a better caregiver for him. The next face he sees will remind him of the ones that were surrounding him when he was in combat. Brad still wears a crew cut and still looks like he's in the military. So the next time Mr. Allimore wakes up in pain and confused, the face that he'll see rushing to his side will be that of a fellow soldier, and not--"

"The enemy," Mel said abruptly.

"Mel, come on," Donna cajoled. "You can't take this personally. It's not about you."

Pointing to her black eye, Mel sighed. "Not about me, huh? So why am I the one getting punched in the face?"

"This is pretty messed up," Haylie said. "Mr. Allimore assaulted a nurse. That's a crime, isn't it? Shouldn't we be calling the police?"

"If it had been intentional, then yes, it would have been a crime. But I don't believe that it was. Do you, Mel?"

Mel paused for a moment. "Not really," she admitted. "I woke him up from a sound sleep to take his blood pressure. He was probably confused and disoriented. It doesn't make my eye hurt any less, but I don't think he was in his right mind when he did this."

"But still, hitting Mel was wrong. If what Mel said is true about him hitting her because she looks like someone from Vietnam, then this is like… a hate crime," Haylie said. "And if we let him off the hook, then it's perpetuating racism. And he's a bigot."

Donna chuckled softly as she continued filling out the report. "I really don't think that this counts as racism or a hate crime, Haylie."

"Why not?"

Donna put her pen down and turned to Haylie. "It just doesn't."

Haylie didn't seem satisfied with her answer.

"Listen," Donna said, trying an alternative approach. "When I was a little girl, I was attacked by a dog and I suffered more than a dozen bites on my arms, legs, and my back. I still have scars from some of them. To this day, I'm fearful of dogs and prefer to keep my distance from them. Does that make me a bad person?"

Haylie blinked a few times and shrugged, waiting for the right answer.

"Of course not," Donna said. "It just makes me Donna LeShay. People are the sum of their life experiences, Haylie."

"Being afraid of dogs is one thing. Hating people of another race is another." Haylie said indignantly.

"Well, to be fair, we're making a lot of assumptions about why we think he punched Mel, but none of us know why it really happened. We have no reason to think that Mr. Allimore hates anyone."

"Right," Mel said with sarcasm. "He just loves me to pieces. No hate here." She pointed to her black eye.

Donna glared at both of them. "Maybe there is something about Mel that makes Mr. Allimore fearful or uncomfortable. Only he knows what it is. When people have to be hospitalized, they're in a very vulnerable place in their lives, and if anything, they need extra patience and understanding. It's not the time, nor the place – nor is it my job or yours – to try to change someone's thoughts or beliefs that they've carried with them their whole lives. We're here to be caregivers and healers, and we have to recognize that sometimes the best way to be therapeutic to another person is to step back and let another nurse do the job."

"So have you been in that position before? In which you've had to just step back?" Mel asked, taking a seat at the break room table between Donna and Haylie.

"I sure have," Donna replied. "I've had patients who refused to let me touch them. They demanded to have another nurse."

"Because you're black? I mean… African American?" Haylie asked, wide-eyed with surprise.

Donna smiled. "I'm sure that the color of my skin had something to do with it, yes. And yes, I'm 'black,' Haylie. That word doesn't bother me."

"But it bothers other people. I had a teacher in nursing school who told us to never say that word. She said she was African American, and that we were supposed to call all people African American instead of black."

"Well, I suppose it's now the preferred term for Americans of African descent," Donna said. "But as for me, you'd have to go a long way back to find African heritage. My own parents were born here in the United States. My fathers' parents came from Jamaica. My mother's mother was a Cherokee Indian and none of us have any idea where her husband came from, or what race he was. He was killed before my mother was born. She never even met him, never even saw a picture of him. He may have been Indian too, or he may have been black, or white or something else altogether. Who knows? All I know is that I'm not from Africa, and neither were my parents, nor their parents. If you trace back my ancestry far enough, I'm sure it would lead you back to somewhere in Africa, but I just don't feel like African is the best way to describe myself. No more than a Cherokee American, or a Jamaican American. When I was a child, my mother used to stand behind me with her hands on my shoulders and make me face the mirror in the morning, and she would tell me to hold my head up high and be a strong, proud black woman. So that's what I do, every day. I know the word 'black' bothers some people, and they might be more comfortable being called African American, but I can't speak for them. I can only speak for myself."

Mel grunted. "And then there's me – the Filipino American. Some people are very proud to be called Filipino American, but I don't like it either."

"Why?" Haylie asked, genuinely confused. "That's what you are, aren't you?"

"I'm both. But I hate being called a 'Filipino American' simply because it sets me apart from everyone else. Why can't I just be an

American? Why do you have to put an extra label on me? If you need to talk about my heritage, fine, I'm Filipina. If you need to talk about my nationality, I'm American. But something about putting the two of them together just makes me feel weird. I don't like it."

Haylie shook her head. "I never know the right thing to say. If I have to mention someone's color or ethnicity, it's like there's no right answer."

"Well, if you're talking about a whole group of people, you're right," Donna chimed in. "Just because individuals belong to a group doesn't mean that they all feel the same way. People have different feelings about how they want to be identified when it comes to their race and ethnicity."

"So what am I supposed to call you, then?" Haylie asked.

"Just call me Mel," Mel grinned.

"And I'm fine with Donna," Donna laughed.

"Come on, guys! I'm being serious. I don't want to have to walk on eggshells all the time, always wondering if I'm going offend you or not."

"We're just kidding with you, Haylie," Donna smiled. "I guess the point we're trying to make is to avoid labels. We have to look at people as individuals and get to know them instead of making assumptions and boxing them into categories. We all have names – not just your co-workers, but our patients, and their families… and we'd much rather be called by our names than anything else. I've been in situations in which I've heard other nurses say things like 'I'm going to check on the Hispanic patient' when they could have just said, 'I'm going to check on Mr. Ramos.' Or we'll tell our patients things like 'Go up to Med-Surg South and look for the black nurse' when we could just say 'Go to Med-Surg South and ask for Donna.' It's always respectful to use names instead of labels."

Haylie nodded. "Yeah, you're right. But there are going to be some times that you can't avoid talking about race. What if someone comes up to me and says 'I know three different nurses named Donna in this hospital. What does the Donna on Med-Surg South look like?' Am I supposed to tip toe around your color and not point out the one thing that would most easily identify you to someone who doesn't know you?"

Donna laughed. "No, of course not. You don't have to avoid talking about my skin color when there's a practical reason, and as long as it's discussed respectfully."

"So I guess you've been on the flip side of that," said Haylie. "You've been called black in a way that was disrespectful, I take it?"

Donna laughed. "I've heard people say things like 'go get that little black nurse' plenty of times throughout my career. And for the record, I've also heard words used in place of black that I don't care to repeat. Anyway, yes, I'm a black nurse, but I have a name. It's Donna. So whenever I would hear comments like that, I would just give my patients and their families a friendly reminder of my name each time I came into contact with them. Sometimes it made a difference. Sometimes it didn't. There are some folks who are just going to say things the way they want to, and there's nothing you can do to change it."

"And it never bothered you?" Haylie asked.

"Sure it did. But as I've matured in my role as a nurse, I've just made a conscious decision to not take things like that personally."

"Okay, we've established that the word 'black' doesn't offend you. But going back to our hypothetical situation, when I'm describing you to someone else, and I say 'Donna is black,' what if it offends the person I'm talking to?"

Donna pursed her lips in thought. "If someone lets you know that they're offended, I think the best thing you can say is something like 'I didn't mean to offend you. Can you tell me a different way to describe Donna that would not be offensive to you?' That way you're showing that you respect how they feel about it, and you're offering them a chance to let you know how to better communicate with them."

Haylie nodded. "That's fair enough. But people don't always let you know they're offended."

"That's true," Donna replied. "It can be uncomfortable and awkward to let someone know that you've offended them, so people will often avoid a tough conversation like that."

"Well, yeah," Haylie agreed. She paused for a moment, deep in thought. "You know, it just dawned on me, I'm guilty of it myself. A few days ago, I was talking to my friend Jaime and she said something that really bothered me. She had just bought a new car, and was telling me that she 'jewed the car dealer down way below sticker price.' I'm Jewish, and she knows that, so it really ticked me off that she would say such a thing. But I let it slide. I guess I shouldn't have."

"She very likely doesn't realize that what she said was offensive," Donna said. "Unfortunately, I hear other people say that exact phrase all the time. There are certain expressions or sayings that we've heard spoken so many times that they just seem to be part of our language, and we don't even realize that they are or could be hurtful. You need to let Jaime know. She's your friend, Haylie, and I can't imagine her intentionally hurting your feelings. So you owe it to her to let her know that what she said bothered you. Otherwise she'll keep saying it, and will probably offend someone else."

"And who knows?" Mel said. "She might offend the wrong person and get punched in the face." She stared at her reflection into the mirror again. Her eyelid had closed halfway over her eye from the swelling.

"I want you to go get that looked at," Donna said firmly. Then she slid the clipboard with the Employee Assault form across the table to Mel. "Write down a description of what happened and sign it. And then head down to Emergency and get your eye examined."

"I hope it can wait," Brad said, as he rushed into the break room. He grabbed Mel by the hand and pulled her to her feet.

"What? Why?" She asked.

"Jenny's out here looking for you. She's having labor pains, and she thinks her water broke. You better get her over to L & D right now because we're sure not set up to deliver babies on this unit!"

"Oh my Lord! I'll have to get back to you on finishing the form, Donna!" Mel called out, as she dashed out of the break room.

Chapter 11
Tuesday Afternoon

Miriam's stomach growled. "How do you know what time it is?" she asked Daphne. Then Miriam heard the bedside table drawer open, followed by the shuffling sound of Daphne searching for something within it.

A computerized voice said, in a choppy, monotone drone, "The time is eleven fifty six."

"What was that?" Miriam asked.

"One guess," Daphne replied.

"Well, it tells time, so I'm going to gamble on it being a watch."

"We have a winner, ladies and gentlemen!" Daphne said with mock excitement. "It's a talking watch. I normally wear it on my wrist, but with all these I.V. thingies stuck in my hands, I took it off."

"Sorry about that," Miriam said. "You have better veins in your hands than you do in your arms."

"Yeah, yeah," Daphne said. "Go ahead and use my lovely hands as a pin cushion. See if I care."

"Hey, I said I was sorry!" Miriam laughed. "But what am I apologizing for? I'm not your nurse today. I'm just a fellow patient. And I'm a hungry one, at that."

"Me too. When does the chow wagon roll around today?"

"Dietary shows up around noon and starts distributing trays. We should get ours soon."

"So you get hospital food and everything?"

"Yes. My boss Donna ordered a tray for me." Then Miriam stopped and sniffed the air a few times. "I smell it," she said, a smile spreading across her face. "Prime rib! With mashed potatoes and green beans."

"I was wondering what that stink was," Daphne said. "I thought maybe a toilet had backed up or something."

Miriam laughed. "Actually, the food here is really good." Then she heard footsteps enter the room.

"Hello," said the visitor. "Are we ready for lunchtime?"

"I certainly am," Miriam said.

"Sure," said Daphne.

The dietary technician gave both of them a tray and left the room.

Miriam reached out in front of her and found the edge of the tray with her hands. She groped blindly for silverware, and upon finding it rolled up in a napkin, removed it from the linen. Then she found the plastic plate shield and moved it aside.

A loud *clack clack clack* filled the room as it tumbled to the floor.

"Whoops," she said.

In the bed next to her, Daphne laughed. "Nice job," she said. "Do I get to throw something on the floor next?"

"Very funny," said Miriam. "I didn't drop it on the floor on purpose."

"It's rather helpful to feel for a surface before you try to put something on it," Daphne suggested. "Use those hands, Miriam. You can trust your sense of touch much better than plain old guessing."

"I'll remember that next time."

Miriam found her fork and stabbed it on her plate. She felt it sink into something soft, and fed the bite of food into her mouth. Then she reached for her napkin and spit it out.

"Ugh," Miriam said, and coughed slightly.

"What's wrong, roomie?" Daphne asked. "You're not choking over there are you? If I have to come and give you the Heimlich maneuver,

I just want you to know that I'm going to send you a bill as big as the one that your hospital is going to send me."

"No," Miriam said, spitting once more into her napkin. "I'm fine. I thought I was getting a mouthful of mashed potatoes, but I actually scooped a big wad of margarine into my mouth. I guess there's a dinner roll somewhere on the plate, and that's what it's for."

Daphne giggled. "Let me help you out," she said. "Touch the rim of your plate at the bottom – the part that is closest to you."

"Okay," Miriam said, putting her finger on the rim of her plate.

"Now think of it like a clock. Your finger is at six o'clock right now. That's where the mashed potatoes are."

Miriam sunk her fork onto her plate, just above her finger. She recognized the creamy texture as her fork cut through it. "Got it," she said.

"Good. Now go up to ten o'clock. That's where your green beans are," Daphne instructed. "And your dinner roll is on a smaller plate, just outside of the green beans at ten."

Miriam moved her fork up the plate and to the left. She touched the food with her fork, and felt a couple of firm green beans shift beneath it. Then she reached for her dinner roll and took a bite.

"Last but not least," Daphne said, "The space between noon and four o'clock is where the prime rib is. Which, by the way, is actually very good. I just tasted it, and you're right."

"Pretty neat," Miriam said. "Is that the standard way that food is arranged on plates?"

"Not necessarily," Daphne said. "Since I'm far more accustomed to eating without sight than you are, I poked around on my plate first to figure out where food was placed, and I assumed that yours would be arranged in the same way. Using the clock to describe the food on your plate is a common practice among the blind, though. I can't take credit for that."

"Nice job, anyway," Miriam said. "Once I imagined the clock, it made perfect sense to me."

A moment of silence passed between the two women as they ate their lunch. Miriam had been hungrier than she had realized, and ate every bite of food on her plate. When she was done, she pushed her tray away, feeling the rolling table glide smoothly away from her bed. She swung her legs off of the bed and found the floor with her feet.

"What's up, roomie?" Daphne asked, hearing the movement from Miriam's side of the room.

"I need to use the bathroom," she said.

"Oh, okay," Daphne said. "Now is when the toilet really gets backed up, right?"

"Give me a break, smartypants." Miriam took a step forward, flailing her hands in front of her, struggling to find her way in the darkness inflicted by the patches over her eyes. She took three steps and smacked her knee into one of the guest chairs in the room.

"Ow!" she cried out.

"Nice job," Daphne said. "Here's your next big lesson – it's okay to ask for help. I ask for it every day. I'm a blind person living in a world full of people who can see, so I don't expect to be able to do everything all by myself."

"Now you tell me," Miriam said. "Okay, Daphne. I'm officially asking for help."

"Sometimes help comes in the form of a person. You could ring your call bell and ask Brad or one of the other nurses to guide you to the bathroom. Or sometimes help comes in the form of a tool, like this one. Hold out your hand and reach toward the sound of my voice."

Miriam reached, and a solid, blunt object grazed her fingers. She moved her hand a bit closer, gripped it and took it from Daphne's outstretched hand. "Your cane," she said.

"Bingo!" Daphne cried out. "You know how to use it?"

"I've seen people using them before, but I've never tried it."

"The loop goes around your wrist so you don't have to worry about dropping it. Let the tip of the cane touch the ground in front of you, and in a sweeping motion, tap it from side to side, making sure that the path before you is clear of obstructions. Keep it low to the ground. If you raise the cane too high while you're sweeping from side to side, you can miss an obstruction. If it's free and clear, you can advance forward."

Miriam shifted away from the chair that her knee had just

struck, moving in the opposite direction. She put the cane on the floor, alternately tapping from left to right.

"Good job," Daphne said. "Try tapping a little bit lighter. If you tap too hard, your hand will absorb all of the impact and it will hurt after a while."

Miriam took several steps in the direction of the bathroom, using the cane to guide her way. "I'm getting the hang of this," she said. When she sensed she was nearing the bathroom, she reached out her free hand. When her fingertips touched the door of the bathroom, she smiled to herself.

"I made it!" She announced excitedly.

"Awesome," Daphne said, as Miriam entered and closed the door behind her. "Don't fall in! I won't be able to help you much then."

A few moments later, Miriam emerged from the bathroom. "Now the fun part – finding my way back to my bed."

"You can do it," Daphne said.

"I know. Give me just a second. There's something I want to try." Miriam took a few steps, advancing slowly from the bathroom toward her bed. "Hello? Hello?" she said. Then, she turned to her right, and repeated the words. "Hello? Hello?"

"What are you doing?" Daphne asked. "If four new people just stepped into the room, I have to admit, I totally missed it."

Miriam turned to her left. "Hello, hello," she said again. Then she turned toward Daphne. "You know there aren't four new people in the room," she said.

"Okay, six maybe?" Daphne asked. "That's how many times you said the word 'hello.' What exactly are you doing?"

"I was just noticing how different my voice sounds, depending on which direction I'm facing. If there's a wall in front of me, my voice sounds louder. Like it's bouncing back at me, like an echo."

"That's because it is," Daphne said with a smile. "And it probably sounds more distant, and just a bit softer when you're speaking into an open space. Like when you're facing the open doorway leading out to the hallway of the unit, right?"

"Right," Miriam said.

"That's called echolocation," Daphne said.

"Echo what?"

"Echolocation." Daphne paused to laugh. "You've heard the expression 'blind as a bat,' haven't you?"

"Yes I have."

"Well, that's because bats are pretty much blind. They have one of the most sophisticated echolocation systems of any living creature. They produce high frequency pulses that they send out into their environment, and they wait to hear how the signals return to them in the form of sound. That's how they get information about the world around them and how they find their prey in the dark. You see, nurse Miriam, some creatures of the nocturnal kind are very well suited to survive in the dark. Others like bats actually thrive in the dark. And then, there are creatures who stand zero chance of survival in the wildness… you know, like human beings who stand in front of walls with patches on their eyes and say 'hello? hello?'"

Miriam couldn't help but smile. "So I'm echolocating. I could actually hear the difference between the walls around me, and the doorway that opens out into the hall," she said.

"I'm rather impressed that you figured that out on your own."

Then Daphne and Miriam stopped talking as they both heard the sound of footsteps approaching. Someone entered the room.

"That's not Brad," Miriam said.

"Nope, it's not," Daphne said. Her smile was evident in her voice.

"Sorry, ladies, it's just me," Donna said. "How could you tell it wasn't Brad, Miriam?"

Miriam grinned. "I've been listening to him walk in and out of here all morning long. I could recognize him from a mile away. Well, maybe not literally a mile, but you get the picture."

"So how has your time with Ms. Wylie been?" Donna asked.

"Daphne," the patient corrected her.

"Like she told me yesterday, Ms. Wylie is her mother," Miriam told Donna as she perched on the edge of the bed.

Daphne laughed. "Actually, Miriam, you're my mother now."

"Uh… excuse me?" Miriam asked curiously.

"I didn't tell you, did I? I'm starring in my own play. Claire in 'Love Is Blind' is none other than yours truly. And I've officially cast you as Claire's mother. So welcome to the show, Miriam. How does it feel to be a star?" She turned to Donna. "Make sure you spread the word. Tell all of the nurses here to come watch Miriam in her debut role as a nosy, overbearing mother."

"Hey!" Miriam cried. "I thought you said that the mother's character was going to go through a nice transformation?"

"I did. But before she gets to that part, she's going to be completely hateful."

"Oh, how nice," Donna said. "Congratulations, Miriam. I would tell you to break a leg, but I don't think your hospitalization for that would be as pleasant as this one was."

"Was?" Miriam said. "The day's not over yet."

Donna hesitated. "I know that, and please don't get mad at me, Miriam, but I need you back on the unit. Could you clock in and work the rest of first shift? Mel just left the floor. Her daughter went into labor. For real this time. And we're also going to need that bed this afternoon. We'll have a patient coming up from the P.A.C.U. very shortly."

"So I'm getting a real roommate," Daphne said. "Better sanitize that bed really good, Miriam. Cranial rectosis is contagious."

"Cranial what?" Donna asked.

"Never mind," Miriam groaned. She reached up to her face and ripped away the tape that was holding the gauze pads over her eyes. She blinked rapidly as she readjusted to the light. "You're going to have to round up some scrubs for me, though. I didn't bring any with me. Because it's – you know – my day off."

Donna gave her a sad smile. "I know, and I'm sorry to do this to you two weeks in a row," she said.

"It's okay. I'm starting to get used to it," Miriam smirked.

"Thanks Miriam," said Donna. "I really do appreciate it. And Ms. Wylie – I mean, Daphne – thank you too. I'm glad Miriam got to spend this time with you."

"Don't mention it," Daphne replied. "I don't know how helpful it was for Miriam, but it was really nice for me to have the company."

"It was tremendously helpful," Miriam said.

"I'm sure it was," Donna said. "If you'll excuse me, I've got to get back to the nurse's station. Thank you both again, and I'm so sorry we had to cut it short." She ducked out of the room.

Miriam sighed loudly. "Back to work now."

"It's all good, Miriam. You've earned your wings. Now fly away, Batgirl. Fly away!"

They laughed.

"Thank you, Daphne."

"Oh, there's nothing to thank me for. I should be thanking you. I not only finagled myself a visitor for half a day to keep me from going crazy from boredom, but I also recruited you for my play. You are going to be in my play, aren't you?"

"Yes," Miriam said with a smile. "I accept. I'll be Claire's mother."

"Good!" Daphne clapped her hands together. "So after I get discharged, and after the hurricane comes and goes, we'll be seeing a lot more of each other."

"I guess we will, won't we?"

"Absolutely."

Miriam rose and made her way to the door. She returned Daphne's cane to her bedside.

"Daphne?"

"Yes?"

"I really mean it. Thank you."

The patient nodded. "You're welcome. And Miriam, try not to worry too much until you see your doctor next week. If you need someone to talk to again, I'm right here. But trust me, one way or the other, you're going to be okay."

"I know," Miriam said with a smile, and left to clock in.

***

Returning from her break, Prateeka and her roommate Anupa stepped out of the elevator onto the third floor of Dogwood Regional Medical Center.

In their native tongue, Hindi, the two young women chattered away. They stopped in the hallway to finish their conversation before Anupa headed to work on Med-Surg North; Prateeka to Med-Surg South.

Just then, Haylie rounded the corner, almost bumping into the two of them.

Prateeka quickly finished her sentence in Hindi, then stopped speaking. Both she and Anupa turned to look at Haylie.

"Hello Haylie," Prateeka said.

"Hi," she responded. She paused, giving a serious look to both Prateeka and Anupa. "Don't let me interrupt you," she finally said, and pushed between the two of them as she continued along her way.

***

Brad was tired already. It had been a crazy day thus far.

He arrived at work that morning to find that he had a very full patient load, and added to it was Miriam in her simulated hospitalization.

Then when Jenny arrived on Med-Surg South, in the early stages of labor and crying for her mother, Brad quickly moved her into a wheelchair, pulled Mel from the break room, and chaperoned both of the anxious women to the Labor and Delivery unit.

Six hours on the floor thus far, and he hadn't been able to take a break yet. He found Donna and Haylie at the nurse's station, and let them know that he was retreating into the sanctuary of the breakroom for a few moments. He turned on the television just in time to watch the news update that Hurricane Fortuna had strengthened to a Category 4 storm, and it was closing in fast on the Carolina coast.

Then Brad logged onto the computer and checked his work emails. There were five emails from the Corporate Communications Department about hurricane safety and preparedness. There was an additional email from Donna reminding everyone to plan for an overnight stay or two, and that Haylie had offered her nearby apartment as a refuge from the storm.

Then there was an email from Haylie herself. It had been sent earlier that morning.

From: Evans, Haylie J.

To: Jackson, Bradley R.

Subject: R U OK???

You don't seem like yourself lately. Is everything okay? I guess the hurricane has everybody stressed out right now, but it just seems like you've got a lot on your mind. I was talking to you at the nurse's station this morning, and you were so spaced out, you didn't even answer. I was just a little worried about you and wanted to let you know that whatever you're going through, if you need a friend, you know where to find me. Hope everything is okay.

Haylie

Brad took a deep breath and exhaled with a groan. He wondered if his distraction had been as apparent to everyone else as it had been to Haylie.

Andrea still hadn't returned his calls, and he was still refusing to speak to Sue. Being the focal point of the bizarre incommunicado love triangle was wearing him out.

Brad opened a browser on the computer and navigated to his personal webmail account. When he logged in, he found that there were two emails from Sue waiting for him. One was dated two weeks after she had arrived in Croatia. The other was dated approximately one month before the day she had returned home to the apartment. They both basically said the same thing, almost word for word, in three short lines:

Brad,

I'm not sure if moving here was the right thing for me to do.

I'm thinking about coming back home to Dogwood. Let me know if you are okay with this.

I hope to hear from you soon.

Sue

He wasn't sure what to make of her words. They weren't an apology for breaking his heart, nor were they a plea to return to the way things were. There was no hidden message, it seemed. She had simply been letting him know that doubt had crept into her mind, and that she wanted to come back home.

She had attempted to give him fair warning by email of her impending return, and he believed her when she said that she had tried to call him. He knew that it was wrong to give her the cold shoulder.

But Andrea was shutting *him* out, and it was just as unfair. He was confused and hurt and angry. And since Sue had set everything in motion, she was going to be the one to pay.

Brad leaned back in the chair and sighed deeply again. He didn't understand women. He still didn't understand why Sue had spent years pressuring him into marriage, and when he finally gave in and proposed, she turned him down and left town.

He didn't understand how he could be so lucky as to meet Andrea and to fall so deeply in love again, fully ready to commit to her, only to see her turn and flee at the sight of Sue. Brad couldn't grasp why Andrea felt so threatened, and why she didn't have more faith in his feelings for her.

He didn't understand Sue and Andrea, period.

And he didn't understand how, after all of their neurotic behavior, he could still love both of them as much as he did.

Feeling a headache creeping up on him, he pinched the bridge of his nose in a desperate attempt to ward it off. He closed his eyes and tried to imagine the perfect woman; one who wouldn't play games and who wouldn't spring surprises on him. One who wouldn't get close and then run away.

He couldn't help but think of Lee. She had all of Sue's charm and beauty, and all of Andrea's practicality; that same humble, down-to-earth personality and great sense of humor. She was lovely, both inside and out.

And while nurses weren't supposed to act upon romantic attachments to patients, Brad knew that Lee wouldn't be his patient forever.

So I know you're new to the area, he imagined saying to her at her discharge. If you're looking for a cool place to hang out, there's a great Mexican restaurant, La Fiesta.

He broke into a smile, keeping his eyes closed, focusing on Lee in his imagination

They have great food, and the best margaritas in town. They have a deejay on Friday and Saturday nights, too. That's where I go most weekends. You should check it out sometime. It would be great to run into you there...

He knew she would recognize it for exactly what it was: a roundabout way of letting her know that he was interested in her and wanted to see her again. And he didn't care. He was tired of having his heart broken, tired of being blindsided with hurt, tired of having no control, no choice. This time, he had the power to do something. He wasn't about to let someone as great as Lee slip away without taking a chance.

Brad heard the breakroom door open. He opened his eyes.

"Hey," Haylie said as she leaned in the doorway. "Your patient is asking for you."

"Which one?" Brad asked, but already knew.

"Miss Matthews."

"Lee," he corrected her as he rose to his feet and made his way to the door.

"You get my email?" Haylie asked. She stood firm in the doorway.

"Oh... yeah. I did. Everything's cool. Thanks for checking on me, though."

After hesitating for a moment, Haylie stepped aside to let him pass. "If you've got any more Reese's cups, you may want to take them in when you go see her." She laughed playfully.

"What?" Brad turned on his heels. He felt a blush of embarrassment creeping across his face. "She told you about that?"

"Yeah. She said she was craving chocolate and asked me if I could get her another pack of Reese's. I told her it wasn't standard fare on the inpatient menu, and that's when she told me that you brought some to her yesterday. Very sweet of you, Brad."

"That was nothing, Haylie. Come on, don't make a big deal out of it."

"I'm not," she insisted. "Seriously though, it was really nice of you to do that for her. I don't see any flowers in her room. She hasn't had any visitors. She's here all alone."

"Yeah, she is. She just moved to Dogwood and things have gotten off to a rough start for her here."

"Poor thing," said Haylie with a frown. "Anyway, aside from the chocolate request, she also said she's having a lot of pain in her belly and she can't urinate."

"She mentioned some pain yesterday. I need to call her doc, now that it has worsened." He moved toward the nurse's station.

"Hey Brad?" Haylie called out to him.

He turned around once more. "Yeah?"

"I mean what I said in my e-mail. I'm here if you need a friend to talk to."

He nodded her way and managed a polite smile. "Thanks, Haylie. I'll keep that in mind."

***

Jenny clenched her teeth and let out a high-pitched squeal as she climbed onto the bed. Tears rolled down her cheeks.

"You still want to deliver this baby without pain meds?" Mel asked.

"I don't think so anymore," Jenny said. "I need an epa... ep..." she stopped talking and cried out loudly.

"Epidural," said her mother. Mel stood on one side of her bed, and a Labor and Delivery nurse stood by the other. Together they locked the guardrails into place.

"My name is Daisy," said the nurse, a young, pretty brunette who appeared to be around the same age as Jenny. "This is your first baby, right?"

Jenny nodded and clenched her teeth through her contraction.

"We'll take good care of you, sweetie," said Daisy. "I actually just had my first one too. Just got back from maternity leave a couple of weeks ago. You're in for some hard work, but it's all worth it." She turned toward Mel. "And your labor coach - is this Mom?"

"For now," Mel said with a nervous laugh. "Guess I'll be Mom and Grandmom shortly."

"You look familiar," Daisy said. "Don't you work here?"

Mel nodded. "I do. My name is Imelda. Or you can just call me Mel. I work on Med-Surg South."

"Well it's nice to meet you, Mel," Daisy said with a friendly smile. She handed her a hospital gown. "I'm going to step out for a moment and let you help Jenny get changed. We've called Dr. Salvo and he's on the way in. Is there anyone else we can call for you? How about the dad?"

"I already called my dad and told him I'm in labor," Jenny panted. "He and his fiancé are on the way. Once they get here, I want them to stay in the waiting room, though. I only want my mom in here with me, not my dad."

Daisy laughed. "Oh, sweetie, I didn't mean your dad. I meant the dad of your baby. Isn't he going to be here with you?"

Mel and Jenny exchanged a sad look. "No," they said in unison.

"I see," Daisy nodded, and smiled awkwardly. She pulled the privacy curtain around them and left the room.

***

"This is Dr. George returning a page," said the voice on the other end of the line.

"Hi Dr. George, this is Brad on Med-Surg South. I'm calling about Lee Matthews, who's got some abdominal pain and difficulty urinating."

Dr. George paused for a moment. "Post-op breast surgery patient – staph infection, right?"

"Yes," Brad said.

"See if you can get a urine sample and send it to the lab."

"She says she can't go."

"You'll need to start a cath for a sample then."

"Ok," he said. "Thanks." He hung up the phone and turned to Haylie, who was perched on the other side of the desk at the nurse's station, making notes on a clipboard. "Hey Haylie, I need a favor."

"Okay. Shoot."

"Can you come into the break room with me for a minute?"

She wrinkled her brow. "I guess."

They stepped into the break room. Brad closed the door behind them.

"Dr. George needs a urine specimen on Lee. I have to start a cath on her, and I'm wondering if you have a minute... could you do it for me?"

She raised an eyebrow. "Why?"

Brad sighed. "I know this sounds stupid, but I just don't want to hurt her. It's such a painful procedure. Every woman that I've ever started a Foley on ends up crying. I just hate it."

Haylie stared at him. "So... let me get this straight. You want me to bring her to tears her instead of you. Right?"

"Well, no. I don't want her to be in any pain, period. But it's kind of unavoidable. I was just thinking that... I don't know, she might be a little less anxious with a female nurse instead of a male nurse starting the cath, and maybe that will make the procedure less painful."

"I don't get it," Haylie said sternly, "You catheterize women patients all the time. You've never had a problem with it up until now. Why start with Lee?"

"Because!" Brad threw up his hands in frustration. "She's young, and she's drop-dead gorgeous, and once I lift up her gown and invade her privacy and inflict horrible pain on her, she's never going to see me as anything other than just a nurse. I'll never even have a chance—"

He stopped abruptly when he realized he'd already said way too much.

Haylie's eyes grew wide with realization. "Brad," she said softly. "You like her."

Brad looked away. He didn't respond.

"What about Andrea?" Haylie asked. "I thought things were going so well with her."

"They're not," he snapped. "I don't want to talk about it right now, but no, things aren't going well at all. Andrea's not even talking to me anymore. It's like Lee came into my life at just the right time."

Haylie blinked. She was too stunned to speak.

"I know that nothing can happen while she's in the hospital," Brad said. "But she won't be here for much longer, and I at least want to be able to have a chance with her when she's not my patient anymore. Please don't say anything to Donna. I don't want her lecturing me about boundaries and all that baloney."

She stared at him. "It's not baloney, Brad. We do need to respect some boundaries with our patients."

"Please," he begged. "All I'm asking is that you go start a cath on her for me, and let's just keep this whole conversation between me and you. You said that if I needed a friend, you would be here for me. So I'm asking you this favor as a friend."

Haylie's face melted into a look of bewilderment. "Alright," she relented. "Fine." She turned and exited the break room.

Brad watched Haylie disappear into Lee's room and close the privacy curtain.

He looked down at the floor, feeling a little bit ashamed of himself. He wasn't completely sure why. Stepping out of the breakroom, he approached the desk at the nurse's station and rested his elbows on the counter. In an effort to distract himself from the situation at hand, he focused his attention on Prateeka.

"How's it going?" Brad asked in the most enthusiastic voice he could muster.

Med-Surg South's newest nurse looked up with a wide smile. "So far, so good," she said. "Except, as you know, my preceptor had to leave for the birth of her grandchild. In the meantime, I am pestering Donna with all of my questions."

"Well feel free to pester me too," Brad offered. "And Miriam, and Haylie. We'll all be glad to help you."

"Thank you," said Prateeka, with a friendly nod. "Tell me, Brad, what is happening with this hurricane? People keep talking about it. Hurricanes aren't very common in India, so I really have no idea what to expect."

He grinned. "We definitely get our fair share of them here in North Carolina. Usually, a hurricane is strong when it hits the coast, but as it moves inland, it loses strength. By the time it reaches us here in Dogwood, it's normally just a lot of wind and rain. We're far enough inland that we usually don't see much flooding. If it is a strong storm, the power will go out for a day or two, some trees may come down, and sometimes roads and buildings are damaged. But after the storm is gone, things usually get fixed quickly. After some cleanup and repair work, life goes back to normal."

She gave a casual shrug. "I suppose that does not sound so bad."

"The most important thing you can do is stay high and dry. Get in a safe place, and stay there until the storm passes."

"Will the storm go north? To Maryland?"

He shook his head. "I seriously doubt it. Hurricane Fortuna started in the south Atlantic Ocean and is headed northwest. It will hit the coast sometime tomorrow in either South or North Carolina, and will keep pushing inland, to the north and west. It will lose strength and speed, and by the time it pushes across the Carolinas, it should die down to a mild storm. Maryland may get some wind and rain, but nothing like the harsh weather we'll see here."

"I just wanted to make sure that my husband will be safe. He should be fine, yes?"

Nodding, Brad smiled. "I should think so. Hey, when will you get to see him, anyway? Are you going to be able to visit him soon?"

"He will visit me here in Dogwood at his next semester break. I'm very excited to see him. I tell him I'm patiently waiting, but the truth is, I'm not so patient. I'm ready for him to finish school so that he can move to Dogwood. I dream all the time about how it will be when Samir and I can finally live together. I imagine that first, we will buy a house. And very soon after that, we will fill it up with children." She smiled, and her face illuminated with the glow of young love.

Brad suddenly felt a wave of disappointment crash over him. He had wanted that, too. But for whatever reason, it wasn't in the cards for him at the moment.

"Brad, I need to talk to you," Haylie said in such as rush that her words almost jumbled together. Dashing toward the nurse's station, she grabbed his elbow and pulled him back into the break room.

"Excuse us a second," he called out to Prateeka, just before Haylie closed the door.

"Sit down," Haylie said.

He wrinkled his brow. "What's going on?"

"Please," Haylie said. "Sit down. I need to tell you something important."

Brad pulled a chair out from under the table and sat. "What is it?"

"It's Lee," she said.

He was instantly concerned. "What? Is something wrong with her?"

Haylie gulped. "Well, that's just it, Brad. Lee isn't exactly a… her."

He shook his head. "What are you talking about?"

She held up the unopened female cath kit. "I can't use this because she… I mean, he is a man. Lee has a penis."

Brad rose from his seat. "Not funny, Haylie. Look, if you're going to play around, I can just do it myself."

"Brad, don't!" Haylie reached for his arm. "I'm not joking around. I went in there to do the cath, and when I lifted her gown, I was pretty surprised. You didn't know either, did you?"

"She's not a man," he snapped back.

"Yes, Brad," Haylie insisted. "Lee is biologically, anatomically a male."

"There's no way," Brad shot back. "She looks like a woman, she talks like a woman, she acts like a woman. What you're saying is just… well, it's just not possible. I don't believe you."

"She's going through the process of becoming a woman," Haylie said. "Doesn't it make sense now, Brad? The breast surgery wasn't just a cosmetic augmentation. She had it because she's going through the process of gender reassignment. It usually doesn't happen all at once, right? It's a step-by-step process."

"No," he insisted. "I know what this is, Haylie. You think I'm all stressed out so you're playing a joke to make me have a good laugh and forget all of my worries. Is that it? Is that what this stupid little stunt is all about?"

She shook her head. "No, Brad, I promise. I'm not joking and I'm not lying."

"I don't believe you." He snatched the female cath kit out of her hand and brushed past her.

Brad paused outside of Lee's room and took a few deep breaths. His mind was racing, and he was angry – not just angry, furious at Haylie. After the long moment had passed, he made his way to Lee's bedside.

"Lee," he began, "I need to start a catheter on you. This is going to be uncomfortable, but I'll be as gentle as I can."

Lee looked terrified. She pulled the bedsheet up to her chest. "I don't understand."

Brad put the packaged Foley cath in her lap and pointed to it. "It's just a tube that I need to insert through your urethra and into your bladder. It will drain the urine out since you can't go on your own."

Lee's eyes grew wide, and her face turned a ghastly shade of white. "I mean, I don't understand why you have to use that one. That other nurse was just in here and she said she had the same thing in her hand. She said it was the wrong kit."

He froze, and his heart skipped a beat. "Haylie? Is that the other nurse that was just in here?"

"Yes, I think that's her name."

"What did she do?"

"She pulled the covers down and looked, and said she needed to go get a different kit."

Brad took a deep breath. His head began to spin.

"Let me see, Lee. I need to see with my own eyes so I'll know if I've got the right kit or not."

Her face turned beet red as she slowly pulled the sheet down toward the foot of the bed. "Do you... want me to take off my underwear?"

"Yes, please," Brad said. He felt himself blushing.

Lee reached down, hooking her thumbs into the waistline of her underwear and slid them down her hips.

Then Brad's heart stopped as he looked down at his patient.

As Lee continued to pull her underwear to her knees, Brad dropped the cath kit and stumbled back into the wall.

Lee sat up with a jolt. "What's wrong?" She asked.

"Oh..," he murmured, then looked up at Lee. "I'm sorry. Ex-… excuse me for a moment," He stammered.

Then he turned and quickly stepped out of the room.

At the nurse's station, Haylie pointed to Lee's medical record on the computer screen. "Right there," she said. "M. For male."

Chapter 12
Tuesday Evening

Brad rested his elbows on the counter and clutched his head in his hands. "I see that now," he said bitterly. "This isn't possible. How could I have had her – I mean, him – as my patient for two days in a row... and not have known?"

"Well, it's understandable," Haylie said. "Unless you specifically went looking to see if there was a tiny little 'F' or 'M' in her chart or on her bracelet, it's easy to see how it could have been overlooked."

He buried his face in his hands. "It makes sense now, why Donna assigned him to me. But no one said anything at report. Her – I mean, his – doctor didn't even say anything. Somebody could have given me a heads up."

Haylie furrowed her brow. "I don't think anyone was intentionally trying to deceive you. I know you've been really distracted lately, Brad. Do you think it's possible that it was mentioned to you at some point, but you weren't paying attention at the time?"

Brad looked down at the floor. "I don't know. All I know is that he could have said something to me himself. Why didn't he?"

"He? Who?"

"The patient. Lee. Or whatever his name is. He had no right to let me think he was a woman, and talk to him like a woman..."

Haylie frowned. "Why should it matter? Lee is here because she's sick and you're supposed to be taking care of her. You weren't supposed to develop feelings for her-"

"Him," Brad said emphatically. "I admit, I was being flirty when I thought Lee was a she. But Lee was flirting right back. She- I mean, he was showing interest too. It was so wrong for him to play around with my feelings like that."

"How do you know she was flirting? Some guys think that if a girl so much as says hello to him, it's flirting."

"I'm not that kind of guy."

"So how did you know that Lee was flirting with you?"

"Trust me, he was. We were being friendly with each other. Talking about our personal lives and whatnot."

"I do that with my patients all the time, Brad. So do you. Do you think it's possible you read more into your interactions with Lee than what was really happening?"

"No," Brad said firmly. "You weren't there. You have no idea what you're talking about."

"But I do know what it's like to feel heartbroken and rejected," said Haylie. "When someone you love suddenly ends the relationship and you have no say in the matter, it's overwhelming. You feel like something's wrong with you, like you're flawed and unlovable, and for whatever reason, not good enough. And in that situation, when someone interesting of the opposite sex comes along, any kind of attention that they pay to you is going lift you back up and make you feel good about yourself again."

"Yeah, great theory," Brad spat at her. "Except for the part about someone of the opposite sex coming along. Lee doesn't qualify."

Haylie threw up her hands in exasperation. "But you thought Lee was a female up until now. And Lee probably assumed that you knew. You do have access to her medical records, after all. It's right here." Haylie pointed at the computer screen once more.

"Just stop," Brad said, raising his voice. "I'm really upset right now. I don't need to be told how stupid I was to miss an important detail like a penis on a pretty woman, and I sure don't need anyone psychoanalyzing my failed relationships with real women."

"Fine," said Haylie. "But your patient needs to be catheterized, and you need to do something about that."

"What's going on?" Prateeka asked, resting an elbow on the counter of the nurse's station desk. She looked at Brad with concern. "Is something wrong?"

Haylie gave her a serious look. "It's Brad's patient," she said softly. "We just discovered that she's a transgender woman."

"Does that mean she is a woman becoming a man, or a man becoming a woman?"

"A man becoming a woman," Haylie said. "She recently had a breast augmentation surgery, which led to a post-op infection, and that's why she's here on Med-Surg South now. Brad has been taking care of her, and he just found out today that she still has male genitals."

"I don't care how much surgery he gets," Brad said angrily. "He was born male. You can change what's on the outside, but he'll always be a man."

"Brad, what's gotten into you?" Haylie asked incredulously, shaking her head from side to side. "Your patient needs to be catheterized, and you need to get a urine specimen to the lab. You've got to put your issues with her gender preference aside and take care of her."

He stood quietly, crossing his arms over his chest. "I don't think I can go back in there," he said. His voice trembled slightly.

Prateeka looked at Brad, then at Haylie. "Let me help," Prateeka said. "I can start the catheter on the patient and send urine to the lab."

"Fine," Brad said. "Lee Matthews. Bed 4-A. Don't forget – male kit." He squeezed his eyes shut and reached up, pinching the bridge of his nose.

"What's wrong now?" Haylie asked.

"Headache," he said.

"Take care of your headache," said Prateeka, "and I'll take care of your patient." She stepped away, disappearing behind the door of Lee's room.

Haylie stepped toward Brad, lowering her voice. "Why don't you take a walk to clear your head? Get some fresh air?"

Brad waited for a moment. "I think that's probably a good idea." He disappeared into the breakroom and came out a moment later with his backpack slung over his shoulder. "I'll be back in fifteen," he said, glancing down at his watch to mark the time.

Shortly after Brad left, Prateeka returned to the nurse's station.

"I got the urine specimen and sent it to the lab for Miss Matthews," she said.

"Good," Haylie said, turning toward the computer and trying to appear busy.

Prateeka sat in a rolling chair and scooted next to Haylie. "Now that Miss Matthews is taken care of, can I talk to you for a moment, Haylie?" She asked.

"About what?" Haylie replied, not looking up from the computer screen.

Prateeka paused for a moment. "I feel as if we got off on the wrong foot," she said.

Haylie looked at Prateeka for a split second. "You think?" She immediately returned her gaze to the computer.

"Yes," Prateeka said. "I feel as if I have offended you somehow. Am I correct, Haylie? Is that how you feel?"

Haylie closed her eyes and took a deep breath, then turned to Prateeka. "Okay," she said. "You want to know I feel? I feel like I've been trying so hard to be nice to you ever since you came to work here, and you don't even care."

Prateeka sat back slightly. "Why do you feel that way?"

"We threw a covered dish lunch for you when you came. I organized that, you know. I was the one who made that whole thing happen. And you didn't even eat any of the food that we had prepared."

"I'm sorry that I hurt your feelings," Prateeka said, "but I'm a—"

"And then, you started talking about how arranged marriages work better than love marriages. Like the rest of us are idiots for wanting to marry people that we actually get to know first, and fall in love with."

"But Haylie, I was just stating a fact—"

"Yeah, but then," Haylie interrupted once again, "You and your friend were speaking a different language when I got off the elevator. And when you saw me, you stopped, and you didn't start again until I walked away. Were you talking about me, Prateeka? Were you making fun of me right in front of my face, and laughing about it because I couldn't understand a word you were saying?"

Prateeka's eyes grew wide. "No, Haylie, we weren't talking about you, I promise. And the reason why I didn't eat the food at my welcome luncheon on Monday is because I'm a vegetarian. I am Hindu. Most of us are. And I'm really sorry if my comment about arranged marriages offended you. I was just stating a fact, and I didn't think that it would be perceived as offensive. I'm sorry if you feel that way, I didn't mean to be rude to you."

Just then, Donna peeked out of her office. She made eye contact with Haylie.

"It's fine," Haylie said, obviously embarrassed that their manager had been tuned into the conversation. She took a deep breath and sighed loudly. "Look, just forget I said anything." Snapping back into nurse mode, she rose to her feet and proceeded to check on her patients.

And Prateeka, although thoroughly dazed and confused, followed Haylie's lead and did the same.

***

Donna peered out of the break room. She had overhead much more than she had wanted to that afternoon. She planned to pull Brad into her office and talk to him when he got back on the unit about his issues in caring for Lee Matthews; that was certainly the more pressing need.

The most recent conversation she'd overheard, however, had been the exchange between Haylie and Prateeka. If not for the fact that Haylie was being completely unfair and inappropriate toward the newest member of Med-Surg South's team, it would almost be funny. Not long ago, Haylie had been the newest nurse, and had been on the receiving end of some harsh treatment by Miriam. The two had both put a great effort into improving their work relationship since that time, but Haylie often felt the need still to remind her colleagues of her rocky start. What a shame, Donna felt it was, that Haylie could so easily recall being a victim of lateral violence and intolerance, but could not recognize that she was now guilty of inflicting the same bad behavior on a peer. She would make some time later that day to talk to Haylie privately as well.

The stress level on the unit was already running high, thanks to the hurricane headed toward them. Things didn't need to get even more out of control than they already were. She turned to her computer and began an e-mail.

To: Dagmar Garrett, Education Services

Subject: Diversity

Hello Dagmar,

I need your help! My unit, Med-Surg South, is experiencing some interesting interpersonal situations right now. I could make a long list of them for you, but I think that the easiest way to describe our need is to say that we are coming into contact with individuals – both patients and staff- who are very different from ourselves. The diversity is creating challenges. I attended a leadership seminar last year in which you spoke about diversity, and you did a very nice job. I would like to invite you to our unit to deliver a brief inservice for my nurses, hopefully as soon as possible. Please contact me if you want to discuss further. I realize that the hospital is in disaster preparedness mode right now, as everyone is getting ready for the hurricane, but there's an even bigger storm brewing on my unit and we need your help!

Donna LeShay

Nurse Manager, Med-Surg South

***

After work, Brad took a detour on the way home. He found himself hovering on the front porch of Andrea's parents' house. He tried to collect his thoughts before knocking.

I've got to get her back, he told himself. *Whatever it takes, whatever I have to say, whatever I have to do. I don't want to keep striking out with women.*

I don't want to be alone for the rest of my life.

He took a deep breath and knocked.

Seconds later, Andrea appeared at the door.

"I miss you something awful," said Brad

She opened the screen door and stepped outside. "Let's sit down on the porch, okay?" Andrea pulled the door shut behind her.

Brad found it odd that she hadn't wanted to invite him inside, as she had every time before when he'd come to visit her at her parents' house. Even if it was just to pick her up to go out on a date, she always held the door open for him and waved him inside. He'd made it a habit to always say hello to her parents and make small talk with them. At first, it had been solely to make a good impression on them, but as he had grown close to Andrea, he'd also become fond of her parents and always looked forward to seeing them. It was quite obvious now that he was no longer welcome in her home, and likely, in her life altogether.

"Are you sure we can't go in for a second?" He asked. "Don't know if you've heard, but there's a hurricane coming." He tried to sound playful to lighten the mood, but failed.

As they settled into the bench-style porch swing that was big enough for three, Andrea planted herself next to one of the armrests, making it quite clear that she wanted some space in between them. Brad obliged and sat at the opposite end of the swing, resting his elbow on the other armrest. He glanced at her sideways as she reached up to push away the layers of dark hair that the wind was blowing in her face.

"What do you want, Brad?" Andrea asked.

"I just miss you. I was hoping we could spend some time together."

She said nothing.

"How have you been?" He asked.

"Good. Busy. I picked up an extra shift this week. I'm exhausted, but I need the money for... you know." She crossed her arms over her chest. "I looked at a couple of places this week where the rent is reasonable."

"Oh," Brad nodded. *No!* He wanted to blurt out. *Don't go rent another place! Just move in with me!*

Andrea faced him again. "So how are things going with Sue back home?"

"Really awkward," Brad felt his stomach suddenly turn into

knots. "She's said she's looking for a job and a place of her own so she can move out."

Andrea simply nodded.

"We're not getting back together," Brad said to her as he reached for her hand. She allowed him to hold it for just a second, but didn't offer her usual reassuring squeeze.

"I don't want to hold you back from Sue if you want to be with her." She gently pulled her hand out of his grasp and rested it in her lap. "If you still love her, Brad, then that's okay with me. I'm not going to be mad at you."

"I don't love her," he quickly said. "I'm over Sue. The thought of getting back together never even crossed my mind." It was a lie, and he sensed that Andrea knew it.

"I think you're fooling yourself."

"Why?"

"I saw the look on your face when you saw her there on your doorstep."

"Whatever you think you saw was nothing more than shock and surprise. And anger. I was mad that she showed up out of the blue like that. It was rude to me, and insulting to you."

"She didn't even know about me, so I don't see how I could find it insulting." Andrea turned her face away from him. "Brad, you couldn't feel anger like that if she didn't still mean something to you."

"She doesn't," Brad insisted. He scooted closer to her and wrapped his arm around her shoulders. "Please believe me, Andrea. I know this all feels weird to you, and trust me, it's weird to me too. I didn't ask Sue to come back. She just did, and it caught me off guard. The only reason she's staying at my house right now is because she doesn't have anywhere else to go. Her name is still on the lease, so legally, it's still her place until the lease runs out. But she's going to move out, and soon. This is just a temporary situation, I swear to you."

"I'm not so sure about that," she said. A tear shot down her cheek.

"I'd never do anything to hurt you."

She nodded. "I know you probably mean that, and I'm sure you think you'd never be able to hurt me," she said, "but sometimes things just happen, even when you don't mean for them to. You and Sue were together for a long time. And as much as you want to deny it, there's still chemistry between you. Even I could feel it when you and Sue laid eyes on each other the other day. I don't want to take you away from her, Brad. I'm afraid that if you let Sue go again, you'll end up regretting it, and you'll resent me."

"Nothing will happen between me and Sue. NOTHING. I promise you." He pulled her toward him and wrapped his arms around her. "The only thing that I could ever regret is letting you go."

She didn't embrace him in return.

"I really do miss you," he said. "How long has it been since the last time we saw each other?"

"About a week."

"Seems like an eternity."

"Yeah, well... how's work going for you?" She struggled to change the subject.

He fell silent for a moment. "I had a crazy day."

"Oh? What's going on?"

Brad sighed deeply. "I've got a she-man patient."

"A what?" Andrea drew back and looked confused.

"A patient who looks like a woman, talks like a woman, acts like a woman... but has a penis."

"So she's transgender," Andrea said.

"Yeah. I went to start a cath on him and it sort of freaked me out when I peeled back the covers and saw what was underneath."

"Him?" Andrea said cautiously.

"Yeah. Well, it's a man. It has a penis. I don't know what people call them these days. Transvestites... transgenders, something like that, I guess."

"It? Them?" Andrea said.

"Yeah."

She stood up, her back turned toward him.

"What? Did I say something wrong?"

"Them," she said, clearly offended. "You say that like they're not human or something."

"I did not," Brad said, growing a bit defensive. "What's wrong with the word them? It's the same word I'd use to refer to any group of people that I don't have anything in common with."

Andrea whirled around. "So you have nothing at all in common with your patient just because she's transgender?"

"He. Anatomically, he's a man."

"But as you said, a man that looks like a woman, talks like a woman, acts like a woman, and prefers to be treated like a woman, right?"

"Well, yeah, but gender isn't something you can choose. His medical record has his gender on it. MALE. He can't change that."

One of Andrea's eyebrows shot up. "So then why was it such a big surprise to you that your patient had a penis?"

"I sort of overlooked that," he admitted. "I mean, if you walk into your patient's room and you see a person that looks like a woman, and who has a woman's name, you don't really need to go to the medical record and verify that she's a woman, do you?"

"I haven't been in that situation just yet. But if I were, it wouldn't be a big deal. She wants to be a woman, so what? It's her life to live, not yours. Why are you so offended?"

"Because you're either born a man or a woman, and it's just plain… freaky… and weird to pretend to be something you're not. I mean, he talked to me like a woman. He smiled at me like a woman. He had me thinking he was a woman."

"It sounds like you and your patient were flirting with each other. Now you're going to tell me that it's okay for a female patient to flirt with you, but not a male patient."

"You're missing the point," he said. "What I'm trying to say is I don't like being deceived. And that's what this guy was doing with me. It was just plain wrong."

Andrea stood quietly for a moment.

"What?" Brad nudged her for a response. "Are you offended?"

"Yes," Andrea said.

"Why?" Confused, Brad stood up from the swing and faced her.

She reached up to her face and slid her index finger underneath the lens of her glasses, wiping tears away.

"Now you're crying?" Brad was confused.

"I need to tell you something," Andrea began. "About my brother."

"Anthony," Brad offered. "You talk about him all the time. When do I get to meet him? And what does he have to do with all of this?"

"Anthony is gay," Andrea blurted out.

Brad felt as if he'd been kicked in the gut. "Why… why didn't you say something before?"

"Why did I need to?" She asked. "Would it have made any difference?"

"No," Brad shook his head vigorously. "Absolutely not. I'm just wondering why it never came up until now?"

"I've spent most of my life protecting Anthony from people like you," she said bitterly. "It all started when Anthony got his first crush on another boy back in fifth grade. The two of them were walking across the playground one day, and Anthony – thinking that the feeling was mutual – reached out and tried to hold the other boy's hand. The kid punched him in the face, knocked him to the ground, spit on him, and then kicked him several times. And once the word got out about what had happened, life as we knew it was over. I'm a year older than him and should have graduated a year earlier, but when all of the bullying started, I failed school that year on purpose so that he and I would be in the same grade after that and could take all of our classes together. On a good day, he'd get vulgar notes in his locker or would get teased mercilessly by his classmates. And on a bad day, he'd get dragged into the locker room or the bathroom and would be beaten to a bloody pulp. I was always on standby, every single day, to be the one to run and get a teacher to intervene, or else jump in and start throwing punches myself to defend him."

"Oh," was all that Brad could say.

"When we both graduated," Andrea continued, "he went off to college while I was getting married and moving out of state. I made him promise to call me every day so that I would know he was alive and well. I made him promise to keep his sexual orientation a secret until he knew for certain that he was in a place that was safe; until he knew that he was surrounded by people who could accept him for who he is."

Brad was speechless. He blinked his eyes a few times, and felt his heart rate speed up.

Andrea continued. "Do you know what that was like for him, Brad? To have to start a new life somewhere, and hide who he really was from everyone else? My little brother has lived in hell for most of his life, because he's been surrounded by people who think and feel just like you do – that men who like other men must be weirdos and freaks and that there must be something wrong with them."

"I... I didn't say that. I said my patient was a freak. I didn't say anything about your brother."

"So gays aren't weird, but transgender people are?"

"Yes. No. I mean... I don't know. I... Andrea, I would never do anything to hurt your brother. I would never do anything to hurt anyone in your family. And I would never do any of the terrible things that people did to Anthony. I never beat up on anyone in school, or even while I was in the military, and trust me, I saw it happen a lot. There are gays in every single branch of the military and life is not easy for them—"

"And what about your patient, Brad? Is life easy for her?"

"You mean, him."

"See? That's exactly what I'm talking about. How easy can your life be when everyone else is telling you what you can and can't be? Who you can and can't love? Or even who you can and can't flirt with?"

"You're blowing this way out of proportion," Brad said. "I didn't mean to get you so upset. You just asked me how my day was, and I was just trying to tell you that I had a patient that I felt really... uncomfortable with."

"So why couldn't you just say that? Why did your patient have to be a freak?"

Brad shook his head. "I'm sorry, Andrea, it just came out all wrong. But I'd never say or do anything to Anthony—"

"I know you won't, because you're never going to meet him."

Brad stood still for a moment, blinking rapidly while Andrea's words registered in his mind. "What?"

Andrea opened the front door. "Please just leave, Brad. This isn't going to work. We're done. Go back home to Sue. She can be the girlfriend you want. I'm sure she doesn't have any gay siblings, and I'm sure that your life with her will be absolutely normal and perfect."

"Andrea, wait!" Brad caught the door with his hand before she shut it. "Don't do this. Don't look for reasons to argue with me just because Sue came back. Sue and I are over, don't you hear me? It's OVER! I love you, and I don't want you to be mad at me. I'll do whatever it takes to make this right."

Andrea looked away. "Just go, Brad, please."

"Let's... let's get married," Brad suddenly blurted out.

Andrea's eyes grew wide as she faced him once again. "Are you crazy? I can't believe you just said that. I can't see you anymore, Brad. It's over. Please just go," she said, as she pushed his hand away and pulled the door closed.

Nice job, idiot, Brad said to himself. *Way to go. That makes the second rejected marriage proposal in just a matter of months. Now you're twice dumped, and you're probably never going to settle down and get married. You're never going to find a woman who loves you and makes you happy. And if you do find a woman who seems to be perfect? Don't get too excited, because she'll probably turn out to be a man.*

Brad stormed off of Andrea's porch and jumped into his car. His tires squealed as he backed out of the driveway and sped down the road that led away from her house.

Chapter 13
Wednesday Morning

"I need to see everyone in the break room," Donna said to Miriam, Brad, Prateeka and Haylie as they lined up to badge in.

They filed in, one by one, and took a seat around the table.

As they settled into their chairs, they noticed that there were index cards taped to the walls, scattered all around the room. Single words appeared on each card, which all of the nurses quickly discovered were descriptive words used to refer to particular 'types' of persons.

Muslim.

Woman.

African-American.

Transgender.

Non-English Speaker.

Mentally Ill.

Deaf.

Overweight.

Single.

Parent.

Jew.

Doctor.

Elderly.

Middle-Eastern.

Gay.

Blind.

Native American.

Uninsured.

Man.

Caucasian.

Immigrant.

And the list went on. There were roughly thirty index cards. The nurses gave each other confused glances as they scanned over them as they settled into the circle of chairs in the middle of the break room.

"What's this all about?" Haylie asked.

"No whining and complaining," Donna scolded. "I invited a colleague from Education Services to do an inservice for us this morning. I've got float nurses covering the unit right now, so there's a lot invested in this hour of training."

The door opened and Mel peered into the room. She was dressed for work in scrubs and her hair was pulled back into a neat bun at the nape of her neck. Her face looked weary, and the dark purple bruise under her eye made her look even more pitiful. Nonetheless, she was smiling. "Hey everyone," she said. "Guess what? I'm a grandma now. Maxton Jeremy Page just made his big debut around one thirty this morning. Seven pounds, four ounces. He and Jenny are both doing great."

"Congratulations!" Her colleagues said, almost in unison. They rose to their feet and surrounded her with hugs and pats on the back.

Donna smiled and embraced her. "That's wonderful news, Mel, but what in the world are you doing here?"

Mel gave a little salute. "Reporting for duty," she said with a smile. "Don't worry about me. I ran home after Jenny delivered so I could get a shower and a few hours sleep. With the hurricane coming tomorrow, all hands are needed on deck. If we're fine on Med-Surg South, I'll be happy to float to another unit that is short-staffed."

"Are you sure? Don't you want to be with your family right now?" Donna asked.

Mel shook her head. "It's okay, really. Jenny's father and his fiancée are visiting with her and the baby today. She's going to have plenty of visitors and I think it will be overwhelming enough without me around. Once things calm down a bit, I can go check in on her during my breaks."

"Well, alright then," Donna smiled. "You're just in time for an inservice."

"About what?" Mel asked. The others looked expectantly at Donna.

"Take a guess," she said. "This week has presented each of us with some unique situations, and there are some things that we should talk about as a team. I think it would be best if we do so with a facilitator who can guide us through a meaningful discussion."

"I'm guessing that this training is about differences," Prateeka said, as she panned around the room and looked at the handwritten signs on the wall. Clutching a brand new legal size notepad to her chest and two sharpened pencils in one hand, she looked very much like an excited child on the first day of school.

Donna nodded. "Correct. It's about diversity."

"Listen, Donna," Brad said, making himself the spokesperson for the group nurses. "Is this really the best time? I know we've all had our share of... uh... diversity over the past couple of days, but is one more training going to fix everything? Why can't we just talk through things like adults? I feel like a kid being sent to school when I don't even want to go."

"The timing couldn't be worse," Haylie chimed in. "We just got here. And every bed is full right now."

Raising an eyebrow, Donna shot both of them a look that very clearly spoke the words that her mouth did not – *Let's change the attitude, please.* "This inservice will only take an hour of your time. And like I told you, the unit is covered for now," she said to Haylie. Then she turned and addressed Brad. "Talking is exactly what we're going to do this morning."

Then the trainer entered the breakroom. "Good morning, Med-Surg South," she said. The nurses recognized her as one of the educators from Dogwood Regional Hospital's Education Services Department. She was a petite, young-looking woman, with long blonde hair gathered neatly into a French twist. She had a glowing smile, which immediately put the group at ease.

"Welcome, Dagmar," Donna said, as she eased into a chair. "We're happy to have you. I just explained to everyone the purpose of our inservice this morning, so I'm going to let you take it from here."

"I'm Dagmar Garrett, from Education Services," she introduced herself, speaking with a slight German accent. She moved toward them in slow, measured strides. Although she was barely five feet tall, she carried herself with pride and seemed much taller. She continued speaking as she walked. "And to the young man who just commented that we should talk about some of the situations you've been facing – just normal adult conversation – kudos to you. Dialogue is a very effective way for us to learn from each other, so that's exactly what we're going to do today. We're going to talk with each other."

Brad grinned as if he had just received a pardon from a serious crime.

Dagmar pulled a chair out from the table and sat between Donna and Mel.

"It's a bit of a tight squeeze," Donna said. "Sorry we didn't have a bigger place to meet."

"It's quite alright," said Dagmar. "As it turns out, this is a perfect setting for our inservice. Even if we were in a larger classroom, I would try to put us all in a roundtable formation anyway."

"Just call us the knights of the roundtable," Brad said in a badly impersonated British accent. All in the group laughed, including Dagmar.

"There you go," she said. "There have been lots of groups of people throughout history who have used a circular structure to hold meetings, in which they've made important decisions, planned strategy, or just had simple face to face discussions, like we're doing today. King Arthur's Knights of the Roundtable is one example. Native Americans and Quakers are others. The circle structure removes the perception of barriers between us and shifts our mindset to one of equality. There's no back row or front row in the circle, and no figurehead. We are all partners sharing in a process, which, in this case, is a discussion about diversity."

Then Dagmar paused for a long moment. She looked at each face in the group, and each of them returned her gaze, watching with an expectant stare. She remained silent until it became uncomfortable for the group.

Finally, Donna smiled. Watching her, Mel couldn't help but smile too. When Haylie saw Mel's grin, she did the same. Brad, Miriam, and Prateeka followed, almost simultaneously.

Then Dagmar grinned. "The fact that you're all smiling right now isn't just a coincidence. It's another phenomena that occurs within a circle. It's called mirroring, which basically means that we copy each other when we communicate with each other. Sometimes it's verbal with words, but most often, it's non-verbal, with body language. Mirroring is a very natural human behavior, and it lets us know that we're giving each other our attention – we're in touch with each other. Yet another reason why discussions work so much better in a circle formation."

"I feel like I'm back in Psych 101," Haylie laughed.

"Well, let's shift gears to Diversity 101," Dagmar laughed in return. "Here's your first assignment. Pair up with the person closest to you and take three minutes to find out three things that you have in common with them. Three things in common, three minutes. Go for it."

Brad and Mel turned their chairs to face each other.

Prateeka was seated next to Donna, and began to turn to her, hoping to avoid pairing up with Haylie, who sat on her other side.

Not so fast, Donna wanted to say, but made a more effective maneuver when she scooted her chair toward Miriam, who smiled knowingly.

Prateeka quickly got the hint and turned to Haylie, who didn't bother hiding her discontent. "Guess we're a group," she whined.

Donna and Miriam immediately began to converse, as did Mel and Brad. Prateeka and Haylie let an awkward moment of silence pass between them before they began to talk to each other as well.

After a couple of moments had passed, Dagmar held her wrist up to eye level, watching carefully as her watch marked the passing of three minutes. "Thirty seconds," she announced as time was running out, then called out "time" after the remaining half minute passed. She instructed the group to face each other in the circle once more.

"Miriam and Donna," Dagmar said, glancing briefly at each of them, "what three things do you have in common?"

Miriam smiled. "This was too easy," she said. "We're both widows, we've both been nurse managers of Med-Surg South – I'm the previous manager, and Donna is my successor and the current manager, of course – and..."

"We both love babies," Donna said with a laugh. "Miriam was talking about her little grandson Timothy and it almost made me tear up. It seems like just yesterday that my own children were crawling around in diapers. They were so much easier to deal with back then."

The group laughed.

"Nice job," Dagmar nodded. "Mel? Brad? How about you?" She looked at each of them with a smile.

Brad chimed in. "For starters, we've both been through some tough times this year when it comes to relationships. Mel got divorced, and I went through a breakup with a serious girlfriend." He was referring to Sue, of course. Brad wasn't yet ready to admit to anyone else that Andrea had called off their relationship. Haylie met his eyes and held his gaze for a moment. She was the only one in the room who knew just how bad things really were for Brad's love life.

"Second," Mel took over the conversation, "Here's a dirty little secret of ours that not many of you know – we've both been smokers before."

Miriam's jaw dropped. "Smokers! You should know better, you two. Haven't you seen enough lung disease patients?"

"Sure we have," Mel said. "But we all do crazy things sometimes."

"And if you didn't hear Mel correctly," Brad said, rolling his eyes, "she said we used to be smokers. Anyway, our third and final thing we have in common – we both LOVE Filipino food."

Everyone laughed again. "Mel and I are best friends," he explained to Dagmar. "And she's a great cook. She got me hooked on lumpia, and I never before knew that I could eat bean sprouts and actually enjoy them."

"Really? What's lumpia?" Dagmar asked Mel.

"It's a Filipino egg roll. It's made with bean sprouts, carrots, and... hey, wait... aren't you supposed to be a diversity expert? Don't you know all about diets from different cultures around the world?"

Dagmar's smile broadened. "I wouldn't call myself an expert in diversity. I'm a diversity facilitator."

"So what exactly does a diversity facilitator do?" Mel asked.

"I'll get around to that in a moment," Dagmar promised. "But for now, we need to hear from Prateeka and Haylie." She read their names from their hospital badges and looked at them expectantly.

As if on cue, both of them exchanged an anxious glance.

"We both failed the assignment," Haylie said.

"Why do you say that?" Dagmar asked.

"Because, you said we had to come up with three things in common between us. We could only come up with one."

"What is it?" Dagmar asked.

"Our blood type," Prateeka replied. "We are both B negative. In searching for things that we have in common, I remember Haylie mentioned earlier this week that she gave blood for the first time ever. The blood bank told her that she has a fairly rare blood type. So I asked her just now what her type is, and she told me B negative. The very same as mine."

"That's an interesting take on what you have in common," Dagmar said. "I bet there's more than just blood type. Maybe it will just take time to figure out the rest."

Haylie shook her head ever so slightly, in subtle protest. She wasn't sure how many of her colleagues caught it.

Dagmar certainly had, but it was time to move on. "Now, as I promised each of you, I will explain what a diversity facilitator is," Dagmar resumed. "I certainly don't want all of you to think that I know every single detail about every culture, group, or individual person in this world. That's not why I'm here. My purpose isn't to dump a bunch of knowledge on you and run off into the sunset; it's to help you become better students lifelong scholars, if you will – of diversity. My hope for today is to create a learning environment that will help you to be better prepared to interact with people who are different from yourselves."

Several heads nodded around the circle.

"So other than being a diversity facilitator, can you tell us a bit more about you?" Donna asked. "We each told you three things about ourselves, so your turn, Dagmar. Tell us three things about you!"

Dagmar smiled. "It's only fair," she agreed. "First thing – I'm not a natural citizen of the United States of America, as many of you have probably already guessed. I was born and raised in Germany. I married an American soldier who was stationed there, and relocated back to the states with him when his tour of duty was finished. He just retired last year and wanted to move back to his hometown of Dogwood, so that's how we ended up here."

"Do you ever miss Germany?" Prateeka asked.

"Every day," Dagmar said. "But at the same time, I love living in Dogwood. I'll always have two homes in my heart."

"As will I," said Prateeka. "Tell us more about you, Dagmar."

She nodded. "Alright. Like all of you, I'm a registered nurse. I worked in Oncology for six years prior to taking a position in the Education Services Department two years ago."

"What was the reason for the move to Education?" Donna asked.

"I had a baby," said Dagmar, "and I wanted to get away from shift work for a while. My position in Education Services is eight to five, Monday through Friday. It's an easier work schedule for a new mom."

"I can certainly understand," said Mel. "A new baby changes everything. My daughter just had her first child early this morning. She and the baby will be living with me for a while. I get overwhelmed just thinking about how much our lives are going to change with this new little person added to the mix!"

Everyone laughed.

"So those are three defining things about me," Dagmar continued. "And look at how much I have in common with the rest of you already. It's easy to see how different we are as individuals, isn't it? But when people take the time to get to know each other, they often find that they are as much alike as they are different. And on that note, let's change gears and think about the many different people that we come into contact with every day. Like our patients and their families. Our co-workers. Our neighbors, our family members and friends." Dagmar reached behind her, grabbing a thick pad of adhesive notes from her tote bag. She handed it to Miriam.

"Each of you, please take about thirty of these adhesive notes."

Miriam separated about a quarter of an inch from the pad, making her best guess at thirty notes, and passed it to Brad. He pulled approximately the same amount, as did Mel, and all the rest of the nurses when the pad was passed their way. When it had traveled throughout the entire circle and had reached Dagmar again, the pad had been reduced to less than half of its original thickness.

"Thanks everyone," Dagmar said. "Do you all have a pen or pencil?"

All of the nurses nodded, reaching for their writing instruments.

"Great. Now, please stand up, and go to one of the four walls in this room. I believe that each of you have already noticed the index cards on the wall. Each card has a word that describes a person. What I'd like for you to do is write down the very first thought that comes to mind when you read that card. Write it down on one of the adhesive notes, and stick the note under the card. Don't censor your thoughts, and don't feel like you have to write something politically correct. Don't write what you think others expect you to think or feel about the particular type of person described on the card; just write the first thing that you think or feel. And when you finish with one card, move to the next so that you cover all of the cards in the room, and end up back in the same card where you started."

The nurses rose from their seats, and went to the wall nearest the door, as if it were the most natural starting point.

Dagmar continued. "Before we start, let's actually spread out throughout the room, so you can give your colleagues some privacy as you're writing your thoughts down. Your responses should be as anonymous as possible. If you'd like to write in all capital letters, that might make it harder for you to recognize each others' handwriting."

As instructed, the six nurses scattered themselves as distantly as possible across the four walls. Each of them wrote their thoughts on the adhesive notes, then posted them under the index cards. Dagmar stood in the middle of the room and observed. As they began to shift and move from one wall to the next, the process slowed somewhat as the nurses paused to read the notes that their colleagues had left before their own. When everyone had made their way around the room, they looked expectantly at Dagmar.

"Stay put where you are," she said. "Haylie, please pick one of the cards closest to you, and read the responses underneath it."

"Uninsured," Haylie said, then focused on the six adhesive notes below it and read them aloud, one by one. "Poor. Unhealthy. Working people pay for their health care. Poor. Will never pay the bill. Feel sorry for them."

Dagmar nodded. "Okay, Prateeka next."

Prateeka pinned her index finger to the card closest to her. "Gay," she said. "Secretive. Good sense of fashion and style. Make me nervous. Feel sad for them. My cousin. Can't get married."

Dagmar turned her attention to Brad. "Brad, go."

"Caucasian," Brad said. "Me. Privileged. Can get jobs easier than minorities. Can't dance," Brad said, and laughed. The group joined him. "Majority," he continued. "Who I am."

"Thank you," Dagmar said. "Miriam? Would you like to go next?"

Miriam nodded. "Muslim," she said. "Covered heads. Prateeka. Terrorism. Women are inferior. The war. Peaceful religion."

"Thank you. Donna?"

"Jew," said Donna. "Religious. Hanukkah. Stingy. Rich. Haylie. Don't celebrate Christmas and Easter."

Dagmar nodded. "And last but not least, Mel."

Mel pointed to a card, as Prateeka had. "Immigrant," she read. "Poor. Don't speak English. We pay for their health care. Need interpreters. Feel sorry for them. Big families crowding the room."

"Thank you everyone," said Dagmar. "If you'd like to read the remaining comments for the rest of the index cards, we'll take a break in just a minute and you can do so then. Let's take our seats for now."

As the nurses returned to their chairs, all could feel that the mood in the room had changed. There was a palpable feeling of tension between them that hadn't been there before.

"Let's talk about what we just did," Dagmar said, taking her seat between Miriam and Donna once again. "What are your first reactions?"

A quiet moment followed. Prateeka was the first to speak. "I'm surprised," she said. "Someone wrote my name under 'Muslim,' but I am not. I am Hindu. I am also an immigrant, yet I am not poor, I am not uninsured, no one else here pays for my health care. And I do speak English."

"I'm irritated," Haylie said. "Okay, fine, I'm Jewish, but I'm not rich, nor stingy. I don't have much, but what I do have, I've worked hard for, and I think I'm a pretty generous person. But someone labeled me Jewish, just like they labeled Prateeka a Muslim. They got the Jewish part right, but I don't like being in the same category with 'stingy' and 'rich.' That's just… stupid. Those are nothing but ridiculous stereotypes." She crossed her arms defiantly.

Dagmar nodded. "I wish I could tell you how many times people have commented about my height and have said to me things like 'I thought all Germans were tall?' I was born and raised in Germany, and I don't remember people being any taller there than they are here in the United States. You're right Haylie," she said with a little laugh. "Those generalized beliefs, or stereotypes, can be pretty ridiculous sometimes."

Prateeka grinned and turned toward Haylie. "At last we have another thing in common. People misjudge us, yes?"

With a halfhearted smile, Haylie nodded. "You could say that."

"At least you are not seen as a terrorist," Prateeka said. "I'm not even a Muslim, but someone in this group thinks that I am, and others in the group associate Muslims with war and terrorism."

"I wrote that," Brad said, sounding a bit defensive. "Not that you're Muslim, Prateeka, but the note about terrorism under the Muslim card. I wrote that, because Dagmar told us to write the first thing that came to our minds. I was in the military for four years, and during that time, I witnessed a great deal of terrorist activity that involved Muslims. I provided aid to Muslim victims of terrorist attacks. The note that I wrote said 'terrorism,' not 'terrorists.' You interpreted it the wrong way."

"So why did you not write the word 'victim?' Why did you choose to write 'terrorism' instead?" Prateeka asked.

"Because it was my first thought," Brad defended himself. "We weren't supposed to censor our thoughts."

"Thank you for making that point, Brad," Dagmar said. "You did exactly what I told you to do – you wrote the first thing that came to your mind. All of you did that, and look at the reactions that it has created already. I think we can all feel the tension in this room, and as Haylie and Prateeka have expressed, there is some offense taken. And as Brad showed us, there is misunderstanding. We'll talk about this a minute, but first I want the rest of you to comment on what you thought about this exercise."

Mel was the next to speak. "Well... I don't know if this is the kind of comment you're looking for, but one thing that I noticed is that a lot of people identified specific people as their first thought. Someone's response to 'Gay' was 'My cousin.' Someone put 'Haylie' for 'Jewish.' And one of us identified 'Prateeka' as being 'Muslim' even though that was incorrect."

"Excellent point," Dagmar said, "Your observation is a very powerful one, Mel. Sometimes we make judgments about entire groups of people based on the interactions or experiences that we've had with only one person, or a small group of people. It's called generalizing, and it can be a very bad thing."

"How so?" Miriam asked.

"Because holding stereotypes or making generalizations about people can lead to biases. A bias is a tendency to think or act a certain way. Biases can affect the way that we behave toward each other."

"I think I get what you're saying," Miriam said. "I have a blind patient right now, so I paid close attention to the 'blind' and 'deaf' cards. And I was really shocked by what I saw. I'm realizing now how it could lead to biases."

"Why don't you go back to the wall where the 'blind' and 'deaf' cards are and read us those responses?"

Miriam stood from her seat and went to the wall where the cards were mounted. "Let's start with 'Blind' first," she said. "Disability. Seeing-eye dogs. Feel sorry for them. Daphne. Missing out on a lot. Don't have normal lives." Miriam sighed, then moved to the 'Deaf' card. "Deaf: Disability. Feel sorry for them. Hearing aids. Missing out on a lot. Don't have normal lives. Have to get an interpreter for a deaf patient."

"So tell us why you're surprised," said Dagmar.

"Well, some of the responses are almost identical," she said. "Blindness and deafness have traditionally been seen as disabilities, and people with blindness or deafness have been lumped into a giant category called 'the disabled,' with people who use wheelchairs, or who have a mental or emotional illness. Someone in our group consistently writes 'feel sorry for them' as their first thought. I noticed it showed up under 'Gay' and 'Uninsured' well. I'm not picking on the person who wrote that, but since this is a learning experience, I just want to share that just because people are different doesn't mean that they want, need, nor deserve pity. People who are blind and deaf… and even people in wheelchairs, and with mental or emotional illnesses do lead normal lives. Like my patient, Daphne. She doesn't feel like she's missing out on anything in life as some of the responses suggest. And she certainly doesn't consider herself disabled."

"Thank you, Miriam," Dagmar said. "So can you explore this a bit and tell us how those kinds of thoughts about a person who is blind, for instance, can lead to biases?"

Miriam paused for a moment to think. "Well, if I have a blind patient, and I feel sorry for that person because I think that she is not 'normal,' so to speak, then I may treat her differently. I may pay more attention to her than my other patients, which would compromise the care that I'm giving to others. Or the pity that I feel for my blind patient may come across in the way that I talk to her and interact with her, and it could make her feel offended and uncomfortable."

"Great," said Dagmar. "Very good example of how a bias can lead to inappropriate behavior. Let me also share a personal example with you. Prior to moving to Dogwood, I worked at a hospital in New York. I was in Germany when I applied for the job, so my interview was done over the phone. My manager asked for my scrub size and ordered a few sets for me. When I arrived for my orientation, I was handed my scrubs, which were way too big for me. My manager had ordered a size up from what I had requested, in tall length instead of regular. When I asked her why she had ordered the wrong size, she said, 'I thought Germans were big people! Tall and wide. You're the first one I've seen that's small.' I wasn't very happy, of course."

Mel's eyes widened. "Wow. Now that was just plain ignorant."

"She was acting on a bias," Dagmar said. "I asked my manager why she thought that all German people were 'big and wide.' It turns out she had a German teacher in high school who was very tall and quite overweight. She met her teacher's family at some kind of school event, and all of the family members were tall and overweight too. Then my manager named several movies that she had seen in which the German characters were played by big people. What all of that added up to in her mind is that all German people were big people. So when she ordered my scrubs, she ordered for a stereotype, not for me."

"I sure hope she apologized to you," Haylie said, shaking her head.

"She did," Dagmar smiled. "And I got new correct-size scrubs very quickly. Now, to get us back on task, are there any other thoughts that any of you would like to share about this exercise?"

The group pondered Dagmar's question for a moment.

"It's pretty amazing to see how one word can evoke such different thoughts from each of us," Donna broke the silence. "I guess what struck me the most is how opposite some of the responses can be. For instance, under Muslim, someone's first thought was 'war,' yet somebody else put 'peaceful religion.' War and peace - they're completely opposite."

Dagmar nodded. "Thank you all. Let's take a five-minute break so that each of you can read the rest of the responses. When we regroup, I'd next like for us to talk about where those 'first thoughts' about these groups of people came from."

***

After the break, the nurses took their seats and resumed their discussion with Dagmar.

"Did any of you look at the other responses on the wall during break?"

Each of them nodded.

"Do you have any new thoughts?" Dagmar asked.

"Some of those are pretty offensive," Donna said.

"Several of them could be perceived as offensive, yes," Dagmar said. "So I have to commend the people who wrote them down. I think that doing an exercise like this one really puts the pressure on us to be careful. Letting down our guard, and sharing what's really going on in our minds can be a dangerous thing to do. We've probably been very afraid of offending each other, but this doesn't work unless we do look at the sincerest of our thoughts that come to mind. We have to be honest with ourselves. When we left off before break, I asked each of you to think about the things that were written down on the adhesive notes and mounted all over the room. So let's talk about all of these first thoughts that came to mind. Where do you think they came from?"

The nurses glanced around them. The walls of the room had been blanketed haphazardly with yellow sticky notes from top to bottom.

"From our own experiences with other people that we've met who fit that description, like you pointed out earlier," Haylie said. "People generalize. Maybe someone else met a Jewish person who was stingy, and now they think all Jews are stingy."

"Sometimes it comes from things that we've simply heard about that particular group of people," said Brad. "Or things that we've seen on TV or in movies. When I was younger, I used to watch old westerns with my Dad. For the longest time, I thought that's what Indians were – people that wore feathered headdresses and loincloths, rode bareback on horses, and lived in teepees. And I guess that dozens of years ago, there were Indians that did. American Indians, anyway. But Prateeka is Indian as well, and she doesn't fit any of those images. She's not even from the same continent. I bet her ancestors had a very different way of life than what I saw on old Westerns."

"Indeed," Prateeka nodded.

"Exactly," Dagmar said. "You're talking about stereotypes. A stereotype is an oversimplified characterization of a person or a group of people. Just like you said, Brad – all Indians wear feathered headdresses and live in teepees, when clearly they do not."

Dagmar raised a finger in the air and pointed at the index card for Jews. "I have a story for all of you, if you don't mind me sharing," she said. Looking around the group, she quickly discerned that there would be no protest.

"Before I worked here at Dogwood," Dagmar began, "I was a critical care nurse at a hospital in Brooklyn, New York, which is a very ethnically diverse area. There's a large population of Hasidic Jews in Brooklyn, and from time to time, we would have a Hasidic patient in our critical care unit. I had never personally known a Hasidic Jew before, but I had heard lots of things about them."

"Like what?" Haylie asked. "That they're rich? Stingy?" She smiled, letting Dagmar know that her message was delivered in good humor, and the group laughed.

"Actually, yes, Those were stereotypes that I held about that group. And I had heard that they were a very private people, and that they kept to themselves, because they thought that they were better than everyone else. So over time, I came to see Hasidic Jews as stuck-up and elitist. Keep in mind, I have never in my life had a personal relationship with a Hasidic Jew. This was all just stuff I heard."

"Stereotypes," Donna said, echoing Brad's comment.

"Right," Dagmar said. "So one day, a Hasidic patient had been admitted to our hospital, and got upgraded from a Med-Surg unit, much like your own, to our critical care unit. I went to get the patient to transport him to our unit. I pushed his stretcher into the elevator, and all of his family followed me in. Once we were inside the elevator, I waited for a moment to see if one of his family members would push the button to the critical care floor for me. But none of them would! I was at the head of the bed with the patient, all the way in the back of the elevator, and I had to shove through all of those people to push the button myself. When I finally got the patient settled in to the critical care unit, I was so angry, I went to a fellow nurse and friend of mine to vent about it."

"Why were you so angry?" Prateeka asked.

"Because those stuck up people wouldn't push the button." She feigned irritation at first; then smiled. "Or so I thought."

"I'm guessing you were wrong?" Haylie said.

Dagmar nodded. "My friend took a teachable moment to explain something to me about Hasidic Jews, which made me feel like a giant fool."

"What was it?" Mel asked, leaning forward in her seat a bit.

"From the book of Exodus, Chapter 35, verse 3. 'You shall not kindle a fire in any of your dwellings on the Sabbath day.' is what it says."

The group exchanged confused looks.

"It was their Sabbath day," Dagmar continued to explain. "And as my friend explained to me, many Hasidic Jews consider electricity to be a form of fire. What I hadn't realized is that the family members' refusal to touch the elevator button meant that they were practicing their beliefs on their Sabbath day. Touching an elevator button would have activated an electrical process, which to them, would have been the equivalent of kindling a fire."

"So they weren't being stuck up. You just made a wrong assumption," Haylie observed aloud.

"Exactly. Can you think about some of the ways that our assumptions might create misunderstandings?" Dagmar asked.

Haylie noticed Donna staring straight at her. She blushed slightly. "Well, yes, actually. We had a 'teachable moment' of our own just yesterday. When we threw a welcome luncheon for Prateeka, and several of us cooked dishes with meat in them. We didn't know that Prateeka was a vegetarian, so when she came to the luncheon and didn't eat the food, I sort of assumed that maybe she was stuck up too."

Prateeka looked down at the floor, as if feeling a pinch of embarrassment. "I am sorry about that, Haylie," she said. "I didn't know that all of you were planning a party with food for me. Had I known, I could have given you fair warning about my special diet."

"We just wanted it to be a surprise," Haylie said.

"I know," Prateeka nodded. "And I was very touched by the gesture. It meant a lot to me, and it helped me to feel welcome. I certainly hope that all of you know by now that I am not stuck up. Many Hindus are vegetarians, not just I."

Haylie nodded slightly. "I understand now," she said. "It's a question that I never would have thought to ask, but now that I know, I'll be careful about assuming things about peoples' diets from now on."

Dagmar jumped in. "Good, Haylie. But the more important lesson is not to assume things about peoples' behavior and what it means."

"You're right," Haylie said.

"If I may," Prateeka began, "I want to share something else that happened yesterday between Haylie and I," Prateeka said. "I do not mean to make this training all about the two of us, but the situation certainly applies. You see, I was talking to my friend Anupa, and we were speaking Hindi. When Haylie approached, we stopped talking. And I believe it made Haylie feel uncomfortable."

Haylie fidgeted in her seat. "Yes, it did. Like I told you yesterday, I felt like you were talking about me since you both stopped your entire conversation the exact same second I showed up."

Prateeka shook her head from side to side. "We weren't. We were actually just talking about what we were going to cook for dinner. We were making our grocery list together."

"So why did you stop talking?"

"Because we thought that it would be rude to continue having a private conversation around you in a language that you cannot understand."

"Then why not just switch to English?" Haylie asked.

Prateeka shrugged. "I know this must sound silly, but sometimes it is hard. Because Hindi is our first language, English does not feel as natural to us."

"And if I can chime in for a minute," Brad cut in, "I think I know what Prateeka means. When I was in the Navy, I was sent overseas for a tour of duty in Panama. I was there for 8 months. Before I left the United States, I had studied Spanish, but it wasn't like I was fluent. When I got there, I was doing the best I could to speak Spanish with the locals, but it was really, really hard. As time went on, I got better at it, but it still never felt completely natural to me to speak a second language. I would have to think in English, then change the words into Spanish in my mind, then say the words aloud. And when someone spoke to me, it was the same procedure, but in reverse. I'd hear it in Spanish, interpret it into English in my mind, and then process what it meant. I found that if I was speaking Spanish for more than an hour or two with locals, my head would literally hurt afterward. That's how much of a strain it would be on my brain. So at the end of the day when I was with fellow servicemen and women from the U.S., all I wanted to do was speak English. And we would sit around and talk and talk and talk until we were exhausted, because it was just so easy to carry on a conversation in English."

Prateeka grinned. "Yes, exactly! When I am talking with people from India, it is very easy to carry on a conversation. Hindi is my first language, and will always be my preferred language. Although I speak English well, it can be hard work to do so, as Brad explained."

"You know," Mel began, "This discussion just made me think about something. We recently had a Spanish-speaking patient, Mr. Gutierrez. I was just thinking about how confused I was about his preferred language. When he was admitted, he said very clearly that he could speak and understand English. And I overheard him speaking it several times on the phone, and with a couple of visitors that came by.

Yet, most of the time when he spoke with us nurses, he always asked for an interpreter. I had to go get Brad since he speaks Spanish and can translate."

"You mean, interpret," Dagmar said.

"Interpret, translate… what's the difference?" Mel asked with a shrug.

"Big difference," Brad jumped in. "Interpretation is spoken. Translation is written."

"How do you know that?" Mel asked.

Brad nodded toward Dagmar. "I took the interpreter training class from Education Services last year. Dagmar was one of our instructors."

"Glad to see you remember your training!" Dagmar said, breaking into a proud smile.

"Well, to get back to Mr. Gutierrez," Mel said, "I just want to know, if he could speak English, why did he choose not to in certain situations? Do you think it gave him a headache or something like that, like it did to you when you've had to speak a second language for an extended period of time?"

Brad laughed. "I don't necessarily think that speaking a second language always causes headaches," he explained. "But it certainly does take a lot of extra effort. And beyond the extra effort, there's also an element of doubt. When I'm speaking English, I'm pretty sure of myself. I've spoken English all my life and I'm confident that the words I say should make sense to another English speaker. On the other hand, if I'm speaking Spanish, it's a totally different story. Spanish is a second language that I acquired later in life and don't speak on a daily basis. Sometimes I'm not completely certain that I'm using the correct words, or that what I'm saying will be understood correctly by a native speaker. Beyond just me speaking, I'm not completely confident that I'll be able to fully understand what someone else says to me in Spanish." He paused for a second, and grinned. "Actually… here's a perfect example for you. When Mr. Gutierrez was here, I tried to ask him in Spanish if he wanted another pillow to sleep with. The Spanish word for pillow is almohada. Instead, I slipped up and used the wrong word. I asked him if he wanted another abogada. I totally screwed it up."

"What's an abogada?" Miriam asked.

"A female lawyer," Brad replied.

Laughter erupted throughout the room.

"You asked him if he wanted to sleep with a female lawyer?" Donna said, as her eyes grew wide and she clamped her hand over her mouth in shock.

"What did he do?" Mel gasped, in between laughs.

Brad grinned. "He just smiled and nodded."

More laughter followed.

"Hey!" Brad cried out playfully. "Almohada, abogada, they sound very similar. It was an honest mistake. I learned most of my Spanish in a classroom, not in the context of real life situations."

"I guess Mr. Gutierrez was disappointed when you showed up with just a pillow," Haylie laughed.

"This makes a great point," Dagmar said. "Mr. Gutierrez may have felt that same fear, that if he tried to talk to one of his nurses in English, he may have miscommunicated his thoughts. And from where he was in a hospital bed, the stakes were pretty high. His comfort and his health, and possibly even his life were on the line. Could you blame him for wanting to communicate with complete confidence?"

The nurses shook their heads from side to side.

"But Mr. Gutierrez really seemed to understand me when I spoke English to him," Mel said. "He would always say 'yes, yes,' and nod his head."

"Because he was probably too embarrassed to let you know if he didn't," Brad countered.

"You know something," Donna chimed in. "In caring for patients from other countries and other cultures, one common thing that I've seen is a huge fear of embarrassment. A lot of patients who are in an unfamiliar setting – like an American hospital – are terrified enough already because they don't understand much of what's going on around them. So when a doctor or a nurse or anyone else wants to talk to them, they don't want to seem foolish. If they don't speak English perfectly, or if they have a heavy accent, they might worry that they won't communicate what they want to say correctly. Or even worse, they fear that they might not understand what's being said to them in English. So even if they do speak English, they might ask for an interpreter to communicate with them in their preferred language."

"The language that we speak and understand the best when we are in pain or in crisis is our own," Prateeka said.

Dagmar nodded. "Which makes it so important for us to have trained, qualified interpreters on hand to bridge language – and sometimes even cultural gaps," she said.

Miriam stiffened in her seat. "Well, I have a small problem with that," she said. "Interpreters cost money, and we can't bill it to patients. The hospital has to pay for it. So if someone can speak English, why should we provide an interpreter? You go to France, and they speak French. You go to Spain, you speak Spanish. You go to Germany, and they speak German. You come here, and you speak English. I mean, that's our official language in this country, right?"

"Good question," Dagmar said. "Miriam has asked if English is our official language in the United States of America. And the answer is no."

All of the nurses exchanged confused looks.

"English is indeed the most commonly spoken language in this country," Dagmar resumed. "It's actually the most commonly spoken language around the world. It is spoken widely throughout Europe, in those very countries you mentioned – France, Spain and Germany."

"And as you know, we speak English throughout India, too," Prateeka said. "I have been studying English in school ever since I was a young child."

"We know," Haylie said, and resisted the temptation to roll her eyes. "You've told us before."

Dagmar continued. "Anyway, English is the most common language that you'll find in any exchange of business in our country, including health and human services. But that doesn't mean that English is our official language."

"So what is our official language?" Miriam asked.

"We don't have one," Dagmar said with a knowing smile. Each of the nurses sat upright, and the room fell silent.

"Come again?" Miriam said. "You're telling me that the United State of America has no official language?"

"That's right," Dagmar confirmed. "An official language was never declared in this country. Several efforts have been made throughout the course of American history to declare English as our official language, but none of them have been successful to date. In fact, one of our founding fathers, John Adams, attempted to establish an official academy of the English language back in the 1700's, but he failed to do so."

"What?" Miriam asked. "Why?"

"It was deemed undemocratic. This country was founded with freedom and democracy as its guiding principles," Dagmar said. "At this time, one of your many personal freedoms in the United States of America is to speak whatever language you prefer. You also have the freedom to seek services from public institutions and businesses, which must make their best effort to do business with you in your preferred language."

"So speaking English actually means that I'm exercising a form of freedom," Miriam said.

"Exactly," Dagmar said. "Just as you exercise the freedom of speech, freedom to worship the faith of your choice, the freedom to vote for the candidate of your choice in public elections, and the list goes on. Speaking a language of your choice in a public forum is one of your personal freedoms. At this time, any organization that receives federal funds to do business – which would include our hospital – has to comply with a set of culturally and linguistically appropriate services, as defined by the Office of Minority Health of the U.S. Department of Health and Human Services."

"Okay, but what if you're not a U.S. citizen?" Miriam asked. "Isn't that our right as Americans? We get patients from time to time that are illegal immigrants."

"And how do you know if they're legal or not?" Dagmar asked.

Miriam shrugged. "I couldn't point out who is here legally or not, but we have non-English speaking people as patients all the time. I know the statistics for illegal immigrant in our state. They can't all be legal when we see them here."

"Whether your patients are legal immigrants or not, you still have the same obligations to them as you do any other patient," Dagmar said. "I want to caution you about bringing that subject up with your patients. You cannot ask them about their immigration status."

"Well we don't, of course," Brad said. "But why couldn't we?"

"Do you ask everyone about their immigration status?" Dagmar asked.

"No, of course not," he said.

"Then you can't single people out just because they appear to be from another country or they speak another language. That's discrimination on the basis of national origin."

The nurses looked at each other, wide-eyed. "I didn't realize that," Brad said.

"Me neither," said Miriam. "But to get back to my question, Dagmar... our personal freedoms that we've been talking about, don't they only apply to U.S. citizens?"

Dagmar shook her head no. "Actually, the personal freedoms that we're talking about at this point are civil rights. Civil rights are not exclusive to just U.S. citizens. As long as you're standing on U.S. soil, you have civil rights. They are rights and freedoms enumerated by our Constitution that are granted to all people. The Title VI of the Civil Rights Act of 1964 specifically prohibits discrimination against people on the basis of race, color, or national origin, when those people are seeking services from organizations with programs or activities that receive federal assistance. Which, as I mentioned, includes services that you provide right here under the roof of Dogwood Regional Medical Center."

"Where can we find that information? On the Civil Rights Act of 1964, Title VI, and the set of culturally and linguistically appropriate services you just mentioned?" Donna asked. She reached for her pen, poised to make notes.

"Go by the hospital library, or log onto the Internet. Do a search for Civil Rights Act, Title VI. Title six appears with the roman numerals – VI. And search for CLAS – with one 's' – it's the acronym for 'Culturally and Linguistically Appropriate Services.' You should be able to find the government websites with reputable information – look for the web address to end in .gov."

Each of the nurses paused to write down information that Dagmar had just given to them. A moment of silence filled the space between them as they busied themselves taking notes.

"Speaking of preferences," Haylie said, breaking the silence a moment later, "there are more than just language preferences."

Dagmar cocked her head curiously and focused on Haylie. "Tell us more, Haylie," she prompted.

Haylie looked at Brad cautiously. "Well," she began, "we have a patient right now who is a transgender woman. She was born a man, and still has male genitals, but is going through a series of surgeries to become a woman. She hasn't completed the surgeries yet, but her gender preference is female."

Dagmar cupped her chin, deep in thought. "And you are already honoring that preference, Haylie."

"What do you mean?" Haylie asked.

"You're speaking about the patient using the words 'she' and 'her.' Even though the patient isn't here, you're speaking about her – and thinking about her – as a woman, which is what she prefers."

"Which is easier for some of us than others," Brad chimed in.

An uncomfortable silence settled among the group.

"Do you want to elaborate on that?" Dagmar asked him.

Brad sighed deeply. "It's my patient that Haylie is talking about," he said. "And I have issues with calling 'him' a 'her.' I mean, he has male genitals. I had to start a catheter, and imagine my surprise when I found out that I had the wrong kit! How can I think of or refer to my patient as a female when I pull back up the gown and there's a penis there?"

"I tried to warn you," Haylie said.

"And I told you, I thought you were kidding." Brad sighed deeply.

"She's going through a process to become a woman," Haylie said. "She just hasn't done that part of it yet."

"Well, until that happens, she is a he. Biologically, physically, my patient is a man."

"But the gender preference is female," Mel said.

"Don't gang up on me," Brad retorted quickly. "What about you, Donna? I know you're religious. Don't you have strong beliefs about stuff like this as a Christian? Isn't it considered wrong? Sinful?"

Donna's eyes bulged. "Don't assume you know what my beliefs are, and don't go putting my faith on trial," she snapped quickly.

"Regardless of what my beliefs are – or yours – or anyone else's in this room, we have a duty to treat our patients with respect and compassion."

"Exactly," Haylie said. "We have an obligation to honor a patient's language preference. How is gender preference any different?"

"It's totally diff--"Brad began.

"Hold on," Dagmar interrupted, sensing that the conversation was about to become even more heated. "Let's see if we can find the common ground. Tell me - when a patient is admitted to your unit, what is your goal for that person?"

"The ultimate goal is for the patient to get discharged and go home," Miriam jumped in. "But to get him to that point, we have to help him heal and regain independence. We have to care for him until he is able to care for himself."

"So let's talk about what's going to help your patient heal and get home faster. How much impact do you – as nurses – have over a patient's progress?"

"A lot," Haylie said. "Aside from the hands-on care that we give them, we control the overall environment in which they're healing. By the things that we say and do - not just directly to them, but all around them, we have the power to make this a place that either helps them or hurts them."

"Go on," Dagmar encouraged her. "Explain what you mean by that."

"Okay," Haylie said. "I'll use my sister Isabel as an example. Between her diabetes and renal disease, she's been in and out of the hospital more times than I could count on my fingers and toes. And while every hospitalization was different, some were far better than others. There's one hospitalization in particular that stands out in my mind. It was horrible. Isabel's room was right across from the nurse's station, and all of the nurses stood outside of her room and gossiped about their coworkers and complained about how much they hated working there. They even complained about their patients. We could hear everything they said! And there was one time that the nurse came into the room and Isabel was crying. She gave my sister a shot, and then left. She didn't ask why she was upset and didn't ask if there was anything she could do to help her feel better. It's like they didn't seem to care about her as a patient or as a person. What a horrible place to try and get well."

"I hope that wasn't here at Dogwood," Donna said. She frowned and shook her head.

"No, thank goodness," Haylie assured her.

"What about a good hospitalization?" Dagmar asked. "Do any come to mind?"

Haylie smiled. "Absolutely. The one that I'm thinking of took place a few years ago. And this one was here at Dogwood Regional Medical Center, a few years ago during Passover. Isabel's nurse read in her medical record that she was Jewish, and that she also suffers from an anxiety disorder. So right away, the nurse wanted to make sure she was doing everything she could to address those special needs. First she came in and sat down with a notepad to ask about what kind of diet my sister needed to follow while she was in the hospital. Isabel explained some of the particulars to her nurse; like why we don't eat bread during Passover, but we have motzah instead. The nurse went out of her way to make sure that Isabel was able to get just what she needed at each meal. And aside from her dietary needs, she just took great care of Isabel in general. It was nothing like the first hospitalization I mentioned. No one gossiped or complained. And this time, when Isabel started feeling anxious and began to cry, her nurse came to her bedside and talked to her to reassure her that she was going to be okay. They cared about her, and it showed in every single thing that they did. She wasn't just a body in a bed – she was Isabel, and the fact that she was different in some ways from the other patients didn't matter."

"What a contrast," Dagmar remarked.

Brad crossed his arms over his chest. "I still don't see how you can compare that to having a transgender patient."

"Well," Dagmar began, "In the case of a transgender patient, there are a couple of things to consider. If the person has male genitals and needs a male cath kit, then that's the one you have to use. Brad is right in that respect. That part of your patient's body is male and the anatomy must receive care specific to a male."

"Exactly," Brad said, smugly.

"However," Dagmar continued, "If that patient's gender preference is female, then you can honor that patient by recognizing her as a woman in every other way. A perfect example is how Haylie discussed this patient, using feminine language – like the words 'she' and 'her.' And 'yes ma'am' or 'no ma'am' when talking about that person. It is possible to do that, correct? As long as the gender of the patient isn't a consideration in a particular procedure or part of the plan or care, then the patient can be, for all intents and purposes, recognized and referred to as a woman."

Everyone nodded, except Brad.

"Fine, if it makes the patient happy, then I can do that," he insisted. "But personally, I just have a problem with the whole transgender thing," Brad said. "I think it's nature that decides that for you – not yourself."

"And you have every right to think so," Dagmar said. "All of you are entitled to your own feelings and opinions in the matter. That's how Brad the person feels. But Brad the nurse has a duty to care for the whole person, not just a disease or diagnosis. And that involves honoring a patient's preferences to the greatest extent possible. Which sometimes means putting your personal beliefs and opinions aside and behaving differently from how you would normally behave outside of work."

Brad sank back in his seat, looking down at the floor. "So even though I have a problem with the whole transgender thing, I just have to pretend that my male patient is a woman and go along with the whole thing."

"You don't have to pretend anything," Donna said. "Your patient disclosed that she was physically a male at admission. She was forthright with our hospital, and if that was overlooked by anyone at any point, that was not her fault." Donna raised her eyebrows and stared hard at Brad. "It is clear to all of us now that her gender preference is female, and while you may be uncomfortable with it, you still must treat her with the same respect and compassion that you would any other patient in your care. And what that means in this situation, Brad, is that you have an obligation to honor who she feels that she is. She feels that she is a woman, and she is undergoing a series of surgeries that will allow her to be recognized – legally, even – as a woman."

Brad nodded. "Okay, okay," he relented. "As long as I'm under the roof of Dogwood Regional Medical Center, she's a woman."

"And," Donna continued, in a stern, motherly tone, "you are responsible for creating the environment that helps her recover and go home. Your job is to make her feel safe and comfortable, not afraid or embarrassed or worried. How are you going to do that?"

"I will honor her preferences," said Brad. "I will treat her as a female, refer to her as a female, and I will treat her with the same respect and compassion I would any other patient."

Donna looked relieved. She seemed satisfied, and nodded in Dagmar's direction that it was time to move on.

Dagmar looked at her watch. "Our hour is almost up," she said. "Before we conclude, there are just a couple of other things I want to ask you to do. The first one is this: please flip your name badge over, and let's read the mission of Dogwood Regional Medical Center together."

Each of the nurses reached for their badges, turned them over, and held them up to the level of their eyes. Miriam was relieved to see that she wasn't the only one squinting to read the shrunken print on the plastic card.

Dagmar led the recitation of Dogwood's mission statement, and the other six nurses joined in. "Our Mission: To provide respectful, compassionate, high-quality care to all people in our community."

Dagmar paused for effect. "Think for just a minute about what that means."

She waited for another minute.

"So according to our mission, what is it that we do?" Dagmar asked. "In your own words."

"We take care of people," said Haylie.

"What kind of people?" Dagmar asked.

"All people," Miriam said.

Dagmar stood and walked to the nearest wall. She began pointing to the note cards on the wall. "Does that include the unemployed?"

"Yes," everyone said.

"Muslims?" Dagmar asked.

"Yes," the group agreed.

"The elderly? Women? African-Americans? The Disabled?" Dagmar pointed to the words on the individual note cards as she read them aloud to the group.

The group nodded.

"Gay? Straight? Middle-Eastern? Men? Mentally Ill?"

They nodded again.

"Who else?" asked Dagmar.

"Jews and Hindus," Prateeka said.

"Blind and deaf," Miriam said.

"People who speak another language," Mel chimed in.

"Transgender," Brad said after a slight pause.

"Each other," Haylie said.

"Everyone," Donna said.

Dagmar returned to her seat. "And according to our mission statement, what kind of care do we provide? Just medical care?"

"No," Prateeka said. "Compassionate, respectful care. Compassion and respect are so important, they are actually positioned before the words 'high-quality' in our mission statement."

"Interesting point," Dagmar said with a smile. "Compassion and respect are part of our duty, then, correct?"

All of the nurses nodded.

"Let me ask just one more thing of you," Dagmar said. "Think about a situation or two that you've been involved in recently, in which differences between you and another person presented a challenge. Next, think about everything that we've discussed today in this hour. If each of you could share one insight with the group about diversity, what would it be? You can take just a moment to think about it."

The six nurses paused to think. They sighed intermittently as they pondered Dagmar's question, and their eyes wandered around the room as their minds collected their thoughts.

"I'll go first," Mel said. "I've been learning lately how important it is not to assume what a person's behavior means. I liked your story about what you learned from caring for your Hasidic patient. I've been in a situation myself with a patient in which I made assumptions about behavior that I'm not sure are accurate. I guess when there is confusion about what behavior means, we need to question it. We need to talk about it."

"Great," Dagmar said. She stood up and crossed the room to a poster-sized piece of paper taped to the wall. With a large black magic marker, she wrote Mel's suggestion down.

"I'll go next," Miriam said. "My insight is that it's important for us to put ourselves in other people's shoes. In order to understand people, we need to see the world through other eyes. That's what you had to do when you tried to see the hospitalization experience through the eyes of your Hasidic patient's family, and that's what I recently tried to do with a patient of mine who is blind. And Brad and Prateeka both helped us understand what it's like to depend on a second language for communication. Both of their perspectives helped me understand how some of our patients may be feeling when they're in the hospital and English is not their first language."

"Good," Dagmar said, writing down Miriam's suggestion.

"I have one to contribute too," Donna said. "Always put the person first. We've done some talking today about how it's important to care for the person, not just the disease or diagnosis. Like the nurse who cared for Haylie's sister; she didn't just care for a patient with diabetes and renal disease, she cared for a person who was Jewish and had an anxiety disorder. She addressed all of the patient's needs, not just her medical diagnoses."

"Excellent," Dagmar said. "Next?"

"My turn," Brad said, looking chagrined. "My big lesson today, obviously, has been to put aside personal biases and opinions and be respectful of differences. That's my duty as a nurse, and that's what our mission statement directs us to do, so... that's what we all have to do, I guess, even if we're uncomfortable with it. We have to put that aside at the bedside."

Dagmar laughed. "I like that – 'put biases aside at the bedside' – good job, Brad." She scribbled his suggestion down on the paper.

"Not just at the beside. We need to do that with each other, too," he said, nodding in Haylie and Prateeka's direction.

Haylie grinned slightly. "I'll go next," she said. "This is very similar to Brad's. One of the recurring themes that I've seen that we need to do is honor preferences of others as much as we can. Whether it's language or gender or even diet, we need to honor not just who people are, but what they want, and what makes them feel happy, and comfortable. And safe."

"Nice job," Dagmar said, jotting down Haylie's suggestion.

"And that would leave me," Prateeka said. "Perhaps my suggestion is a bit different, but I think it is important to focus on what we have in common. That is what Dagmar's first activity made us do when paired up with each other to talk. If we focus on how we are alike, it is easier for us to relate to each other. We may not know everything about our patients, but we know that as human beings, we all want to be treated with respect and compassion. There are universal needs that are bigger than the diversity among us. Like in the case of Haylie and I…"

Haylie, who had been staring absentmindedly at the floor, looked up at the mention of her name.

"I could talk all day long about how different we are," Prateeka continued, "but in reality, I think we are more alike than we realize. Yes, we have the same blood type. But we are also young women who are new to our profession. We are doing our very best to learn and succeed as nurses. It could be a lonely place to be – just starting out in a new career; just starting out in life. Which is why I'm glad that I'm not there alone." She looked at Haylie and smiled. "I think that in all the ways that really matter, we are not so different after all."

Haylie shrugged. "When you put it that way… maybe not," she said.

Dagmar added Prateeka's comment, then turned to Donna. "I'll take down everything else on the wall, but I'm going to leave this one piece of paper. You can use this as your ground rules – or guidelines – when it comes to diversity. This comes from your own wisdom that you've shared with each other, and it's all good advice, so keep it visible for a while. The next time you're dealing with a difficult interpersonal situation, take a look at this list and see if it holds any answers for you."

Dagmar stepped aside to reveal the writing on the poster-size paper. Each of the six nurses read the bulleted points silently to themselves:

- Don't assume that you know what the behavior of others means. When in doubt, talk it out.
- See the world through other eyes.
- Always put the person first.

- Put personal biases aside at the bedside – and among each other.

- Honor the preferences of others as much as possible.

- Focus on what you have in common with others.

"Thank you, Dagmar," Donna said. "This was a wonderful inservice, and this list is going to stay on the wall in our break room."

All of the nurses of Med-Surg South applauded as they rose from their seats.

"Thank you," Dagmar said. "I've learned a lot from all of you today. And if you ever want to have another discussion about diversity on your unit, please call me to facilitate. I'd be happy to come spend more time with your unit."

"Well, first things first, let's all get through this hurricane and then we'll talk," Donna said.

Each of the nurses responded with a forced smile or a nervous laugh as the attention was refocused on the approaching storm.

Chapter 14
Wednesday Afternoon

During a break, Mel dashed to Labor and Delivery unit. She peeked her head into the room to find that there were no visitors at the moment, and Jenny was fast asleep. Mel stepped inside long enough to kiss Jenny on the cheek, then tiptoed out of her room. She made her way to the nursery.

Mel smiled as she peered into the window, marveling at the six beautiful new babies that were napping in their bassinets. They were all so precious and perfect.

But Maxton Jeremy Page is the cutest baby in the whole nursery, yes he is! Mel almost said aloud.

One of the babies beyond the glass window had awakened. It was writhing in its tiny bed, trembling and crying. Mel wished that she could reach through the window and take the crying child into her arms to give it comfort. She looked at the baby's name, written on an index card and taped to the front of the bassinet. Taylor, Shanelle.

"Welcome back, Grandma," said Daisy as she approached Mel and stood beside her. "I knew that Med-Surg South couldn't keep you away for too long!"

"It's been a heck of a day," Mel said with a weary smile. "But it's my break time and nothing could keep me away from coming to check on our little angel."

Baby Maxton slept soundly in his bassinet while newborn Shanelle screamed beside him.

"You got some great lungs, little girl!" Daisy said to the baby through the glass.

"She may be a crybaby, but she's just precious," Mel cooed.

"Yeah," Daisy agreed. "It's just a shame, the way she is." She shook her head from side to side.

"What do you mean?"

Daisy shook her head disapprovingly. "Black father, white mother. Not married, either, so it's a double whammy. We see it all the time. I can't believe how common it is these days."

Mel literally took a step back. She felt anger rising in her chest, and her heart began to thump loudly. "I'm sorry. I don't think I'm understanding you. What's wrong with the child having unwed parents that are two different races?"

Daisy rolled her eyes. "It's just not fair to the child. People just aren't very accepting of it. Those kids get ridiculed all their lives and they'll never fit in anywhere. It's just not natural to mix races, and it's unfair to bring a child into the world out of wedlock. That's what's wrong with our society today. People have just lost their moral compass. No one has values anymore."

"You really think so?" Mel cocked an eyebrow.

"I know so. It's a tough world that we live in, and people can be cruel. I don't know why parents would want to make it any harder on their child than it already is. It's unnatural. And the rest of the world knows it and sees it, you know?"

Mel took a deep breath, collecting her thoughts as she exhaled. "You really should be careful who you make comments like these to," she said coolly. "I happen to be the mother of two mixed race children. And my grandson that you just helped deliver was born to parents who aren't married. He is a mixed race child too."

Daisy's eyes bulged with surprise. "Oh... but... you and your daughter look just alike. So I guess you and her father don't look that different. And the baby looks like both you and your daughter. Same skin, same eyes. He can't be that mixed. You're all not that different."

"So you're saying that different is bad. Different is unnatural."

Lowering her voice, Daisy leaned toward Mel. "Look, it's not like I just made it all up. It's not like I'm the only person in the world who feels that way."

"Of course not," Mel said as she narrowed her eyes. "That whole line of thinking has been around for a very long time. I fell asleep in history class a time or two, but I was wide awake on the day that we were learning about the Holocaust in Nazi Germany. They thought different was bad, too, and they did their best to get rid of an entire race of people who were different."

Daisy's jaw dropped. "How dare you compare my beliefs and feelings to the Nazis and the Holocaust?"

"And how dare YOU condemn mixed race couples for having babies?" Mel's voice rose an octave. "You're supposed to be caring for these babies and their mothers, not judging and criticizing them!"

"I do take care of them," Daisy said. "I've never hurt anyone. I'm not a Nazi, and I keep my opinions to myself."

"No you don't, otherwise we wouldn't be having this conversation. I want to talk to your nurse manager, and I want a different nurse assigned to my daughter. I don't want you coming near her again, knowing that's how you feel about her and her child."

"You know what? I'm done talking to you," Daisy sneered and held up her hand in front of Mel's face. "Wherever you're from… maybe you should just go back there. Go home to where you belong."

"I am home," Mel said. "And this won't be the last you hear from me."

"Whatever," Daisy said, and marched away in a huff.

As Mel watched the nurse storm down the hallway, she felt red hot anger boiling up through her body and into her head. She was almost certain that if she looked in a mirror, steam would be shooting out of her ears. She turned in the opposite direction and began to walk.

With each step, Daisy's words repeated themselves in her mind like a broken record.

The whole world knows it and sees it…

It's just not natural to mix races…

I'm not the only one who feels this way…

She stopped walking, suddenly frozen in place.

I'm not the only one who feels this way…

And suddenly, Mel knew what she had to do.

***

Brad paused in the break room, his eyes fixing on the written list that he and his fellow nurses had prepared in their diversity inservice earlier that morning.

- Don't assume that you know what the behavior of others means. When in doubt, talk it out.
- See the world through other eyes.
- Always put the person first.
- Put personal biases aside at the bedside – and among each other.
- Honor the preferences of others as much as possible.
- Focus on what you have in common with others.

His eyes went back to the fourth bullet point: Put personal biases aside at the bedside. He thought about Lee, and how badly he had failed her in that respect.

Stepping down the hallway, Brad lingered just outside of her doorway for a moment before entering. His heart was pounding as he stepped inside. "Hi," he said meekly.

Lee was sitting up in bed, reading a paperback book. "Hi," she replied as she looked up, and then very quickly returned to her book.

As Brad took a step closer, Lee visibly tensed up.

"Are you feeling better today?"

She nodded. "Karen, the night nurse said that my labs came back and showed a prostate infection. She called the doctor and he prescribed some new medication last night. I'm better today."

"I know," he said. "She gave me a report on you this morning. I'm glad you're feeling better."

"Thank you." She looked away nervously.

"Lee," he began, "I also came to apologize for the way that I acted yesterday. It was totally inappropriate, and I'm sorry."

Shrugging, Lee looked up momentarily. "It's fine," she said.

"No," Brad replied. "It isn't." He sat down in the chair next to her bed. "I did some thinking today and I feel horrible about the way that I acted yesterday. I'd like to talk to you about it, and explain some things. About me."

Lee pondered Brad's words for a minute, then nodded, inviting him to continue.

"What happened the other day was all about me. It had nothing to do with you."

She raised an eyebrow. "Huh?"

"I guess I need to tell you a few things about me. I hope it will help you understand why I acted the way I did."

Lee nodded. "Okay. Go ahead."

Brad sighed and looked down at the floor. "I used to be the kind of guy who didn't believe in love," he said. "But I finally got the point that I thought I was in love with a girl. I asked her to marry me. She said no, and left me. Shortly after that, I met another girl that I thought was really special. I was hoping that maybe she would be the one I would marry. But she just broke up with me too."

"I'm sorry," Lee said. She drew her knees to her chest and wrapped her arms around them, leaning forward slightly. Her eyes softened into an expression of sympathy.

"So I've been moping around since that happened last week. I've been confused and sad and angry at the whole world. And then you came along."

Lee sat up straight. He had her full attention.

"The morning that you were admitted and I walked in on you and saw you lying here sleeping, I couldn't help but think about how beautiful you were, and how perfect you were, and I didn't understand why in the world you would go all the way out of state for a surgery on your… you know…"

"It's called 'breast augmentation,' Brad," Lee said. "It's okay, you can say the word 'breast' out loud. I'm not going to get offended."

"Right." Brad blushed. "Breast augmentation. Anyway, when you woke up, and we started talking, I thought you were really cool. I enjoyed being with you, and I started looking forward to seeing you. And I just felt really lucky that I got to be your nurse. A lot of my patients are grumpy and annoying but you were so nice." He looked down and paused for a moment. "This next part is hard for me to say."

"Go on," Lee urged him.

"I started to have feelings for you," he finally said, after a long pause. His gaze was still on the floor. "And I guess I was thinking that maybe someday...not now, obviously, not while you're a patient in my care, but..." he paused for a long time, then pinched the bridge of his nose as his head began to pound again.

Lee waited. "Are you saying that before you knew I was transgender, you wanted to ask me out?"

He nodded. "I guess there's something I should explain before I go farther. As nurses, when we get a new patient, we look at the person, and the name, and if it registers as "female" or "male" in the brain, we just leave it at that. It was probably mentioned to me at some point that you are transgender, but my mind has been all over the place this week, so that information likely went in one ear and out the other. I looked in your bed and I saw a beautiful woman, and your bracelet and your chart said 'Lee Matthews,' and that, in my mind, registered as 'female.' I had no other reason to assume that you weren't. I mean... I had no reason to think that you still had male organs. True, there's a letter 'M' in your medical record where I assumed there would be an 'F,' in the section reserved for gender. But it's sort of buried, somewhere between social security number and date of birth and patient ID and all those other numbers and letters that just sort of merge together in an alphanumeric mush after you look at bracelet after bracelet and patient chart after patient chart and... oh, crud, I'm just babbling right now and I'm not making any sense, am I?"

"Actually, you're making perfect sense," Lee said. "Please, go on."

He nodded. "When I looked underneath your gown yesterday and I saw your... your..."

"Penis," she said. "It's okay for you to say it."

Brad looked down again, and his face turned bright red.

She laughed softly. "Sorry. I thought you were worried about embarrassing me. I guess it's you who feels embarrassed."

He nodded. "I'm doing the best I can," he said, making eye contact with her again. "But yes, I saw your penis, and as you know, I flipped out. I had feelings for you, and finding out that you were a man – biologically – I mean, it was a big shock to me."

Lee watched his face, and there was sadness in her eyes.

"It was like having the rug pulled out from under my feet. For the third time in just a few months. I thought I had found happiness with my first girlfriend, but I was wrong. Then I thought that my second girlfriend was the one for me, but I guess I was wrong about that too. And then, after meeting you, I felt hopeful that you might be someone I could get to know, and maybe be close to someday. And when I found out that you're not a woman – biologically, I mean – I felt that rug getting ripped out from under my feet once again."

They sat in silence for a moment.

"We just had an inservice in which we spent a lot of time talking about how we have to put the person first in patient care. We talked about how important it is to treat our patients like people, not like a disease or a diagnosis. And it made me realize something. I wasn't thinking about, nor treating you like Lee the person, or Lee, my patient. I wasn't even thinking about your diagnosis. I was thinking about you as Lee, the beautiful girl that I wanted to ask out on a date. And it was completely inappropriate. I was wrong, and I've been really angry about it since yesterday. I just didn't realize until today that I was angry at myself. I failed you as nurse, and I owe you an apology."

He watched Lee for a reaction. She just stared back at him.

"I am so sorry," Brad told her. "I am ashamed that I made you feel uncomfortable, even for a second."

At last, Lee smiled. "It's okay, Brad," she said. "The way that you acted makes more sense now. Sometimes I forget that the outside of me is catching up to who I am on the inside, and that it won't always be obvious to people that I'm transgender."

"What do you mean?"

Lee suddenly looked sad. "It took a lot to get to this point. I've spent most of my life fighting to be a girl. It's been a tough battle, and it has been painful every step of the way. After more than ten years of counseling, my entire family finally realized that I can't be fixed, because I'm not broken... I'm just a woman that was born with a man's body. They've disowned me because they can't accept me this way. I've endured everything from mockery to violence, once I started transitioning to life as a woman. I've been through risky hormone therapy, and surgeries that have been painful and expensive, and I'm obviously not through yet."

"Why?" Brad asked. "Why fight that hard if it hurts you so much?"

"Because this is who I am," Lee said. "Imagine waking up tomorrow and finding that you had female organs instead of male organs."

Brad's eyes widened and he grimaced.

"What would you do?"

"I guess I'd start looking high and low for my man parts," he said. "Surely they'd turn up eventually."

They both laughed.

"But it wouldn't change anything else," Lee said, speaking slowly to make her point. "You'd still be a man, wouldn't you?"

"I guess. Yes."

"You'd still be attracted to women. You'd still want to wear men's clothes, and you'd still want to wear your moustache, and do all of the other things that would define you as a man."

"I guess so. But I'd still be looking for my..."

"Penis," Lee completed his sentence for him. "You wouldn't feel complete if your body didn't match who you are on the inside, would you?"

"No."

"That's how I've felt all of my life. The reason why I went out of state for my breast surgery is because there's a center for transgender health in Florida that specializes in gender reassignment. I wanted to go somewhere that I knew I would be treated compassionately, by people who understand how much I've had to endure to get to this point. And I would have gladly told you all of that from the very beginning, had you asked about it."

Brad nodded. "I realize that. I assumed very wrongly that you were a woman – biologically, I mean, and instead of thinking and acting like Brad the nurse, I was thinking and acting like Brad, the guy who was really interested in you. And it was very wrong of me."

"It's okay," said Lee. "I accept your apology."

"Thank you," Brad said. He exhaled deeply, as if a great weight had been lifted from his shoulders. "You really are a special person. And I... wish things were different, Lee. I feel so bad saying this, but I want to be able to have children someday with the woman I marry..."

She laughed. "Brad, it's okay. You don't owe me any explanation, and you don't need to feel bad about anything. I guess I have an apology of my own to make."

"What do you mean?"

"I'm sorry if I gave you the wrong idea," she said. "I'm not single. I have a serious boyfriend."

Brad sat upright, as if he had just received a mild electric shock. For a moment, he was speechless. A strange feeling washed over him. He couldn't discern what it was, but marveled at how it felt a little bit like rejection.

Lee leaned over and grabbed her purse from the bedside table, reached in, and withdrew her wallet. She opened it and pulled out a photo, which she handed to Brad. It was a picture of Lee with her boyfriend. He was a handsome twenty-something, with short dark hair and a goatee. He was wearing sunglasses and a tacky Hawaiian shirt, and the ocean filled the background of the picture. His arm was around her. Brad wasn't sure what he had been expecting her partner to look like, but he was surprised at how normal they appeared. Just two everyday people, just a young couple in love.

"Oh," Brad said. "Cool. How did you meet him?"

"We met online. It's a long distance relationship, for now. He lives in California, but he's trying to find a job here in Dogwood so he can move out here to be with me."

"Long distance relationships are tough, I hear. How long have you been together?"

"A little over two years," said Lee. "We visit each other every couple of months. That picture was taken last summer when I went to see him in San Diego."

"This may sound like a dumb question, but does he know that you're transgender?"

Lee nodded. "Of course. He knew before we even met in person. It was only fair, you know. It's not like he had a hospital bracelet or medical record to look for my gender status." She smirked.

"Ouch," Brad said. "Nice shot. Guess I deserved that."

"It's okay," Lee said with a playful smile. "Ted is a great guy. We're very happy. I'm not looking for anyone right now, and I'm sorry if I did anything to give you that impression."

Brad smiled and handed the picture back to her. "Apology accepted," he said. "But totally unnecessary. In looking back over the past few days, you didn't really say or do anything misleading. I think you were just being polite and friendly, probably just being the same Lee that you are to everyone else, and I misinterpreted it. I guess it's a guy thing."

"So I've heard. Anyway, truce? I'm really glad you talked to me. I understand you much better now. And hopefully you understand me better, too."

"I do."

"So… friends?"

"Friends," Brad said with a smile. "Unless Ted is the jealous type. Is he?"

Lee laughed. "Not too jealous," she said, her eyes twinkling.

***

"Now you listen to me, Darius," Donna said sternly into the phone, "Don't you dare drive home. You just leave your car parked there on the street. This weather is far too dangerous for driving."

"You don't have to tell me twice, mama," Darius yelled into his cell phone.

"I can barely understand you," Donna said. "The signal is breaking up. You need to get in a place that's safe and dry, and get out of the storm! The job hunt can wait for another day."

"Trust me, I'm way ahead of you," Darius yelled back. "I'm waiting for the bus. I'm in a coffee shop right now, and the person at the counter told me that they're going to close down all businesses in downtown Dogwood and stop all of the bus routes at five o'clock today. It's fifteen minutes after four, so I should be able to catch the downtown bus into our neighborhood. It was scheduled to come at five minutes past the hour, but it's running late. It will come eventually, though. I think I'll be able to make it home safely."

"Good," Donna said. "This is no time to be driving. Pray hard that the bus will be a safe way to get home."

"I will, Mama. Everything will be okay."

"Be safe," she said.

"Bye for now," he replied. "I'll call you when I get home."

He pressed the 'End' key on his phone and dropped it in his pocket.

Darius looked outside of the coffee shop just in time to see headlights approaching on the street that ran parallel to the long strip of downtown storefronts. The Dogwood Area Rapid Transit bus slowed to a halt at the bus stop just outside of the coffee shop.

Darius sighed with relief. He stepped outside, feeling the hurricane force wind and rain pounding against him as he fought his way to the bus.

The doors opened, and Darius climbed the stairs into the vehicle. He dropped two quarters into the farebox and settled into an empty seat three rows back from the front.

"Hold it, hold the door!" A male voice cried out. Darius watched as another young man made his way up the stairs of the bus. He paid his fare and started down the center aisle.

Darius suddenly felt sick to his stomach as he recognized the newest passenger on the bus.

"Hey, D! Long time no see!" The young man called out. He slid into the empty seat next to Darius as the driver closed the doors of the bus and pulled the vehicle back out onto the street.

Darius looked down, refusing to make eye contact with his seatmate. "How's it going, Money?" He asked quietly.

"It's all good, all good. I heard you got paroled four months ago.

How come you didn't call me?"

Darius stared out the window. Although it was just minutes before noon, the sky was as black as midnight. "Things are different now," he said solemnly.

"What are you doing all dressed up in a suit and tie?" the young man asked.

"Job hunting," Darius replied.

Laughing, the young man elbowed Darius sharply. "Job hunting," he repeated with disdain. "You know, you've got a job, D. They don't call me 'Money' for nothing. I've been holding your job for you ever since you left. Now that you're back, you're in luck. It's hiring time again. I can get you set up with a car, and I can hook you up with a place to live. I hear you're living back home with your mama these days. Never would have pegged you for a mama's boy."

Darius cut his eyes toward Money, then looked out the window again. "No thanks," he said. "I'm straight now."

"I'm sure you think you are," Money said with a laugh. "But let's be real. How long have you been out?"

"Four months," Darius said. "You heard right."

"Four months," Money said. "Seems like an honest, straight man like yourself should be able to find something in four months' time. But you're not having any luck, are you?"

"Not just yet."

"And you won't," Money replied. "You're a felon. Branded for life. Your past is all that matters. Doesn't matter how well you can put on the good-boy act now. No one's going to buy it."

"It's not an act," he insisted. "I'm not the same person that I used to be."

Money laughed. "That's too bad," he said. "I think you're fooling yourself. As soon as you figure out that no one's ever going to give you a chance again, you can come on back. I'm not holding any grudges, D. I'll be here when you're ready." Money reached into his coat pocket and pulled out a wad of cash. "Tell you, what. Here's a little advance. I know you're good for it, so whenever you're ready, you know where to find me. That raggedy suit of yours is looking like it came from the thrift store. At least go get yourself some new threads."

Darius didn't budge.

"Come on, man," Money said.

Darius shook his head. Money laughed and tucked the cash back into his pocket. "Okay then," he said. "I'll just hold onto it until you're ready."

The bus slowed to a halt, and the driver opened the doors.

Money slapped Darius on the shoulder. "This is where I get off," he said, standing up from the seat and stepping into the aisle. "My ride may be sitting in a flooded lot, but I'm still out taking care of business. Rain or shine, I come through every time," he laughed. "That's customer service, D. That's what it takes to run a successful business. That, and good associates. So you come on back when you're ready."

Darius stood up, and grabbed Money by the arm. "I'm done with all of that," he said. "And if you ever see me again, you don't know me. Do you understand?"

Money looked down at Darius' hand gripping his arm. Then he looked up at Darius again, narrowing his eyes. "I'm just going to pretend like I didn't hear that," he said. "When you get tired of hearing the word 'no,' you know where to find me."

"I can live with hearing 'no' for the rest of my life, and living with my mother, if that's what it takes," Darius said. "But I can't – and won't – ever go back to living the life I lived before. I'm done with that, and I'm done with you. Like I said, you don't know me. We're done, Money. This is your stop, and this is goodbye."

Money brushed Darius's hand off of his arm. "We'll see about that," he said, and sauntered off of the bus, laughing louder with each step that he took.

Darius sighed. He rested his elbows on the headrest of the seat in front of him, clasped his hands together, and bowed his head in prayer.

Please... let it not be true... that my past will haunt me forever, that I'll never be given another chance again...

"May I have a seat?" a man's voice interrupted, prompting Darius to finish his prayer with a hasty, unspoken Amen.

Darius looked up, and literally felt a shiver travel down his spine.

"Mr. Williamson," he said, recognizing the man as the person who had interviewed him the week before. "Sure."

Darius shifted, making plenty of room for Mr. Williamson to slide into the aisle seat next to him.

"Thank you," he said.

Darius nodded. "No problem."

Mr. Williamson stared down at the floor for a moment, then turned and faced Darius. "So... it's nice to see you again," he said with a quick nod.

Darius smiled politely. "Likewise." At that moment, he wasn't sure which seatmate had made him more nervous – Mr. Williamson or Money.

"I haven't taken the bus in years," Mr. Williamson said. "But I was downtown for a late lunch meeting, and the rain and the wind picked up so heavily that I wasn't sure I could drive home safely."

Darius nodded. "I had to leave a vehicle downtown also. Apparently a lot of people did, judging by how full the bus is today. Anyway, it stops four blocks from my mom's house, so I'm going to get off there and hope the wind doesn't blow me away before I can make it to her door."

Mr. Williamson nodded. "I'm guessing you're still out and about, looking for a job?"

"Yeah," Darius said. "Haven't had much luck yet. Although I did put an application in at the coffee shop on Second Street today. They said they'd have the store manager call me. We'll see what happens. I suppose serving coffee could be a fun job."

Mr. Williamson smiled. "Fun, maybe, but I'm sure it wouldn't pay as well as the supervisor job at my warehouse."

Darius wrinkled his brow. "Probably not," he said. "But I wasn't.... qualified for that job, if I understood correctly. So, I've got to find something else."

"Oh, you're qualified," Mr. Williamson said. "More than qualified. I think you'd do a wonderful job, in fact. And if it's not too late, I'd like to make an official offer to you right now. We can talk about the salary and benefits if you'd like to come into my office again, preferably on your first day of work. I'd really like it if you could start work as soon as this hurricane has passed through."

Darius sat up straight in his seat. "I... I don't understand. I must have missed something. When I was in your office earlier this week, you basically told me that you weren't willing to hire me because of--"

"Your past," Mr. Williamson said. "And I just now realized what a huge mistake I made."

Darius raised an eyebrow.

"I've been sitting in the seat behind you since you got on the bus in front of the coffee shop, and you were joined by that other fellow who came on the bus. And I couldn't help but overhear your conversation with him."

Darius took a deep breath.

"I'm sorry if it was an invasion of your privacy," Mr. Williamson continued, "but as I heard you talking with that other man, I realized that I had made a huge mistake in not hiring you."

Darius exhaled loudly. "You heard all of that?"

"Yes I did," Mr. Williamson said. "And I'm glad that I did. I had my mind made up about you, Darius, and I realize now how wrong that was. What you did – and the person that you were – is in the past, and that's where it all belongs. I see that you're a different man now, and you're someone that I think would fit very well on my leadership team at the warehouse. And if you're willing to forgive my poor judgment, I'm willing to give you a chance." Mr. Williamson held out his hand.

Darius looked down at it and smiled. He reached out and gripped Mr. Williamson's hand in his own, and shook it vigorously.

"Sounds good to me," Darius said. "You won't be sorry."

"I know," Mr. Williamson said, smiling broadly. He reached into his pocket and drew out a business card, which he handed to Darius. "Let's get through this storm, and then I want you to call me. Okay?"

Darius took the card and smiled. "Alright, Mr. Williamson. I can do that."

"Congratulations, Darius, and welcome," Mr. Williamson said, patting him on the back. "I look forward to you being a part of my team."

***

With Jenny's purse tucked under her arm, Mel retreated to Med-Surg South and quietly sequestered away in the break room, where she knew she'd find the privacy that she'd never get in the waiting room of the Labor and Delivery unit. Once inside, she closed the door and dumped the contents of Jenny's handbag onto the table.

Mel sifted through them until she found Jenny's phone. She scrolled through the list of names until she found the one she was looking for: Jeremy Henderson. There were two entries for him. Dorm, and Mobile phone. Although Jenny had assured her mother that she'd called both numbers only to find that both lines had been disconnected, Mel used Jenny's cell phone to dial them both once again. She wasn't surprised to hear "please check the number you have dialed, as this number is no longer in service" recorded messages when she placed both calls, but felt like it had been worth the effort to try anyway.

Mel recalled Jenny mentioning that Jeremy was from a small town in the western part of the state, and that his family owned a sporting goods store. She turned to the nearby computer and pulled up a search engine. After several minutes of browsing, she had made a list of fourteen sporting goods stores in North Carolina, all west of Dogwood.

Mel placed the first call.

"Hi, I'm looking for Mr. or Mrs. Henderson. Do I have the right store? No? Okay… you wouldn't happen to know of another sporting goods store in the area that's owned by the Henderson family, would you? No? Okay… well thank you anyway."

Mel tried three more of the numbers on her list, repeating the same words as if reading from a script, each time, with the same results.

But when Mel placed the fifth call, the results were different.

"Yes, this is Anna Henderson speaking," the voice at the end of the line replied.

Mel hadn't expected success so quickly. She gulped, and took a quick minute to form the words in her mind.

"Hello Anna. By chance, do you have a son named Jeremy?"

"Yes, I do. Do you need to speak to him?"

"No, actually, I'm calling to speak to you."

There was a pause on the other end of the line. "What is this concerning?"

Mel inhaled deeply. "My name is Imelda Tagaro, and I'm Jenny's mother. I'm assuming Jeremy has mentioned her to you?"

Silence on the other end of the line.

Mel took it as an invitation to continue. "I'm calling because your son and my daughter are now parents, Mrs. Henderson. The baby was born this morning. His name is Maxton Jeremy Page. Congratulations. You're a grandmother."

More silence.

"I'm not sure why Jeremy dropped out of school, disconnected his phones, and refused to return Jenny's calls, but it doesn't change the fact that he's now a father."

On the other end of the line, Anna Henderson took a deep breath. "I'm not sure this is the best time…"

"Oh, it's not the best time for me either," Mel said curtly. "When my daughter came to me a few months ago and announced that she was pregnant, and her plans were to leave school so that she could have her baby, I didn't think that the timing was so great for me personally. But, Mrs. Henderson, we didn't really have a choice at the time. Whether I liked it or not, I had to accept that a new baby was going to be a part of our lives. Jenny says that your son is the father, and if that's what she says, then I believe her. I need to know what's going on. Why did your son drop off the face of the earth when he found out that my daughter was pregnant?"

Mel waited for a response. She thought that she heard Anna sniffle on the other end of the line. When the silence continued, Mel grew frustrated. "Are you still there, Mrs. Henderson?"

"Yes," she said. "Jeremy came to us a few months ago also, probably around the same time that Jenny came to you. My husband didn't take the news so well."

Finally, Mel thought, almost sighing audibly with relief. She knew that Anna Henderson's forthcoming words might not make her very happy, but they would at least provide the answers to her many questions. She remained quiet and allowed Anna to continue.

"He was very upset, and very disappointed in our son," she said, as she lowered her voice to almost a whisper. "If this is about money, we'll provide for the child. Jeremy will pay child support, I'll see to that—"

"Are you serious?" Mel almost yelled. "You think this is about money? Jenny doesn't want or need your money. She needs a father for her child."

Silence again.

"Why?" Mel asked, fighting tears of rage. "You and your husband pulled Jeremy out of college so that Jenny couldn't find him, and you forbid him to contact her, didn't you? Why did you do it?"

On the other end of the line, Anna whimpered. It was obvious to Mel that she was crying.

"I didn't want to," she said. "But my husband, he's so severe in his ways…"

"Why?" Mel demanded. "It's not like Jeremy and Jenny are the first young couple to ever deal with an unintended pregnancy. Why did you and your husband cut your son off from my daughter?"

Anna sniffled. "Jeremy showed him a picture of Jenny-"

"And he saw that she was different," Mel said, finishing Anna's sentence for her.

After hesitating for a moment, Anna simply said, "Yes."

"Let me guess. When he saw the little Asian-looking girl in the photo, and when Jeremy told him that Jenny is the child of a Filipina mother, your husband couldn't handle that."

"I tried to reason with him," Anna offered. "I explained to him that the baby will be his own flesh and blood – our flesh and blood - regardless of what race it may be. But he wouldn't listen."

"So your husband's solution was to make your son sever contact with Jenny? Ignore the problem and hope it goes away, right?" Mel's tone grew angrier with each word she spoke. "You agreed with his scheme to pull Jeremy out of school, and shut off his telephone, and forbid him to talk to Jenny. You just went along with the whole plan, thinking that it would keep the baby out of your lives and you wouldn't have to deal with it. Right?"

"I… I tried," she pleaded. "He's a good man, and he loves his family, but God knows, he is so stubborn. When he makes up his mind about something, you simply can't change it."

"What about your mind, Mrs. Henderson? Anna? Don't you have one? Can't you make your own decisions? And haven't you taught your son to think for himself?"

Anna wept loudly. "We went to counseling at our church. Our pastor insisted that my husband had the biblical authority to make decisions for our family. The Bible says, 'wives, submit yourselves unto your husbands.' I'm a Christian. I have to. I can't just pick and choose which parts of the Bible to believe in."

"Well I'm a Christian too! How godly and righteous do you really think you are, turning your backs on your own flesh and blood? How do you think God feels about young men who carelessly father babies and then abandon them?" Mel spat.

"Don't judge me," she choked on her words. "You have no idea how hard I tried to reason with my husband."

"Not hard enough, apparently." Mel said. "I don't really know what I'm supposed to say at this point. I just thought you might want to know that you're now a grandmother, and your son is now a father. And if you stand firm in your husband's choice to reject this child because it's just a fraction Filipino, then frankly, you don't deserve the blessing of having this beautiful, perfect baby in your lives."

All that Mel could hear was the muffled sound of sobbing. The woman on the other end of the line sounded genuinely tormented and deeply upset, but Mel still couldn't muster any sympathy for her.

"Dogwood Regional Medical Center, in Dogwood, North Carolina," was all that she could say. "That's where I'm calling from, and that's where your grandchild is, on the Labor and Delivery Unit, if you even care. I won't bother you again."

Mel pressed the "end" button on Jenny's phone just as Donna entered the break room.

"I thought I heard yelling in here," Donna said. "What's going on?"

Mel burst into tears, cupping her hands over her face. Donna grabbed a tissue from the dispenser on the wall and placed it in front of Mel as she took a seat across from her at the table. "Mel, honey, what's wrong?"

Mel took the tissue and pressed it against her face, pausing for a long moment to regain her composure. "Donna, I've lived in Dogwood for twenty years. And I've never in my life felt more like an outsider than I do now."

"Why?" Donna leaned forward, resting her elbows on the table.

Mel pointed to her face. "What's so wrong with looking different from everyone else?"

Donna arched an eyebrow. "You're feeling like an outsider because you're Filipina?"

Mel nodded. "You don't understand, Donna. I look different. I sound different. Patients don't want me to take care of them because they think I'm going to kill them; nurses talk about my children like they're some kind of unnatural half-breeds, and everyone else frowns upon my grandchild coming into the world because they're so offended by the legacy of a tainted bloodline." Mel sunk her face into her hands and wept again. "You don't understand. You don't know what it's like."

Donna reached out and touched her arm. "Honey," she said soothingly, "Look at me. Look at these brown eyes, and this brown face, and this head of hair that's never going to shimmer and bounce around like it does for the women in shampoo commercials."

Mel looked up, blotting her eyes.

"I've had patients refuse to let me take care of them because they thought I was the housekeeper. I've had people call me all sorts of terrible names – behind my back, AND to my face – without knowing anything else about me other than what they saw on the surface; the color of my skin. I remember taking my own children to the doctor when I was a younger woman. The receptionists would stare at me in the waiting room and shake their heads. They'd make comments to each other about how wrong it was for unmarried 'colored' women to keep having children on public assistance. I wasn't unmarried; I was a widow, and I've never received a penny of public assistance in my life. But when they looked at me, that's all that they chose to see. So don't tell me that I don't understand, Mel." She reached across the table and took Mel's hands into her own.

"I guess that was a pretty stupid thing for me to say," Mel said, looking embarrassed.

"I know what it's like to be different. Throughout my life, there have been people who have tried very hard to make me feel that way. But for your sake, Mel, let's do a reality check," Donna said. "It's not every single patient that doesn't want you to take care of them, it's one. Mr. Allimore. That's it, Mel. Just one patient, and he never even said that he thought you were going to kill him. That was an assumption on your part. When you make assumptions about other people, you're just as guilty of judging them as they are of judging you."

Mel took a deep breath, sighed, and nodded. "You're right."

"About the nurses who talk about your children... is it really nurses, or a nurse?"

"Just one nurse. Daisy from Labor and Delivery. She and I got into a heated discussion today. She started it when she said that it's unnatural for people to have mixed race children. And I ended it when I basically called her a Nazi."

Donna's eyes grew wide. "Tell me you didn't say that," she said.

"Well, not in those exact words, but--"

"You can't say things like that to other employees of the hospital, Mel."

"I know I was wrong, but Daisy didn't have the right to say what she said, either."

"No she didn't. I think I should arrange a meeting between the two of you, myself, and the nurse manager on Labor and Delivery to discuss this."

"Fine," Mel said with a nod. "I'm okay with that."

"Now this comment you made about a 'tainted bloodline'—"

"Has to do with the father of Jenny's baby, and his racist parents," Mel finished Donna's sentence.

"What happened?"

"I just got off the phone with the boy's mother. She told me, in no uncertain terms, that the family was against having a relationship with the child because Jenny is Filipino. Or technically half Filipino, not that they care. I suppose it doesn't really matter to them what she is, whole or half or whatever. They took one look at her picture and made up their minds that they weren't willing to accept a mixed race baby into their family."

Donna remained quiet for a moment.

"You talked to the mother?"

"Yes."

"And she told you all of this? She told you that this is how she feels about the situation?"

"She said that this is how her husband feels about it, and apparently, he makes the decisions for the whole family."

"So Jeremy and his mother just agreed to it, and that's that. Right?"

"Apparently so," Mel said curtly. "She said she tried to change his mind but she couldn't do it."

"Well if she tried to get her husband to change his mind, it sounds like maybe she's not so against the idea of the baby being a part of their lives."

"And if that was the case, then she could have stood up to her husband. She and her son could have walked away from him, and they could have shut him out of their lives just like they did Jenny. She could have taken a stand, Donna, and I don't have any sympathy for her not doing so. She used the Bible as a crutch. 'Wives, submit to your husbands,' is what she said. Can you believe that?"

Donna took a deep breath. "Ephesians. Chapter five, verse twenty-two."

"How lame of her to hide behind the Bible and use it as an excuse. If her husband wants to be a bigot, then fine. But you'd think she could grow a spine of her own. And so could their son! What nerve they have to call themselves a Christian family!"

Donna grew tense. "Careful, Mel. I happen to believe in the scriptures too, and I take them very seriously."

Mel threw up her hands in frustration. "Don't tell me you agree with that woman and her lame excuses!"

"Of course not, but it's not my place to judge them. If Jeremy and his parents refuse to accept the baby as part of their family, then that's just the way things are, Mel. You don't have any control over that. Maybe you should focus your energy on things that you do have control over.

Even though Jeremy might not want to have a relationship with his child, he does have an obligation to support the baby financially, and there are enforcement agencies that can help you with that--"

"Jeremy is a college kid. He probably doesn't even have an income. Even if he did, it would only be minimum wage, considering he has no degree yet, and no career experience." Mel sighed. "It's up to Jenny, whether or not she wants to fight that fight." Mel dabbed the tissue at her eyes. "As for me, I'm done fighting."

Donna touched Mel's shoulder.   "People can be cruel, Mel. No matter where you go in this world – Dogwood, North Carolina or anywhere else – there will be people who will do everything they can to make you aware of how different you are, and they'll want you to believe that different means less. But in the words of Eleanor Roosevelt, 'no one can make you feel inferior without your consent.'"

Mel looked up at Donna and was surprised by the intense look on her face.

"So don't you dare let them, ever," said Donna.

Chapter 15
Wednesday Evening

At the end of their shift, Donna, Miriam, Brad, Mel and Haylie lined up to clock out.

"I'm so excited," Haylie beamed. "You guys are going to be the very first overnight guests in my new place." She marched down the hallway toward the exit, proudly leading her colleagues to the refuge of her nearby apartment.

"We really appreciate you letting us spend the night," Donna said. She reached into her overnight bag for an umbrella. "Darius called me about an hour ago and said that it's raining cats and dogs, and the roads are absolutely treacherous right now. There's no way I'd want any of us out on the road tomorrow morning, trying to fight our way in to work."

"Wait a second," Miriam stopped short. The other nurses stopped and turned to face her. "We're missing Prateeka. Isn't she coming?"

Donna's eyes grew wide. "Oh no," she said. "I forgot to tell her that we were all going to Haylie's apartment tonight. I told her about the hospital's regular preparedness plans, with the temporary shelters in the conference rooms and all, but it completely slipped my mind to tell her that Haylie had offered us a place to stay as an alternative."

Haylie's face reddened with embarrassment. "I forgot to mention it to her too," she confessed. "I should have said something, I know, but it's been pure chaos on the unit over the past few days."

"Maybe she hasn't left yet. I'll run back to the unit and see if I can catch her before she clocks out," Mel said as she sprinted down the hallway.

"Do you have her number, Donna?" Asked Brad. "Maybe we can reach her by phone."

Donna groped around in her bag for her mobile phone and flipped it open. "Yes, thank the Lord I had the presence of mind to add her number in on Monday." She dialed the number and waited, then shook her head from side to side. "I'm getting voice mail," she mouthed to the group.

"Leave her a message," Miriam said. "Maybe we can catch her in time."

"Prateeka," Donna began, "this is Donna. I was hoping to reach you before you left the hospital today. We just wanted to let you know that the rest of us are going to spend the night at Haylie's apartment. It's walking distance from the hospital, and we're all concerned that it won't be safe to drive to work tomorrow. If you get this message while you're still at the hospital, or if you'd like to meet us at Haylie's this evening, call me back. Wherever you are, be safe, okay? Bye now!" Donna snapped her phone shut.

"I feel so bad," Haylie said, hiding her face behind her hands.

"It was my fault, not yours," Donna insisted. "I should have been the one to tell her."

"No use wigging out over it," Brad said. "I'm sure she'll be fine."

"Yeah, but I feel rotten now that we left her out," said Haylie. "I mean, she just came to work here, and we've forgotten about her already."

Brad grinned. "All this coming from the same person who met Prateeka two days ago and said she was stuck up and rude?"

"Oh, leave me alone," Haylie said with a frown. "I don't know, maybe I was being too harsh. Maybe I was making too many assumptions about her."

"Sounds like the inservice this morning made you do some thinking," Donna said with a grin.

"Something like that," Haylie said.

Then Mel made her way back down the hallway and rejoined

them. "No luck," she said. "She's already gone. I also zipped by the temp shelter in the conference room. She's not there either."

"Well, we've done all that we can do," Donna relented. "Haylie, lead the way."

Together, the five nurses made their way to the exit. As they pushed through the double doors to exit the facility, the wind pushed back with strength that rivaled their own.

The nurses raised the hoods on their raincoats and braced themselves. The sky was already dark, and rain was coming down in sheets. Donna hoisted her umbrella above her head, attempted to open it, but the wind whisked it out of her hands. They watched as it tumbled through the air until it was out of sight.

"Walk fast!" Haylie said. She bolted ahead, her colleagues following at her heels. Moments later, they entered the Dogwood Park Apartment Complex and trailed Haylie to her apartment. Gathering in a circle, they huddled together until she opened the door.

They entered in a rush and peeled off their wet coats and shoes.

"That was wild," Brad said. "I don't even want to know how much worse it's going to be in the morning when we're all trying to get to work."

"Seriously," Mel said. "Did you see the way that Donna's umbrella went flying?" She doubled over in laughter, and the others joined her.

"That was pretty funny," Miriam said. "I hope you weren't too attached to it."

Donna chuckled. "It can be replaced. All of you, on the other hand, can't."

"Donna, can you check your phone?" asked Haylie. "See if Prateeka called."

Donna reached in her bag and found it. She flipped it open and shook her head. "No calls."

***

When her shift ended, Prateeka clocked out and made a beeline through the wind and rain to the employee parking lot. As she piled into her rental car, she struggled out of her soaked coat before settling into the driver's seat. She put the key in the ignition and turned the engine on. Her teeth chattered while she waited for the car to warm up.

In her handbag, her phone beeped. She took it out and saw the icon of a closed envelope on the screen. Underneath it were the words NEW VOICE MAIL.

She listened to the message. It was Donna. *The rest of us are going to spend the night at Haylie's apartment,* she said. *If you'd like to meet us at Haylie's this evening, call me back.*

Prateeka thought for a moment.

They are inviting me to be polite, she told herself. *Haylie would not really want me there. She has made it quite clear that she doesn't like me.*

Prateeka thought for a moment, then typed a text message to Donna.

I got your voice mail and I am on my way home this evening. Thank you anyway.

Chapter 16
Wednesday at Midnight

Haylie awoke to the smell of smoke.

She sat up in a panic.   Lightning shone through her bedroom window for just a split second, followed by a crash of thunder that rattled the walls around her. She inhaled a deep breath and again, she smelled smoke.

Cigarette smoke.

She stumbled out of bed, reaching for her bathrobe and slippers. Miriam, Donna and Mel were bunking in on the queen bed and futon in the room next to hers. Hard as she tried, she couldn't imagine them breaking into a pack of cigarettes for a late night smoke.

Haylie stepped out of her room and into the hallway. She heard Miriam snoring through the door of the guest room.

As she moved toward the living room, the smell of smoke grew stronger. As did the sound of the wind and rain. When she reached the living room, she turned on a lamp to check on Brad. A pillow and rumpled blanket were there, but Brad was not.

"Brad?" Haylie said softly. He couldn't have gone far, she knew.

Thunder exploded outside once again, and rattled the sliding glass door to the patio. It was open, by just a hair. She stepped toward the patio, sliding the door all the way open.

Outside, Brad sat under the covered deck on the concrete floor, his back resting against the stationary panel of the sliding glass door. He clutched a lit cigarette in his right hand.

"Busted," Haylie said. "After you told all of us in the inservice this morning that you're an ex-smoker!"

Brad shook his head woefully. "I know, I know," he muttered. "I'm a hypocrite. What in the world are you doing up at this hour?"

"I smelled the smoke and it woke me up."

He took a long draw off of the cigarette, then flicked it to the concrete floor and crushed it with his shoe. He picked up the butt and rose to his feet. "Don't worry, I'm headed straight back into your apartment for the trash can. At least I'm a considerate smoker."

Brad stepped inside and threw away the remains of the cigarette in the kitchen trashcan. Haylie slid the door closed behind, then cornered him as he was making his way back to the sofa. "Brad, are you okay?"

He let out a long sigh. "No, not really."

"Do you want to talk about it?"

Brad shrugged. "No," he said. "But I guess you're not going to let me off the hook if I don't say something, huh?"

"It's the price you have to pay for getting busted smoking at my place," Haylie joked.

They sat down on the sofa. "I'm sorry about that," Brad apologized. "I only started smoking again just recently. Literally just a few days ago. It's a terrible habit, I know, but that's just what I do when I get stressed out."

"What's got you so stressed?" Haylie asked.

After a long moment, Brad opened up. "All kinds of things. Sue came back home last week, for starters."

"Oh... wow," was all that Haylie could say. "How do you feel about that?"

"Honestly? Confused. When I saw her, I was both happy, and angry. She showed up when Andrea was there. So Andrea panicked and took off, and she's been giving me the cold shoulder ever since. I went to see her yesterday evening, and it didn't go well. She was looking for any excuse she could find to start a fight with me. I know she's just pushing me away because she's afraid that I'm going to get back together with

Sue and break her heart. So to show her how sincere I was, I… kind of popped the question."

Haylie shrank back. "You asked her to marry you? In the middle of an argument?"

"I know," Brad said. "Not very romantic, but I was desperate."

"So what did she say?"

"She said, 'I can't believe you said that,' and slammed the door on me. Now I look back on yesterday and I can't believe I said it, either."

"Brad," Haylie said softly, "you and Andrea have only known each other a few months? Don't you think it was a little soon to ask that?"

"I don't know," he said. "I'm completely confused right now. For the longest time, I thought that I didn't want a wife and children and the whole nine yards. But I know now that I do. I want the whole American dream, Haylie. I want to get married. I want to buy a big house with a white picket fence, and I even want a kid or two."

"That doesn't sound unreasonable. Maybe it's meant to happen for you, but you just haven't met the right person yet."

He sighed deeply. "Apparently not. And the whole thing with Lee… that really messed with my head too."

"I know."

"This is all between you and I, right? You swear you won't say a word to anyone else?"

"My lips are sealed," Haylie said.

He nodded. "I was starting to like her, Haylie. Really like her. It was like someone took all the great things about Sue and all the great things about Andrea and combined them into one person, and it was Lee. When I found out that she was transgender, it threw me for a loop."

"Brad, if you like her, you know she is going through gender reassignment to physically become a female--"

"And she has a boyfriend," he said. "She showed me a picture of him, and as crazy as this sounds, all I could think was… lucky guy. But then again, Lee is a guy too. Or used to be a guy. And it's something that I don't fully understand, and certainly something I'm not comfortable with. But at the same time, I had feelings for Lee, and I don't know how to just make those go away."

"Oh, Brad," Haylie said. "I wish I knew what to say."

"I wasn't sure what to say either, but I knew I needed to say something. To Lee, anyway. She's better now, and she'll probably get discharged this evening. Since I may never even see her again, I needed to let her know that I was sorry while I had the chance, for acting the way I did yesterday. She accepted my apology."

"Good," said Haylie. "Maybe that will help you feel some peace over the situation."

He nodded. "There's someone else I need to make peace with," said Brad. "I owe you an apology as well, Haylie. I was wrong to ask you to start the Foley on Lee. She was my patient and my responsibility and it was wrong for me to ask you to do it. I'm sorry."

"It's okay," Haylie insisted. "Don't even worry about it. I had offered to be there for you if you needed a friend, and you did."

"But it was manipulative of me to put you in that situation and call it a favor of friendship. I'm very sorry, Haylie. I've been so wrapped up in myself that I didn't think about how my selfishness was affecting other people. Like you and Lee. And..." his voice trailed off.

"Is there someone else?" Haylie nudged him.

"Sue," he said.

"What about Sue?"

"I'm refusing to speak to her."

"Why?"

He shrugged. "To punish her, I guess. She really hurt me, Haylie. And now that I have the chance to hurt her, I guess I'm taking full advantage of it."

"So is it making you feel better?"

He shook his head. "No. I've never felt worse in my life."

Haylie turned toward him. "So stop punishing her. Talk to her, Brad. She came back home. That must mean that she wants to work things out with you. Would you ever consider giving her a second chance?"

"I don't think so," he shook his head. "I still care about Sue a lot. I'd even say that I still love her. But I don't think that we're right for each other. She doesn't know what she wants out of life just yet. On the other hand, I do know what I want, and too much of it doesn't line up with who Sue is. The time that we spent apart after Sue left gave me some room to breathe, and a chance to live my life my way for a change. I could watch sports on TV all day long, for instance, and no one complained about it. And then there's Bella. I love having a dog, but now that Sue is back, she can hardly stand her. She makes a face every time Bella comes near her."

"So what's the plan? Will one of you move out? If you and Sue aren't going to be together, it's not very practical to keep living under the same roof."

"I know," he said. "I guess after the hurricane passes, I'll talk to her."

"I know it will be hard, but if you go ahead and deal with it, you can start healing and move on with your life."

"You're right," Brad said.

They sat without speaking for a moment. Outside, the chorus of wind, rain and thunder continued its noisy performance.

"How about you? How are things going with Dan?" Brad finally asked.

She sighed. "They're not. He resigned from Dogwood to be a travel nurse. And he resigned from our relationship, too."

"Aw, man... Haylie I'm sorry," Brad said with sympathy. "Here I am running my mouth all about my love life problems. I didn't mean to make this all about me."

"It's okay," Haylie said. "I haven't talked to anyone else on the unit about it either. I'm still hurting and I guess I'm not yet ready to share the story. And I'm definitely not ready to get bombarded with women giving me those horrible 'hey girl, it's his loss' pep talks."

Brad laughed softly. "I know what you mean."

"Breakups stink."

"Yeah, they sure do."

Haylie yawned. "I'd love to keep venting about our sad love lives, but I'm afraid we're both going to be zombies tomorrow if we don't get some sleep."

"You're right. Since this is my bed for the night, I'm afraid I'm going to have to kick you out," Brad said.

"No problem," Haylie said, rising to her feet. "But if I catch you smoking again, I'm going to wake up Miriam, Mel and Donna, and let all three of them sit you down and lecture you till dawn about lung disease."

"Fair enough," Brad laughed.

Haylie started toward her bedroom.

"Haylie?" Brad called from behind her.

"Yeah?" She turned around to face him.

"Hey girl," he said in a playfully feminine voice, "It's his loss."

She laughed, covering her mouth with her hand as not to wake her sleeping colleagues in the guest room.

"In all seriousness, though, thank you," said Brad. "For giving us all a place to stay during the hurricane. And for being a good friend to me. Thanks for listening."

"You're welcome," she said as she turned off the lamp on her way out of the living room. "Sleep tight."

Chapter 17
Thursday Morning

"Ready," said Haylie, watching the anxious faces of each of her fellow nurses as they lined up at her front door. "Set," she said, as they zipped their raincoats and raised the hoods over their heads. "Go!" She flung the door open and the five nurses stepped outside into the wind and rain. There was no question about it; Hurricane Fortuna had arrived in Dogwood, North Carolina. The sky was pitch black, even though it was just a few moments before seven o'clock in the morning.

They linked arms and started their mad dash out of Haylie's apartment complex, fighting their way through heavy wind and rain. The power was out for as far as the eye could see, so Haylie brought a flashlight from her apartment to light the way. Moments later they arrived at the employee entrance of the hospital. Security guards draped in plastic ponchos were waiting at the entrance, struggling to hold the heavy doors open against the forceful winds. The nurses peeled off their wet coats and rubbed the muddy soles of their shoes on floor mats that the guards had placed just inside the entrance.

"That was rough," Donna said. "No question about it, Hurricane Fortuna has arrived!"

"You know, we've still got a few minutes before we clock in," Mel said, glancing down at her watch. "Do you all want to go meet my grandson?"

By a unanimous vote, the five nurses headed toward Labor and Delivery. At the window of the nursery, Mel pointed to her grandson.

"There he is," she glowed. "Our little Maxton Jeremy Page. Isn't he precious?"

Brad was the first to envelop her in a hug, and Donna, Miriam and Haylie were standing by to embrace her when they were done.

"Congratulations, sweetie," Donna said, squeezing her tightly.

"He's so adorable," Haylie said.

"Congrats to the coolest grandma that I know," Brad said with a smile.

"Just you wait, little Maxton," Miriam said to the baby through the nursery glass. "We're going to spoil you rotten as soon as you get out of there and come home."

"What a blessing," Donna remarked, giving her a hug. "I know you've been through some tough times, Mel, but this beautiful baby boy is going to bring you and Jenny so much joy."

"Yeah," Mel agreed, "You're right. I am very blessed. I just wish..." she stopped speaking, and then shook her head sadly.

"You wish what?" Miriam asked.

"That Jenny didn't have to be... oh... never mind. You're right, I'm not going to stand here and think about what's wrong with this picture. I'm just going to be thankful that I've got a beautiful, healthy grandson."

"So, tell us how Jenny picked the name," Haylie said in an effort to change the subject.

"Maxton was Bruce's father's name," Mel explained. "Jenny and Michael were really close to him and when he died, they both agreed that whoever had a son first would name him after their Grandpa."

"And what about the middle name?" Miriam asked. "What did you say it was – Jeremy?"

Mel nodded. "The baby's father," she said. "If he never gets anything else from his father, he at least gets his name. Not that his father deserves a namesake child, but... hey, not my decision to make."

Donna and Miriam exchanged a sad glance. "Honey," Donna cajoled, as she put her arm around Mel's shoulders and pulled her close, "Don't go beating yourself up over that. You tried your best, and you just have to accept that it's beyond your control. That baby's not going to miss out on a thing, Mel. You and your family are going to love little Maxton Jeremy enough to make up for his father not being around--"

"Did you say Maxton Jeremy?" A woman's voice called out from behind them.

When Mel turned around, she wouldn't have recognized the woman if not for the handsome, blonde young man with her. Mel recognized him from the pictures that Jenny still kept in her wallet.

It was Jeremy.

"Anna?" She asked the woman at his side.

The woman, who was tall and slender, with shoulder-length graying hair and tired-looking eyes, nodded in affirmation.

Mel's jaw dropped.

"Did you say that the baby's name is Maxton Jeremy?" Anna asked. She and her son stepped forward and looked through the nursery window.

"Which one is he?" Jeremy asked. There was a nervous warble in his voice. "Which one is my son?"

Mel pointed. "That one. You see his name card?"

They leaned in for a better look. Anna put her hand on her son's shoulder.

Donna, Miriam, Haylie and Brad looked at the two visitors, then at Mel. It was obvious that no introductions were needed, and that the two grandmothers and the new father needed a moment alone.

"Mel, it looks like you've got some company, so we're going to head back down to Med-Surg South," Donna said, and shot Miriam, Haylie and Brad a *let's get out of here* look. She left with the three of them trailing behind her.

"Thanks, everyone," Mel said, and smiled at her colleagues as they made their way to the elevator and disappeared behind the sliding doors. Then she approached Anna and her son.

"Mel," she began, "This is Jeremy. My son, and the father of our grandchild."

Jeremy smiled awkwardly, and extended his hand to Mel. Instead of returning his gesture with a handshake, she stepped forward and hugged him. "Thank you for coming," was all that she could say. Jeremy hesitated at first, but then wrapped his arms around Mel and hugged her back. Resisting the urge to cry, Mel fought hard to regain her composure. "Jenny is in room 5. Go ahead and see her, Jeremy."

When he started down the hall toward the patient rooms, Mel and Anna faced each other.

"How in the world did you get here?" Mel asked.

"We drove.   After you and I talked on the phone, something in me just clicked, and I decided that this is what I had to do. So I went to Jeremy and talked to him about it. We made the decision to come to Dogwood. We packed overnight bags, got in the car, and just started driving."

"You literally drove into a hurricane," Mel said, bewildered.

Anna nodded. "The weather wasn't so bad when we left home. It started getting rainy and windy about an hour to the west of Dogwood. By the time we got here, the roads were really bad."

"Where did you stay last night?"

"The Dogwood Guest Inn," Anna said, referring to the hotel across the street from the hospital. "We would have come over here last night to see the baby, but it took us hours to get our car parked, and then get a room. The Inn is completely full right now."

"What about your husband?"

Anna shook her head from side to side. "He didn't come," she said. "I made one final plea to him to have a heart, and come to Dogwood to meet our grandchild. But he wouldn't. When I told him that Jeremy and I were going anyway, he pitched a fit, and nearly blew the roof off the house yelling at us as we walked out."

Mel raised an eyebrow. "What does that mean for you?"

"I don't know. It may mean that my marriage is over. I hope not, but if that's his choice, then so be it. I had to make a choice of my own, and whatever happens, good or bad, I can and will live with the outcome."

Mel was at a loss for words.

"I know you must think that Ed is a horrible person," Anna said. "He's not. He's a good man. He's been a wonderful husband and father – loyal and loving – and there's nothing he wouldn't do for Jeremy or I. He worked two and three jobs at a time for the first ten years of our marriage to come up with the capital for us to open our store, which has been a very successful business, and he's invested our income wisely, so that Jeremy will have a very secure future. He's been in church every single

Sunday since we met, and he supports all kinds of charitable causes and civic groups... and..." Anna began to tear up.

"You don't have to explain," Mel said.

But Anna continued. "He's a good man, Mel. A very good man, with a good heart. And he's not the terrible person you probably think he is. He has close friends of every different color of the rainbow. He just has very strong beliefs against interracial relationships and marriages and children of mixed race. I honestly don't know where it came from, and I don't know if those attitudes will ever change. It's just who he is, and it's just very unfortunate that those beliefs would be strong enough to come between him and his family."

Mel frowned. "I understand," she said. "I debated for a long time about even sharing the news of Jenny's pregnancy with my mother. She's a devout Catholic and has very strong feelings about unwed women having babies. But in the end, I decided to tell her. It's not like we could hide it forever. She was very upset for several weeks, but she finally accepted it. And now... believe it or not, she's starting to warm up to the idea of being a great grandma. I'm going to try to fly her over from the Philippines to see the baby soon."

Anna forced a sad smile. "I wish Ed could just get over it that easily. "

"It wasn't easy to accept," Mel insisted. "Not for my mother, and not for me, either. Our kids have made their own choices, which are much different from what we would have chosen for them, had we been in control. But we're not, and we haven't been in a very long time. We're mothers of adult children, and they're choosing their own paths. There is only one choice that we really have left as parents; to give them our unconditional love and support, or to withhold it."

"I know," Anna said. "And I'm so sorry that my husband is withholding his for now – possibly forever. I thought that standing by him was the right thing to do. But it wasn't."

Mel put her hand on Anna's shoulder. "Anna... you don't have to sacrifice your marriage over this. You can go back to Ed and smooth things over with him. Jeremy and Jenny and the baby will be fine. They can all stay here with me, and I'll do everything I can to help them until they can make it on their own. And you can keep in touch and see the baby whenever you want. Ed doesn't need to know about it."

"I don't want to live my life sneaking around and keeping secrets," she said. "I set up a savings account for the baby when Jeremy broke the news to me about Jenny being pregnant. I insisted that Jeremy start making deposits to it, and we just kept it secret from my husband. Just doing that much made me really uncomfortable. I'm a big fan of honesty, even when it hurts." She reached up to her face and swiped a tear away with her index finger. "I love Ed, and I always will. But I've made my choice and I'm not looking back. I did what I had to do, and the rest of our lives – as a family – is entirely up to him. If he wants to divorce me and disown his son and grandchild, then we will be a family without him."

"Oh," Mel gasped, surprised at her own voice giving sound to the anguish she was feeling inside. It was only at that moment that she was able to see the situation through Anna's eyes, and finally understand the weight of her burden. "Anna, I'm sorry. I never realized what I was asking you to do when I made that phone call yesterday."

Anna reached forward and put her arms around Mel. "You have nothing to be sorry for," she said. "I feel like I should apologize to you, for taking this long to do the right thing."

Mel hugged her back. "I'm very sorry for any pain that I've caused you, or your family. You and Jeremy are welcome to stay with me for as long as you need to. You're part of my family now." She brushed tears away from her cheeks.

Anna squeezed her tight, then pulled away. "Let's quit all of this crying nonsense, Mel. I've driven a very long way, and I'm ready to meet my new grandbaby."

"Come with me," she said. "Let me forewarn you, this kid has a healthy set of lungs on him. He came out screaming at the top of his lungs, and he tends to cry if anyone except for his mother holds him. So if he screams at you, don't take it personally. I don't know who in the world he gets it from."

"Probably his grandfather," Anna said. "My Ed. He'd be proud, if only he knew."

***

Andrea left home nearly an hour early for work, even though the hospital was only two miles away. The morning weather report mentioned that Hurricane Fortuna had arrived. It had been downgraded to a Category 3 storm, which was still quite serious, and probably too dangerous for driving. However, she felt confident that if she drove slowly and carefully, she would make it.

She flicked the windshield wipers to the highest setting, and watched as the blades doubled their speed in back-and-forth sweeps across the glass. She wasn't at all surprised to see that it barely made a difference. Visibility was so low that she could just barely make out the headlights of vehicles in oncoming traffic. She did her best to keep a safe distance from the taillights on the cars ahead of her – most of them flashing frantically in hazard mode.

Carefully, she continued toward the hospital. Making a turn off of the main highway, she slowly made her way into the right lane and pushed ahead at a snail's pace. Squinting her eyes through the darkness and heavy rain, she searched for taillights in front of her. And as quickly as she found them, she noticed that they were not moving. The car ahead of her own was stopped in the middle of the road. She tapped her brakes lightly so that she wouldn't hit the vehicle nor hydroplane off of the pavement, and slowed to a stop. Ahead of her, she could make out the silhouette of a young woman standing by the driver's side of the car, clutching an umbrella that the wind had blown inside out.

Reaching into the glovebox, Andrea pulled out the flashlight that Brad had left there for her. It was a bulky piece of military equipment, left over from his days of active duty in the U.S. Navy. Her heart felt a pang of sadness as she recalled the day that he'd placed it there for her.

"Why are you putting that in my car?" She had asked.

"Just in case. Everyone should carry a flashlight in their car. You never know when you might need one."

She had laughed. "I've never needed one before, but I'll keep it there if you say so."

"Hey," he had said playfully, "I'm just trying to take care of my girl."

Andrea swallowed hard, feeling a knot in her throat, the familiar first sign that tears would follow next. She fought back against her emotions, bracing herself as she stepped out of the car and approached the woman ahead of her.

"Are you broken down? Do you need help?" Andrea cried out, hoping that her voice would carry over the harsh weather. She shined the light on the stranded woman as she walked toward her.

"Help, yes, please!" cried the high-pitched female voice, as the woman turned to face Andrea.

When the stranger's face was illuminated by the flashlight, Andrea stopped walking. She felt her stomach do a flip-flop. "Sue?" She called out.

The woman took a step toward Andrea. "Yes, it's me, Sue!" She yelled. "Do I know you? I can't see you!"

Andrea pointed the flashlight toward her own face as she made her way to Sue's side, and could almost feel the tension mount as the other woman's eyes lit up recognition. "Remember me?" Andrea asked.

"Oh," said Sue. "Yes, you're... Brad's girlfriend. Andrea, right?"

Andrea nodded awkwardly. "What's going on with your car?"

Sue shook her head frantically. "I don't know. I hydroplaned as I was making the turn down this road, and I think it flooded the engine. It just coasted for a minute or two, then shut off in the middle road. Now I can't get it to start again."

"Where are you headed?" Andrea asked.

Sue glanced into the car nervously. "I was going to the hospital. Brad left his backpack at home yesterday, so I wanted to bring it to him."

"All this just to bring him a backpack?" Andrea muttered, mostly to herself, then shook her head in disbelief. "Let's push your car off of the road and lock it up. Get Brad's bag and I'll give you a ride to the hospital. You might be stuck once you get there, but I can at least get you out of the rain and to a safe place."

Sue nodded. "Thank you," she said, with true gratitude.

The two of them managed to move Sue's vehicle to the shoulder of the road, and quickly retreated to Andrea's car.

Inside, Andrea started the engine again and turned the heat all the way up.

Sue rubbed her hands together, then held them over the passenger's side vent. "Thank you," she said.

"You're welcome," Andrea nodded.

They sat in silence for a moment, staring straight ahead at the rain pounding the windshield.

"I'm sorry to put you in an awkward situation like this," Sue apologized.

"Don't worry about it, Sue. It's okay."

"I guess you think I'm a horrible person, for what I've put Brad through..."

"No, I don't think you're a horrible person," Andrea said. "You don't have to explain yourself to me. Let's just focus on getting somewhere safe, okay?" Carefully, she pulled her car back onto the road and proceeded to the hospital.

"Okay," Sue agreed.

"So," Andrea began, in a desperate attempt to lighten the mood in the car, "what's Brad got in that backpack that's so important that you'd journey out into a hurricane to bring it to him?" She attempted a polite laugh.

"Oh... let me see..." Sue said as she rifled through the bag. "His favorite hoodie sweatshirt, his mp3 player, and his cigarettes. I think he's probably got a pack in his locker at work for breaks, but once he runs out, he's going to be in trouble."

"Cigarettes?" Andrea asked with concern.

"Yeah. I hate that he's smoking, but he's convinced that he needs to. He says that smoking somehow calms him down. I'm not fighting him on it. I just want him to be happy."

"I just can't believe he's smoking again," Andrea murmured. "He was smoking when I first met him, and he quit just a couple of weeks later. He said he felt so much better when he did."

"Well that makes sense," Sue observed. "Brad smokes when he's got a broken heart. When he's happy again, he quits."

Another awkward silence.

"I'd rather him be happy than smoking," Sue said. "And all that's missing from that equation is you."

Andrea remained silent.

"I'm not staying at the apartment with him," Sue said. "I just leased an apartment of my own. I was supposed to move in today, but thanks to the hurricane, I guess tomorrow is the earliest I can hope for. I'm packed and ready to move in. Brad and I are over, Andrea. I'll admit that I still love him, but I recognize that I did some damage to our relationship that I can't undo. I can't win him back, and I don't even want to try if he's already moved on and found someone else who makes him happy. He loves you, and if you love him, then the two of you should be together."

Andrea glanced at Sue out of the corner of her eye, but still didn't speak.

"I didn't mean to break you guys up," Sue said. "I'm sorry. Brad is so mad at me, he's still giving me the cold shoulder. He stays holed up in the bedroom with the door shut, and won't even talk to me. I'm losing my mind. This trip to the hospital isn't just to bring him his backpack. I've got to talk to him and make him listen to what I have to say. I guess the only way I can do it is confront him in a place where he can't run away from me."

Andrea took a few deep breaths before responding. "It's not your fault, Sue. You didn't break us up," she said. "I did."

Sue stared out the window. "I can't see how it's not my fault. You guys were happy together. And then I showed up, unannounced at the house..."

"Sue, please," Andrea begged. "I was the one who chose to break up with Brad. It felt like things were just getting way too serious between us, and I was so scared of getting hurt, and I was honestly just looking for an excuse to break up with him."

"I don't understand. Why?"

Andrea gripped the steering wheel as a gust of wind blew hard against the car, nearly pushing it onto the shoulder of the road. Once she regained control of the vehicle, she sighed loudly. "He just doesn't know what he wants right now. I was the one in the relationship who pursued him and asked him out, and made all the first moves. So I've always wondered if he's with me because he wants to be with me, or if he's with me because I want him to be with me. The whole time that he's been with me, he hasn't ever used the 'L' word. Three months together, and there's no mention of love. And I was okay with that. I didn't want anything serious. But he was getting so serious, so intense, that I was feeling the need to back off even before you came back into the picture. When I saw him the other day, he panicked and made a half-hearted marriage proposal."

"He asked you to marry him?" Sue said, obviously a little hurt.

"Yeah - in the middle of an argument. I was literally walking into my parents' house, and closing the door on him when he blurts out, 'let's get married!' It was so sad, so desperate," Andrea said, shaking her head. "He sees his friends falling in love, settling down and getting married. He thinks he's supposed to be doing the same thing."

"So did I," Sue said. "That's why I nagged him and pressured him the entire time we were together. I got so sick of being the bridesmaid, never the bride. It started to dawn on me that while I was completely fixated on having my own fairytale wedding, I wasn't so sure if I wanted the marriage that came with it. And by the time he was ready to ask me, I knew for certain that it wasn't what I wanted anymore."

"I just got divorced," Andrea said. "My marriage was anything but a fairytale. I married my first husband six months after meeting him, which is why it didn't last. A year into the marriage, and we finally figured out just how incompatible we were. All we did was fight. I've only been with Brad half of that time, and we're still getting to know each other too. We're still finding out things about each other."

"Like what?"

"Like me just finding out that he's taken up smoking again," Andrea smirked. "And he just found out the other day that my brother is gay. I never mentioned it before, because I didn't think it was important. Brad tried to pretend like it was no big deal, but I know he was uncomfortable with it. Anyway, the bottom line is, we certainly don't know each other well enough to make any big commitments right now. The last thing I want to do is jump back into another knee-jerk marriage. That's why I asked for a break."

"It sounds more like a break up," Sue said.

Andrea nodded. "It was," she said.

"Poor Brad," Sue said. "We both chased him until we caught him, only to find out that we didn't want to settle down and commit to him after all. He must be the most confused person on the face of the earth."

"I'm sure he is," Andrea said. "And that's why I don't want to do any more damage to him. I tried to tell myself that breaking up with him was the right thing to do for his sake, because he had so much history with you, and he needed to give your relationship a second chance since you came back home. But the truth is, the breakup was the right thing for me to do for me."

"You don't have to explain yourself. I did the right thing for me too. I don't know what I was hoping to find in Croatia," she said. "Myself, I guess. I went because my sister, Sandra, was working in an orphanage, and she would write me these heart-wrenching letters every week about how wonderful and rewarding it was. And when I arrived and starting working with her, I expected it to be wonderful and rewarding too. But it wasn't. Not for me. It was hard, and it was sad, and every day, all I could do was cry. I tried to toughen up and adapt, but I couldn't. Sandra finally sat me down one day and told me to go home. She and everyone else could see that I was just not meant to do this kind of work, so they pooled their money, bought me a plane ticket, and sent me home early."

"Oh," Andrea said. "I'm... sorry, I guess."

"No need to be," Sue replied. "I came home because once again, I'm starting over. I need to figure out who I am and what I'm supposed to be doing with my life, but the very valuable lesson that I learned in Croatia is that I need to stop looking toward other people to define all of that for me."

Andrea glanced at Sue for just a moment, then fixed her eyes back on the road. "I know exactly what you mean. I'm living with my parents right now and I swear, it's like I'm a child all over again. They have something to say about everything I do. My dad criticizes the clothes I wear. If he thinks my skirt is too short or if I'm wearing a sleeveless shirt, he lectures me about dressing more modestly. I'm a grown woman, for crying out loud! I haven't even told them about the breakup with Brad yet, because they adore him. 'He's a keeper,' my mom is always saying. 'You need to marry that one!' They're making me lose my mind," Andrea groaned. "I've got to get my own place and move out."

Sue paused for a moment. "I don't know how you'd feel about this, but I just leased a two bedroom apartment. I'm going to be looking for a roommate soon... just in case you might be interested."

"You know," Andrea said thoughtfully, "that just may work."

"We don't have to be best friends or anything, no pressure,"

Sue said with a little laugh. "I just need someone to share the rent and utilities, who can help me keep the place clean, and doesn't make a lot of noise. We could try it out. You could come and be my guest in the extra bedroom for a week or two, and if it seems to be working out for the both of us, I could get you added to the lease."

"I'd like that," Andrea said, "but one of us is going to have to tell Brad." She made a turn and pulled into the employee parking deck of Dogwood Regional Medical Center, shifted gears into park, and cut the engine. The inside of the car had suddenly become very quiet inside the shelter of the parking deck, even though the storm continued to rage outside.

"I'll tell him," Sue said. "But before I do, are you sure about this? Are you sure it's really over?"

Reluctantly, Andrea nodded. "I wouldn't close the door on it permanently, but I know that for now, I don't want to be in a relationship. Not just with Brad, with anybody. He's a good guy and maybe someday, things could work out. But I don't expect him to sit around and wait for me. He's got his life to live too."

"I'll talk to him then," Sue said. "And hopefully he'll listen this time."

"You know, maybe it would work best if I come with you. It would be hard to ignore both of us. I wasn't very kind to him the last time we spoke, and I definitely didn't go about ending things the right way. I have some apologizing to do."

Sue turned to look at Andrea. "I'm sorry," she said. "I know breakups aren't easy, and I still can't help but feel like this is my fault, and that I set it all into action."

"Maybe your return set things into motion, but you should know by now that it's not your fault," Andrea assured her. "It would have happened sooner or later. And in spite of the bizarre circumstances, I'm glad we met and got to talk this morning. Had we not, I never would have known how similar our situations are."

"I would have just been Sue, the crazy ex girlfriend to you," she laughed.

"Nah," Andrea insisted. "One thing I know for certain is that Brad has great taste in women. Obviously," she said, pointing to herself.

They both laughed.

"It's going to be one heck of a day," Sue said. "I've got to figure out what to do about the car on the roadside. I've got to track down Brad and talk to him. And I've got to figure out how to get back home after the storm is done."

"I'll take you home when I get off from work," Andrea said. "Provided that the weather is better and not worse."

Sue nodded. "That would be great."

"I've got an umbrella on the floorboard under your feet," Andrea said. "I think it's big enough for both of us. Unless the wind turns it inside out, we can make a break for it and hopefully not get too wet."

Sue retrieved the umbrella and held it in her lap. Then she reached for the door latch, but paused before opening it. "Brad's probably going to have a heart attack when we both come to him to talk, and when he finds out we're going to be roommates."

"Well if he does... at least he'll be at the hospital already."

***

Prateeka's hands trembled as she turned the key to start the ignition.

As she pulled out of her driveway, her heart began to pound, and she couldn't help but recall the monsoon rains that had flooded Mumbai several years ago. Nearly the entire city had flooded, and hundreds of people had died. Her grandmother had been one of them.

Samir had remembered that tragic summer as well, and upon hearing the news of Hurricane Fortuna rushing toward North Carolina, had called Prateeka that morning. He had begged her to stay home from work that day, but his plea had been in vain.

Prateeka pressed the gas pedal slowly, cautiously. The car jerked forward, and a spray of water shot into the air along the passenger side of the car. The streets were flooded on the shoulders, so Prateeka moved slightly to the left of the dotted line dividing the road into two lanes. She drove approximately a mile, and since the roads were deserted, she moved to the middle of the road once she determined that it was much safer than staying in her own lane. If any oncoming traffic appeared, she knew that she could react quickly enough to slow down and slide into her lane again.

The rain continued to pound her car, but she forged ahead at a slow and steady pace. She suddenly felt very proud of herself for taking control of the situation and for facing her fear of driving. She knew that she would be needed at work today, and couldn't let the hurricane keep her away.

A strong gust of wind blew her to the left, and for a moment, her car swerved completely into the opposite lane. A spray of water crashed against her driver's side window from the flooded shoulder, but she quickly corrected the direction of the car and found her way to the middle of the road again. Her heart pounded, but Prateeka convinced herself that she didn't need to worry.

She kept driving, putting mile after mile behind her, feeling more sure of herself with each passing minute. She pressed the gas pedal a bit more as her confidence grew.

Then she saw lights approaching from the opposite direction. Instinctively, she pulled her foot from the gas and tapped her breaks to slow the speed of her car. She glided carefully from the middle of the road and into her lane, slowing down as flood water sprayed into the sky on the passenger side. Slowly, she proceeded ahead.

As the oncoming vehicle approached, she could see that the headlights were mounted much higher than hers. Shortly after that realization occurred, the outline of a tractor trailer rig appeared before her. It looked frightfully menacing, like the shadow of a monster emerging from the fog.

She gripped the steering wheel tightly.

Just speed up, she told herself. *The sooner I can move past the truck, the sooner I will be the only vehicle on the road again, and it will be safer.*

She pressed the gas pedal.

The truck drew nearer from the opposite direction.

She pressed the gas pedal harder, hearing the engine growl in response, and feeling the car lunge forward.

Almost there! She smiled.

But from out of nowhere, it seemed, a strong gust of wind blasted at her car. Prateeka shrieked as she felt the vehicle being pushed into the opposite lane. She fought back, swerving her steering wheel to the right. Then she felt herself spinning, spinning, spinning out of control, and heard the loud noise of the truck's horn blaring down...

Her mind was bombarded with the wildest thoughts as she spun round and round.

Thank goodness I took the extra insurance when I rented this car at the airport.

When was I supposed to turn in the rental car, anyway? Was it today? I must get my own car soon.

Why is that truck on the road in a hurricane?

Why am I on the road, driving in a hurricane?

Will Samir be mad at me when he finds out about this?

What will Haylie say about me when I don't show up for work on time?

Is it the car spinning, or is it my head spinning...?

When her vehicle slammed into the truck, she never felt nor heard it. She passed out just a split second before, completely oblivious to the head-on collision; and the subsequent rolling of her vehicle over and over again on the highway, until it settled upside down in a flooded ditch.

Chapter 18
Thursday Afternoon

Mel lingered in Mr. Allimore's doorway, watching him sleep. The lights were off, and he seemed to be enjoying one of his rare moments of rest. It was shortly after two o'clock in the afternoon, but the sky was so dark that it felt more like midnight. Outside the wind howled, punctuated by an occasional roll of thunder.

Next to Mr. Allimore's bed, a visitor napped in the guest chair. Mel hadn't been formally introduced to the patient's family members since Brad had been reassigned to care for Mr. Allimore. However, Mel was certain that the man was Mr. Allimore's son. Even sleeping, he looked like a carbon copy of Mr. Allimore, minus a couple of decades of age. His arms were crossed over his chest and his head tilted to one side. Mel imagined that he would feel very uncomfortable when he woke up from sleeping in such an awkward position. She sighed deeply, and wondered where all of her concern for Mr. Allimore and his family had come from. Considering that her only interaction with the patient thus far had been a punch in the face, her compassion seemed out of place.

Still, Mel felt as if there were more to this man's story than what she knew, and her heart continued to ache for him.

Mr. Allimore's son shifted slightly in his chair, mumbled something in his sleep, and went back to snoring. He tilted his head slightly to the other side.

Mel stepped away to the linen cart and found a blanket and a pillow. She tiptoed back into the room and covered Mr. Allimore's guest, doing her best not to wake him. Then carefully, gently, she wedged the pillow between his face and the chair. When she was done, she turned and stepped quietly out of the room.

When she reached the door, she was startled to hear him speak. "Thank you," he said softly from behind her.

She spun around. "I'm sorry to wake you," she said.

"It's okay," he assured her. "We're all very light sleepers in my family. Mostly because of my father," he said, pointing to the patient next to him.

"Yeah, I've heard... and seen," Mel said, "that he has a very hard time sleeping."

"It's always been that way," he replied.

Mel nodded. "I'm sorry about that," she said.

"Are you the one that my father hit in the face?" The man asked.

Mel hesitated for a moment. "Why are you asking?"

"I heard he gave one of the nurses here a black eye. I can't see very well in the dark, so I can't tell if it's you or not."

Avoiding his question, Mel changed the subject. She felt that she was making a connection with Mr. Allimore's son, but knew that the conversation would take on a different tone if she confessed to being the victim of the assault. "Do you have any clue why he may have done that?"

The man sighed, and readjusted in the seat. "I do," he said. "I'm quite sure I know exactly why he did it."

Finally, Mel thought to herself with a deep sigh. At last, she was going to get some answers.

"Did it have anything to do with his time in Vietnam?" She approached the subject carefully, worried that the mention of the words might bring Mr. Allimore out of his sleep, swinging fists and ready for another assault.

"It did," Mr. Allimore's son replied.

"Okay," Mel said. "Was he a prisoner of war, by chance?"

"No," the man replied.

"Oh." Mel took a small step back. "So what about his amputated finger? How did that happen?"

The man sat up, gathering the pillow in his arms and hugging it to his chest. "Some of the Vietnamese were friendly to the U.S. Troops, and some weren't, as I'm sure you've heard."

"Of course," Mel nodded.

"Sometimes it was hard to tell the two apart, so for survival reasons, there were times when soldiers had to assume that everyone was unfriendly."

"Right."

"My father and two other soldiers were passing through a Vietnamese village that had been attacked. It was supposedly abandoned. They were sweeping through to see if any weapons and live ammunition had been left behind. From out of nowhere, it seemed, a young Vietnamese woman appeared. My father said that she smiled and waved to them, and called out something that sounded like a greeting. She started walking toward them. Then she started reaching into a military-issued knapsack that she was holding in her arms."

Mel's eyes grew wide. "Oh my," she said. "How did the woman get a military knapsack?"

The man shrugged. "There's no way to know. It could have been given to her by a soldier. It could have been found on the ground. Maybe it was taken from the body of a soldier who had died in combat. It's hard to guess how she got it. But when she started reaching into it, my father and the three soldiers panicked."

"What happened?" Mel asked. She found that she was wringing her hands together nervously.

"None of them could speak much Vietnamese, so they all yelled 'No! Stop!' in English. The young woman didn't understand, and she kept advancing toward them. They had to assume the worst."

"What… that she was unfriendly? That she was reaching into the bag for a weapon of some kind to kill them?"

"Exactly. So they drew their guns, and my father was the first to fire. He shot her in the head and killed her instantly."

Mel shuddered.

"They rushed over to the woman and reached into the bag to see what was inside."

"What was it?" She felt her pulse begin to race.

"Three oranges."

Mel blinked. "Oranges," she repeated. "Oh my God. No guns, nothing harmful?"

"Right."

"So... she was friendly."

"They figured out – after she was dead – that she had been left behind in her village, probably very lonely and scared. So when she saw American troops, she may have assumed that they were coming to her rescue. I imagine she was trying to offer them something to show her gratitude. She reached for oranges and got a bullet in the head."

Mel shook her head. "I can't believe it."

"Neither could my father. It wasn't the first life he had taken. He had killed men in combat, but I guess it's different when you're shooting at people who are trying to shoot you first. This time, he had killed an innocent young woman, and he went into a deep depression over it. He started to hallucinate and claimed that he could see the woman during the day. At nighttime, he would dream about her. A few weeks after it had happened, he took out a machete and cut off the finger that he had used to pull the trigger. That's why he's missing the index finger from his right hand. Then he tried to kill himself."

The man stood up next to his father, and pointed at a jagged scar that started just below Mr. Allimore's thumb and traveled halfway up the length of his forearm. The scar tissue was thick and raised from his skin, indicating that the self-inflicted wound would have been deep enough to have severed the blood vessels in his wrist. Death should have come quickly after that cut had occurred.

"A fellow soldier found him very shortly after he cut himself," explained Mr. Allimore's son. "He was stitched up in the combat hospital and sent home right after that. Mental health discharge. My father was convinced that the ghost of the woman whom he had killed had kept him alive so that she could make him suffer and pay for his crime for the rest of his life. He didn't try to kill himself again, for fear of angering the ghost even more."

Mel felt tears sting her eyes. "Oh," she gasped. "It wasn't his fault. He was just a scared young man, acting on orders, trying to protect himself and his fellow soldiers, and he had no way of knowing..."

"I know that. And my family knows that too. But no one could have ever convinced my father of that. He's harbored this unhealthy obsession with it, and after years of counseling and medication, and having been committed for psychiatric treatment three different times, nothing has changed. He still carries that guilt around with him every day." He stared down at his father, with sadness in his eyes. "This must sound horrible, but I was thankful when I found out my father had cancer. I know the doctor said that his outlook is hopeful once he gets chemo, but all that's going to do is slow things down. The end will come eventually for him, and I think we'll all be thankful when it's his time to pass away," he said.

Mel felt tears spring to her eyes.

"He's lived a miserable existence since that fateful day in Vietnam," Mr. Allimore's son continued. "He's never been able to forgive himself. Sometimes I wonder if the ghost of that young woman really is haunting him, and that's what keeps him tossing and turning and crying out in his sleep most nights. He won't be able to rest in peace until he's dead. And even then, who knows? He's already convinced himself that he's beyond forgiveness and he's going to hell. I just hope that he's wrong about that part."

"I'm so sorry," Mel said. "I'm sorry for everything that your father – and your whole family have endured."

He nodded kindly. "Thank you," he said. "But you never answered my question. "Was it you that he hit in the face?"

Mel shrank back through the doorway, easing herself out of Mr. Allimore's room. "Don't worry about any of that," she said. "That nurse knows that it was just an accident... and she forgives him."

***

"Oh, this is not good," Donna said, shaking her head with worry as she hung up the phone.

"What's wrong?" Miriam asked.

"I just got a call from the Ryan Memorial Center," said Donna, referring to the newly built, small children's hospital on Dogwood Regional Medical Center's campus. "The backup generator isn't responding for some reason. They've lost all power throughout the entire building. They just called to ask for any available staff that we can spare to come and help move patients over to the Medical Center."

"Oh that's horrible," Miriam said, shaking her head slowly.

"From what I just heard over the phone, it sounds like a nightmare. They're all in a panic over there. Security is trying to get some emergency lighting set up over there but in the meantime, they've only got a few flashlights and they're trying to use cell phones to move around in the dark, and it's not working. The kids are screaming and crying, the families are scared to death and are trying to comfort the little ones, and the nurses on the units are all flipping out because they feel like they've completely lost control."

Miriam paused for a moment. "I think I can help."

Donna looked even more worried. "Miriam... I'm not sure I can do without you right now. We've got every bed full on this unit, and Prateeka hasn't shown up for work today. I don't know if you should go."

"We can manage. Between Mel, Haylie and Brad, I'm sure you guys can cover for a little while. Let me go to the Ryan Center, Donna. I can help."

Reluctantly, Donna agreed. "Okay. Be safe. And get back here as soon as you can."

"You bet I will," Miriam said, and grabbed her umbrella as she left the unit.

She made her way down to the employee exit door, and shuddered as she watched heavy sheets of rain slash across the sky. The strong winds howled eerily like ghostly banshees crying out from the depths of the sea. A chill went down her spine. She zipped her coat and pulled the hood over her head, attempting to obscure her face as much as she could from the dangerous weather. Bravely, she stepped through the double doors of the hospital exit, and braced herself.

Outside, rain pelted her face, each drop stinging her skin like a sharp needle. She clutched an umbrella but didn't dare open it, knowing that the wind would rip it straight out of her hands and send it flying. Sure, she could have hiked to the far side of the hospital, taken the elevator three stories up to the crosswalk, but that would have meant at least a ten minute walk, and a climb down three stories to the lobby at the Ryan Center once she arrived. She wasn't sure if her arthritic knees could handle it or not. The walk to the entrance of the children's hospital was a straight path across a paved courtyard, and on a day with perfect weather, it usually took Miriam no longer than two minutes.

She wasn't sure how long it would take her to make the journey today.

Taking a few cautious steps forward, she left the shelter of the awning over the hospital entrance, and stepped into the full force of the storm. A gust of wind blasted against her at just that moment, and it was strong enough to make her teeter in her steps.

Come on, old girl, she coaxed herself. *You can do this. A lightweight like Haylie or Mel couldn't make this walk without getting picked up and blown away in the wind, but not you, Miriam Simpson. God bless these thunder thighs and this huge old woman hiney, for they must be there for a reason. Maybe this is it.*

She advanced a few more steps, wincing as the rain stung her face. The wind blew against her with such force that she felt as though she couldn't breathe. She blinked frantically, struggling to make out the entrance of the Children's Hospital.

Oh, forget this. I can't see it anyway. Miriam cupped her hands over her face, took a deep breath, and then broke into a sprint that would have put Olympic hopefuls to shame.

Huffing and puffing as she ran, she leaned forward against the rushing wind. She ran until she was sure that she had reached the entrance, and then she removed her hands from her eyes. The glass double doors were directly in front of her. Had she taken three more steps, she would have crashed into them.

"Whoa," she said aloud, impressed at her own intuition. A security guard held the door open for her. As Miriam entered, she was temporarily blinded by the beam from a flashlight.

"Hey," she said. "That's bright! Who is that?"

"Sorry," a female voice replied from the darkness behind the beam of light. "I'm Patricia Emery. I'm the nurse manager on Pediatric Oncology. And you?"

"Miriam Simpson. I'm from Med-Surg South at the Medical Center. We got a call that you all needed assistance moving patients. I'm here to help."

"We had a whole bunch of volunteers show up all at once, so I think we're in good shape at the moment. I just sent out several teams of people to move the children. However, we've got a more pressing issue that has just come up. We're missing a patient," Patricia said in a panic. "Her name is Brandy Bryant and she's five years old."

"How did she go missing?"

"She must have left her bed. We've got search parties looking the unit over, but she hasn't turned up yet."

"What's she here for?"

"Her heart. She was scheduled to have a pediatric pacemaker put in yesterday, but then the hurricane hit and all surgeries were canceled."

"Oh my God, Patricia… if that kid is wandering around in the dark, alone and afraid with a heart problem… that's bad."

"You don't have to remind me."

"You don't think she tried to go outside, do you?"

"I doubt she would have made it that far, and surely someone would have seen her. There are security guards all around the entrances and exits."

"So where could she have gone?"

Patricia paused to think. "The only other place she could be is in one of the two wings of the hospital that aren't open yet. It's not likely, though. The doors to the unit are locked."

"But the doors are secured electronically, right? Since the power has failed throughout the building, she may have been able to get in."

Pausing again, Patricia sighed deeply. "You're right. My brain is so frazzled right now that I didn't even think about the obvious."

"Well then let's start searching there. I'll take the Hematology-Oncology unit. I vaguely remember seeing it during one of the tours. Can you send someone else down to the N.I.C.U./P.I.C.U. wing?"

"Sure," Patricia said. "But don't go alone."

Miriam looked around, straining her eyes in the darkness. "Who can I take with me? I don't see anyone else around at the moment."

Patricia reached for her walkie-talkie. "Let me call security and see if they can send someone else over."

"There's no time," Miriam said. "We can't let anything happen to that little girl. Every second counts. I'll be fine, but she may not be. Let me go search."

Looking worried, Patricia glanced at her watch. "Okay," she said. "Take one of these walkies with you," she said, pointing to three of the devices on the counter of information desk.

Miriam picked one up and tested it to make sure that it was fully functioning.

"Just one problem," Patricia resumed. "We're   all   out   of flashlights. Do you have one with you?"

"No, but I've got my cell phone. I'll turn it on and use it for lighting." She reached into her pocket and powered it on. The device cast just enough light for Miriam to see Patricia, as well as her surroundings.

"Good. Be safe. Do you remember how to get to the unit?"

Miriam nodded, and turned toward the direction of the Hematology-Oncology unit. "Everything will be fine, Patricia."

"Be safe. Use that walkie if you run into any trouble. Oh, and you can leave your umbrella here if you want."

Miriam looked down at the curved handle of her blue and white golf umbrella, which she had sandwiched between her arm and her side. "Actually, I think I'm going to keep it with me."

"You don't have to go outside to get to the unit," Patricia said. "Are you sure you remember the way?"

Nodding, Miriam smiled. "It's not for the rain." Waving the umbrella over her head as she walked away, she took brisk strides toward the wing of the Hematology-Oncology unit. As she left the lobby of the Ryan Children's Center behind, the emergency lighting faded from her view, and darkness took her in.

She reached for her cell phone and pressed the menu button to light up the display. A fluorescent green haze spread out a few feet surrounding the phone, just enough for Miriam to find the handrail on the wall. She reached for it and slowed her steps as she moved forward. She found the double doors of the Hematology-Oncology unit, and pushed them open.

As she entered the unit and the door closed behind her with a loud thud, the last traces of light disappeared completely from her peripheral vision.

"Brandy?" She called out. "Brandy, honey, are you in here?"

Only silence followed.

Miriam stepped forward, keeping a close grip on the handrail. She followed it until she stood at the opening of what was to be the first patient room on the unit. Leaning into the doorway, she called out again for Brandy. There was no reply.

Outside, lighting illuminated the sky and for just a split second, brightened the inside of the room. Miriam could see the outline of a few pieces of medical equipment that had been stored in the room, and boxes of medical supplies stacked in the corner.

Moving along, she reached for the handrail again and made her way to the doorway of the second patient room. She called out for the girl again. She repeated the process in each one of the rooms until she rounded the unit and found herself back at the entranceway.

"Brandy?" She called out one last time.

Then she heard a sniffle. Miriam spun in the direction of the noise. She pressed the menu of her cell phone button again. Then her phone beeped to signal that the battery was low.

"Great," Miriam muttered. "You couldn't have picked a better time to die, you stupid battery. Please hold on for just a little bit longer."

Again, she heard a sniffle, and a high-pitched whimper. The sounds were muffled, but it was obvious that Brandy was close-by. Miriam grinned.

"Brandy, sweetheart, don't be afraid. My name is Miriam and I'm here to help you. Can you tell me where you are?" Miriam paused and waited for a reply. All that she heard was another beep from her mobile phone, reminding her that the battery was almost completely dead.

Miriam heard yet another faint sniffle. Then she realized that there were a couple of other places that she hadn't checked on the unit. She turned away from the double doors leading back to the lobby of the Ryan Children's Center, and began to make her way into the dark unit once again. She pressed a button on her cell phone for lighting, but the phone chimed its power-off tone as the last of the battery power was exhausted.

"No!" Miriam cried out, and resisted the urge to fling the phone across the room out of anger. She reached in the front pocket of her scrubs shirt and found her penlight. She pressed it and was disheartened to find that although it was working, the light that it cast reached only a few inches ahead of it into the darkness. It would be no help whatsoever in navigating around in the dark. She slid the penlight back into her pocket with a sigh.

Then, she heard noises again. The faint sounds of a child crying drifted toward her from somewhere ahead of her, somewhere in the dark unit. She reached her walkie and pressed the button.

"Patricia, you there?" She spoke into the unit.

After a brief pause, a burst of static sounded from walkie-talkie, and Patricia spoke. "Yeah. Did you find her?"

"I think so. I hear crying. Can you get someone to bring a wheelchair to the door of the unit?"

"Will do."

Miriam began moving forward toward the sound of the crying child, and away from the rail on the wall. Grabbing for the handle of the umbrella, she lowered it until the tip of it tapped the floor with a soft click. Then she tapped it from side to side, sweeping to check for obstructions in her path before she moved forward.

She followed the sounds until the tip of the umbrella tapped against a solid surface. Miriam reached forward to touch it, and felt it give way slightly when she pressed her hand against it. Realizing that it was a door, she slid her hand downward until she found the handle. From the grand opening tour of the children's hospital, she recalled that there was the unisex guest restroom in the middle of the unit. Miriam opened it slowly.

"Brandy? Honey, is that you in there?"

The sounds of crying continued. "Yes," a frightened voice finally replied. Without being able to see her, Miriam heard the voice rise up from a low spot on the floor. She could tell that the girl was cowering in the corner.

"Oh thank goodness," Miriam said, all of the words spilling out of her in an ecstatic rush. "Honey, my name is Miriam. I'm a nurse over at the grown-ups hospital. Why don't you come with me, and we'll get you someplace safe and sound?"

"But I don't want to get into trouble," she whimpered.

"You're not in trouble, Brandy. Why would you think that?"

She began to wail loudly. "I did a bad thing," she said.

Miriam knelt down on all fours and began to crawl toward the crying little girl. "Whatever you did, sweetie, it's going to be okay. I promise you, nobody is going to be mad. We just want you to be safe. Tell me what happened."

"I was sleeping," Brandy said. "And when I woke up, all the lights in my room were off. And so was the TV, and all of those machines and stuff that normally make noises. Everything was quiet and dark. I'm soooo afraid of the dark," she said.

"That's okay," Miriam said. "You're not the only person that has ever been afraid of the dark. Tell me what happened next."

Brandy sniffled. "Well, I called out for somebody to help me, but nobody came. My mom is normally in the room with me, and the nurses are coming in all the time, but no one was there. So I went looking for someone to help me get the lights back on. I had to pull of all those stickers with the wires on them on my chest. And my V.I., too. I took it out of my hand."

"V.I.?" Miriam asked. "Do you mean I.V.?"

"Um… yes. I think that's what it's called. I pulled out my V.I.…. I mean, my I.V. And then I crawled out of my bed at the bottom, 'cause I couldn't get over those hard things on the side."

"The guardrails," Miriam said. "That's what they're there for, to keep you safe in your bed."

"But I was alone and scared. I didn't want to stay. I wanted to get out of bed," Brandy said. "I wanted to find a grown-up. And I wanted to get away from the window. There was a lot of thunder and lightling."

"Lightling?" Miriam said with a chuckle. "That does sound pretty scary."

"It was. So I got on the floor and I was trying to find my way around. And I was bumping into stuff and getting scared. I couldn't see anything. But I got to the door and I went out. I heard people talking, so I tried to go to where they were. But I couldn't find anybody. They all left."

"They didn't leave, sweetie. You just walked onto another unit," Miriam explained. This part of the hospital isn't open yet. That's why nobody is in here."

"Well I got scared because it's so dark, and I couldn't find anybody. And then I had... I had to..." The child began to wail again.

Miriam advanced slightly toward her on her hands and knees. She felt her hands come into contact with wetness on the floor.

"I had to pee-pee," Brandy wailed. "But I couldn't find a toilet. I kept walking around in the dark until I found this room. I felt the toilet, so I sat down on it to potty. But when I did, my pee-pee went all over my legs and all over the floor. I don't want to get in trouble for going potty on the floor."

"Ah, I see." Miriam lifted her hand from the wet spot on the floor and wiped it on her pants. Recalling the view of the guest bathroom from the tour, she remembered seeing the newly installed toilet that Brandy was cowering next to in the darkness. In her mind's eye, Miriam could vividly see the plastic sleeve still fitted over the brand-new toilet seat. Apparently, it had not yet been removed.

"The toilets aren't really working just yet, Brandy. The one that you tried to use is actually still wrapped up in some of the plastic that they put it in when it came from the factory. That's why the pee-pee went all over you and the floor instead of into the toilet."

"How come they put plastic on toilets?"

"I guess too keep it from getting damaged or dirty while it was being shipped from the factory out here to the hospital."

Brandy suddenly giggled. "I never thought about where toilets come from before," she said. "Have you ever been to the toilet factory, Miss Miriam?"

"Nope, I can't say that I have."

"I would not want to go inside a toilet factory. It would probably smell bad with all those toilets everywhere."

Miriam laughed. "Maybe so. But you know what, Brandy? You're not in trouble for trying to use the potty back here. I promise. No one is going to be mad."

"I'm supposed to be a big girl now," she said. "Big girls don't pee-pee on themselves. Or on the floor."

"Oh, honey," Miriam said, trying to suppress a laugh. "I'm a nurse for grown-ups, and trust me, big girls and big boys pee-pee on themselves and the floor all the time. It happens a lot in the hospital, especially at times like this, when somebody isn't feeling good or they're just plain scared."

"But when somebody comes to clean it up, they're going to laugh at me."

"No they won't. But I tell you what," Miriam said, "If it will make you feel better, we can tell everyone that it's my pee-pee, not yours."

"Really?" Brandy's tone brightened.

"Sure. I'll say it's my pee-pee, and I'm proud of it!"

The little girl laughed.

"Come on, sweetie. We need to get out of here. There are lots of people who are worried about you right now."

Miriam reached forward and waved her hand slowly until it came into contact with the child. Brandy jumped slightly. "It's okay, it's just me," Miriam said. "That's just my hand. Why don't you grab onto it?"

Miriam felt tiny fingers wrap around her own.

"Can you stand up, Brandy?"

"Yes ma'am."

Together, Miriam and the little girl slowly rose to their feet.

"I'm standing in my pee-pee," Brandy said.

"Nope, it's my pee-pee, remember?" Miriam said.

Laughing, Brandy squeezed her hand. "Can you make the lights come on, Miss Miriam?"

"No, sweetie, I can't. The storm made the electricity go out in the whole building. But there's electricity in the grown-ups' hospital, so we're moving all the kids over there. Would you like to come over to the grown-ups' hospital with me?"

"Is it a long way in the dark? I'm really scared of the dark," Brandy replied.

"It's not very far. Listen, why don't you take a step closer to me and let's walk out of the bathroom together. Can you do that?"

"Don't let go of me," Brandy said fearfully. "I'm real afraid of the dark. I bumped into stuff when I was walking around before and I got hurt."

"Everything will be okay," Miriam said. "I'm right here. Don't be scared. Just because you can't see the world around you doesn't mean that it's any different. Things are exactly the same in the dark as they are in the light."

"Are you sure?"

"I'm positive. And you know what else? I know how to walk in the dark without getting hurt."

"How?"

"A friend taught me how. Come with me, and I'll show you. Just stay close to me and let's get out of the bathroom."

Brandy moved forward, and together they advanced out of the restroom. Miriam kept hold of her hand.

"Here's what you need to do," Miriam said. "Give me your other hand."

Brandy reached forward, and Miriam placed the handle of the umbrella in it.

"What's this?" she asked.

"It's an umbrella. We're going to use it to help us find our way around." Miriam moved her hand down the length of the umbrella until she found the tip. She touched it to the floor. "Give it a tap or two."

"Okay." Brandy lifted the umbrella and tapped it twice.

"Good job. Now I want you to keep tapping, but do it from side to side."

Brandy followed the instructions.

"What do you feel when you tap?"

"The floor," Brandy said. "Tap, tap," she said out loud, and giggled.

"Right. Just the floor, and nothing else. So we know that if there's nothing but floor in front of us, we can take a step ahead. We'll be safe and we won't bump into anything."

"Okay," the girl said. "You won't let go of my other hand, will you?"

"No, I won't let go. Because you're leading the way, Brandy. Let's tap-tap our way out of here. What do you say?"

"Okay," Brandy said. And together they took a step forward.

And then another, and another. Slowly, they advanced through the unit toward the double doors, one step at a time.

"I think I'm getting good at this. Tap tap," said Brandy.

"I think you are too!" Miriam encouraged her.

Then the tip of the umbrella hit a solid surface, with a dull thud. "I hit something, Miss Miriam," Brandy said.

"And I believe that would be the door." Miriam reached forward and found the horizontally mounted metal push bar with her free hand. Then she placed Brandy's small hand upon it. "Ready? Push!"

They pressed on the heavy door, and it opened. On the other side, a bright light shone in their faces. A security guard pointed a flashlight at them. He waited with a pediatric wheelchair.

"Whoa!" Miriam said, covering her eyes with her hand. "How about moving the light out of our eyes?"

"Oh, sorry!" The guard said, and lowered his flashlight till it pointed at the wheelchair.

"Hey, wait," Brandy said. "Can you please shine it on Miss Miriam again? I want to see what she looks like."

"Okay," he said, shining the beam on her, but not directly in her face. Miriam looked down and saw Brandy for the first time as well. She had dark, curly hair and doe brown eyes. "Hi," she said to the little girl.

"Hi Miss Miriam," she smiled. "Can I keep your umbrella or do you want it back?"

"You can hold onto it if you like."

The security guard jumped in. "Would you like to take a ride, young lady?" he asked Brandy.

"Yes sir," she said, climbing into the wheelchair. "Are you going to take me to the grown-ups' hospital with Miss Miriam?" She drew her knees up under her in the seat, and placed the umbrella across her lap.

"I certainly can," the guard told her.

Miriam took the flashlight and pointed it ahead of them. Together, they made their way down the hallway and back to the lobby of the Children's Center, where a small crowd of hospital staff and concerned parents, including Brandy's mother, waited. They applauded as the three of them approached.

Patricia breathed a sigh of relief and hugged Miriam. Brandy's mother knelt to hug her in the wheelchair.

"Mommy," said Brandy, "This is my new friend, Miss Miriam. Guess what? She teached me how to walk in the dark. I know how to walk with the lights off now, without bumping into anything!"

Everyone laughed. Brandy's mother stood to hug Miriam. "Thank you," she whispered. "I was in the cafeteria over at the Medical Center getting a to-go plate for lunch when the power was lost. And when I got back here and found out that Brandy had wandered out of her room, I was worried sick! Thank you so much for bringing my baby back, safe and sound."

"You're a hero, Miriam" Patricia gushed.

"I'm glad I could help," Miriam said. "Brandy was a very brave girl. She did great."

"Let's get her moved over to the Medical Center," Patricia said. "There's an empty bed on Med-Surg South, so they're holding it for her."

"That's my unit," Miriam said cheerily to Brandy. "You get to come hang out with me until the power comes back on in here."

"Sounds great," Brandy's mother remarked. "You lead the way and we'll follow." She took the security guard's place behind the wheelchair, and together they began their trip toward Med-Surg South.

"Mommy, do you want to know a secret?" Brandy said, tilting her head back and looking up at her mother. Her big brown eyes were sparkling with amusement.

"What's that, baby?"

"When we were in the dark, Miss Miriam pee-peed on the floor." The little girl doubled over laughing, as did Miriam.

***

"Brad?" said Sue, as she and Andrea approached the nurse's station at Med-Surg South.

Brad looked up from the computer screen. "Sue... Andrea?" He said with confusion.

At the mention of their names, Donna peeked out of her office, and Mel leaned out of her patient's room to see what was going on. Haylie pretended not to notice and shuffled away, leaving the three of them alone.

"Can we talk?" Andrea asked.

"All three of us?" He asked.

Sue nodded. "Please, Brad."

"You couldn't have picked a worse time and place," he said, looking back and forth at the two women.

"We know," Andrea said. "We promise we won't take long."

"Fine," he said. "Let's go." He rose to his feet and stepped into the break room. Sue and Andrea followed. He closed the door behind them.

***

Mr. Allimore had pressed his call bell. Mel looked at the clock.

Come on, Brad. Break time is over, Mel thought to herself. *I'm dying to hear what the story is with Sue's return, and why she and Andrea walked onto the unit together, but your patients are waiting.*

Miriam was gone. Haylie was changing a dressing in Mr. Crowell's room. Prateeka still hadn't shown up. The door to Donna's office was closed.

"Help me," Mr. Allimore called. "P..p..please, help."

Great, Mel sighed. *Maybe he'll blacken my other eye for me. Round two, here we go!*

She stepped toward Mr. Allimore's room cautiously. Mel was a bit worried to see that none of his family members were there. She would have preferred to deal with Mr. Allimore with other people present to restrain him if need be.

But it was just Loren Allimore, curled up in fetal position on his right side, shivering and whimpering. The call button was still in his hand, and his thumb flicked at it nervously.

Mel approached him slowly.

"Mr. Allimore?" She said in the most soothing voice that she could muster. Her black eye throbbed for a split second,

"C-c-come closer," Mr. Allimore stuttered. His pain was evident in his voice. "P-p…please."

Stepping lightly, Mel made her way to the side of his bed and faced him. He was drenched in sweat, trembling from head to toe, and his eyes were bloodshot and watery.

Remembering the story that his son had shared with her, Mel's heart wrenched, and she was overcome with sorrow.

"What can I do for you, Mr. Allimore?" She asked.

His eyes, which had been focused on nothing in particular, followed the sound of her voice, and his gaze settled on her face. A shiver went through Mel's spine. She felt as though he were looking not at her, but through her.

Mr. Allimore raised his trembling arm and made a weak fist. He was in no shape to throw a punch, Mel could tell, but instinctively, she took a step back.

Then the patient extended his index finger from his fist, and pointed at Mel.

"You," he said softly.

She braced herself, wondering what would come next. "What can I do for you, Mr. Allimore?" She repeated her previous question.

"Forgive me," he whispered. "Please…forgive me."

Mel felt a knot in her throat and swallowed hard, hoping to chase it away.

"I never wanted to do it," he continued. "I never wanted to hurt you. Please… please, forgive me."

She wasn't sure if he was speaking to her – the nurse he had punched in the face, or a ghost from his past on whom he had unleashed a far worse crime. It didn't seem to matter. His sorrow was real enough for both offenses, and Mel was overwhelmed by it.

Gently, cautiously, she reached forward and took his trembling hand into her own. "I forgive you."

Loren Allimore closed his eyes, sending a cascade of tears down his cheeks. He exhaled deeply.

"I forgive you," Mel said again, fully convinced that her words were the only medicine that he truly needed at the moment.

His hand became still in Mel's grasp, and the stillness traveled up his arm, into his chest, into his shoulders, and down through his torso and legs. As if Mel's touch and her words had healed him, his entire body went limp. His whimpering ceased, and his labored breathing became regular – deep and slow. He opened his eyes, blinked a few more times, and then closed them.

For a moment, Mel worried that something was happening to him, and that the sudden drastic change may have meant that he was going downhill. She checked his BP and took his vitals, all of which indicated that he had slipped into a comfortable, sound sleep.

"I forgive you," she said once more. She reached for a tissue and as gently as she could, touched it to Mr. Allimore's eyes to wipe his tears away while he slept.

***

The unit phone was ringing off the hook, it seemed. Haylie felt like someone had changed her job title to a switchboard operator, and had somehow failed to notify her.

Several of the patients' family members were calling to let their loved one know that the weather was so nasty they wouldn't be coming to visit that day. Even more of the docs had called to check in over the phone, and report that they wouldn't be able to make rounds until after the hurricane had passed. The Pharmacy and Lab had called a few times, and Emergency had called at least four times, looking for beds to admit patients to.

"Med-Surg South, this is Haylie," she greeted the next caller, trying her best to remain friendly. From the caller identification display, she could see that the call was coming from the nurse's station in the Emergency Department.

"Haylie? Haylie Evans?" A frantic voice cried out on the other side of the line.

Haylie sat up with a jolt, realizing that a personal call from Emergency was not good.

"Yes?"

"This is Alisa in Emergency," replied the fellow nurse. "I need for you to come down here right now."

"What's going on? I don't know if I can get away."

"It's Prateeka Patel. She was in an accident."

"Oh no," Haylie gasped. "Is she okay?"

"You know I wouldn't be calling you if she was. I need for you to come down here as soon as you can."

"Why?"

"I need for you to sign some consent forms for surgery and blood transfusion."

Haylie felt as if the wind had been knocked out of her. "You need me to what?"

"Sign off on surgery and blood transfusion. She's got you listed as her next of kin. Didn't you know?"

"What? Are you sure?"

"I'm looking at her medical record right now. Samir Pratel is listed first, but there's an out of state number. When I call it, it's a pager, and he hasn't returned the page yet. You're listed as number two. So you're it, Haylie. Get down here now."

Haylie hung up the phone. Her hands were trembling.

Chapter 19
Friday
The Calm After the Storm

When the pink-coated volunteer pushed a cart full of flowers to the nurse's station at Med-Surg South and placed the largest bouquet on the counter, all of the nurses gathered to find out who the lucky recipient was.

Donna removed the tiny envelope pinned to the ribbon tied around the vase. "To the nurses of Med-Surg South," she read aloud. "Looks like these flowers are for all of us to enjoy."

"That's just what the envelope says," Miriam pointed out. "Read the card inside."

Donna withdrew the folded card. She opened it and squinted to read the small print.

"Dearest nurses of Med-Surg South," she began. "Thank you so much for taking such good care of my husband, Loren Allimore. He has endured many hospitalizations over the past few years, but I must say that out of all the nurses who have ever cared for him during this time, you all have been the most compassionate and understanding."

Mel's eyes grew wide, but she refrained from speaking.

Donna continued. "I wanted to let you know," she said, still reading from the card, "that since my husband returned home, he has somehow managed to sleep peacefully through every night since the day he was discharged from your hospital. There have been no sleepless nights. Not even one."

Mel rested her elbows on the counter of the nurse's station. She cupped her face in her hands as her eyes grew wide.

"My husband and I had a long talk yesterday," Donna continued reading. "We spoke about his cancer, his treatments, and his prognosis. He was in good spirits. It seems that regardless of how much longer he has to live, he has finally found the peace that he has been missing for most of his life. He awakens each morning, smiling and rested, and no matter what each new day holds for him, he is able to navigate through it with a calm in his soul that I have never seen before. And when he falls asleep at night, sometimes I stay awake just to watch him sleep."

Tears began to spill from Mel's eyes. She sniffled loudly, and Donna looked up from the note. " Mel, honey, are you okay?"

Mel nodded. "I'm fine," she said. "Keep reading."

Donna returned to the note. "I want to thank all of you for your kindness and your compassion. It has made all the difference in the world for my husband, and for my family. Sincerely, Bea Allimore."

Mel smiled. "That's a beautiful note," she said.

Donna reached for her, wrapping her arms around Mel in a tight embrace. "I know how hard this past week has been for you," she said. "I'm really proud of you. For the way that you handled the incident with Mr. Allimore, and for being Jenny's labor coach, and for accepting Anna and Jeremy into your family. You're just plain amazing, Mel. You know that, don't you?"

Mel laughed. "You're the boss. If you say so."

"How are things going at home anyway?"

"It's a crowded house for now. Jenny and Jeremy and the baby are staying in her room, and I've got Anna camped out in Michael's room. Michael's staying with Bruce and seems to be pretty happy there for now. I might just let him stay with his dad for a while, if that's what he wants."

Donna cocked her head. "How do you feel about that?"

"It's fine," Mel said. "All of my attention is on Jenny and the baby, and the Hendersons right now. I'm glad that Bruce is really stepping up and being a good dad to Michael."

"Speaking of dads, how is Jeremy doing with his new role as proud papa?"

Mel smiled. "Wonderfully, as a matter of fact. It took some time for him to smooth things over with Jenny, but once they got past that, everything is going well. I'm impressed with him. He's really doting on Jenny and the baby. I can tell he loves them both very much."

"What about Anna's husband? Is he still out of the picture?"

"So far, yes. Anna is leaving tomorrow to go back home. Her plan is to try and work things out with her husband, but if that doesn't pan out, she'll be packing the rest of her and Jeremy's things and coming back to Dogwood to come up with a new plan. I know that Anna and Jeremy are both hurting over it right now, but I don't believe that either of them have regretted their decision. Maybe things will be different someday. Maybe they won't. It is what it is."

"It can't be easy for them," Donna said. "Maybe that hurt will heal as time passes by. And speaking of healing, it looks like your black eye is going away."

Laughing, Mel reached up and touched the tender spot beneath her eye. "It went from black to purple, to a lovely shade of green. Maybe I can color coordinate with my scrubs as the colors continue to change, you think?"

"Go for it," Donna laughed.

"Well how about you, Donna? How are things going with your family?"

Donna's eyes lit up. "They're great. Darius got a job!"

"Wonderful!" said Mel. "Please pass on my congratulations. What's he going to be doing?"

"He'll be working as a supervisor in a warehouse. I have to tell you the story, Mel. He interviewed last week and the man who spoke with him told him that they were concerned with his criminal record. He all but said no to Darius. Then the strangest thing happened. Darius took the bus home on Wednesday, and ended up sitting next to the man who interviewed him. I don't know what happened, but something on that bus ride made him decide that Darius was worthy of the job. He made him an offer on the spot."

"Wow," was all that Mel could say. "That's amazing, Donna."

"I never stopped praying for him to get the job, even after the interview seemed to tank. You know how we were talking about the Bible the other day, and how some folks take scripture very literally?"

"Yeah," Mel nodded.

"Well, I'm one of those folks. Luke chapter eleven, verse ten. 'For everyone who asks receives; he who seeks finds; and to him who knocks, the door will be opened.' I asked, and the door was opened for my Darius. I had no idea it would be the door to a crowded city bus, but the Lord works in mysterious ways," said Donna, with a twinkle in her eye.

***

Brad hoisted the last storage box full of clothes and miscellaneous items into the back of Andrea's car. He took a step back as she closed the hatchback.

Sue finished stuffing a storage crate behind the passenger's seat, then stepped behind the car where Andrea and Brad stood.

"Thank you," she said, stepping forward and wrapping her arms around Brad. "For everything."

"Ditto from me," Andrea said, seizing both of them in a group hug. Brad wrapped one arm around each of the women and squeezed them tightly.

"Are you going to be okay with this, Brad?"

He shrugged. "At some point, I'm sure I will. What are the rules of this strange arrangement, anyway? Do I get to come over and visit?"

"Absolutely," Sue said.

"I know it sounds like a horrible cliché, but we can still be friends," Andrea said.

"All three of us," Sue said.

"Four of us," Andrea said. "Bella too. Would you mind if I come over every now and then and take her out for a run at the dog park?'

"I see, now you're just going to use me for my dog," Brad whined playfully.

Andrea chuckled. "Thank you, Brad. Seriously. For being so understanding about all of this."

"We need to get going," Sue said, looking at her watch. "Sorry to rush, but I've got a job interview later this afternoon."

"Then let's go," said Andrea.

They hugged Brad again, and made their way to the front of the car.

"Hey... just one favor?" He asked.

"Yeah?" Andrea replied, pausing to look over her shoulder before she sat down in the driver's seat.

"If either of you meet any other guys and start dating someone new... can you just not let me know about it for a while?"

Andrea smiled. "I don't think either of us are planning on that happening any time soon," she said.

"But just in case it does?" Brad said sadly.

"Brad," Sue said, touching his shoulder, "Other guys are the last thing on our minds right now."

As Andrea and Sue loaded into the car, he blinked several times, making his best effort to chase away the tears that were forming in his eyes. Then he forced a brave smile. "Bye," he said very softly.

"Take care of yourself," Andrea nodded out the window before she drove away.

For a moment, all that Brad could do was stand still.

Women, he thought to himself. *I'm done with them. All of them. It doesn't matter if they're high maintenance or low maintenance. Doesn't matter if they're tomboyish or ultra-feminine. Doesn't matter if they're blonde or brunette. And now it doesn't even matter if they have male genitals, I suppose. They all do the same thing – they break hearts. I'm done.*

Then Brad's phone rang. He reached into his pocket for it, glancing at the caller ID display before he answered.

It was Haylie.

"Hello?"

"Hey," she said. "Are you busy?"

"Not at the moment. I just finished helping Andrea and Sue move all of their things out of my apartment. Can you believe it? Both of my exes are now roommates. They literally just left my place to move in together. I'm still just standing in the parking lot in a state of shock."

Haylie sighed. "I'm sorry, Brad. I really am."

"Thanks, Haylie. What's up with you today?"

"I'm headed to the hospital to see Prateeka. Donna called me and said that her surgery went well yesterday and she's up to having visitors, so I want to go check on her."

Brad laughed. "Well that's pretty sweet of you, considering you hate her."

"I don't hate her," Haylie said.

"I know. I'm just kidding."

"Yeah. So anyway I was wondering if you'd like to go visit her with me?"

Brad turned and began to make his way back into his apartment. "Yeah, I guess I could do that."

"I'll be passing by your neighborhood. How about I pick you up?"

"I guess that would be fine. Is it safe for you to be driving around right now? How are the roads?"

"So far, so good. There's still some minor flooding around town, but from what I can tell, most of the trees and debris were removed by cleanup crews this morning."

"Wow. That was fast."

"Yeah. Power is back on all over town, and everything is open. So I was thinking, after we stop by the hospital, would you like to go get a pizza with me? Maybe catch a movie after that?"

Brad grinned. He turned and began walking toward his apartment. "What is this, Haylie, a sympathy date?"

"Yes. That's exactly what it is."

Brad laughed as he opened the door walked inside. "Am I that pitiful?"

"It'll be fun," Haylie said. "Certainly more exciting than spending the rest of the day having a pity party for yourself."

"So what are the rules for sympathy dates? Do I need to wear anything fancy? Are we going dutch?" Brad made his way to his bedroom closet, searching for a change of clothes.

"Attire is up to you" Haylie said. "My treat this time. Next time, it's yours."

"We're planning for a next time already?"

"Unless you want me to go ahead and break up with you as soon as this date is over."

"No," Brad said. "I've been dumped enough lately. I'm not going out on any real dates or getting myself into any new relationships any time soon."

"Brad," Haylie scolded, "Relax. It's just me. I don't want to fall in love right now, I don't want to move in with you, and I don't want to get married… I just want to have pizza and a movie with you. That's all. Think you can handle that?"

"I think so."

"I'll pick you up in about an hour."

"See you then."

Brad disconnected the call and flopped backward on his bed. He closed his eyes, sighing deeply, and feeling the familiar pressure between his temples of an oncoming migraine. He reached up and pinched the bridge of his nose. Then his phone buzzed, alerting him that a text message had arrived. It was from Haylie.

Take an aspirin. Sympathy dates are better without headaches.

In spite of how hard he tried to resist it, a smile slowly spread across his face.

And in spite of having convinced himself that that all women were out to mess up his mind and break his heart, he was thankful to learn that he was wrong.

He was thankful for Haylie.

***

"I hear that congratulations are in order," said Dr. Salvo, Miriam's Ophthalmologist.

"For what?" Miriam picked her head up slightly from the headrest of the tilt chair and faced her doctor.

"I read the article in the paper this morning about how the hospital fared during Hurricane Fortuna. There was a mention about you and how you found the little girl who was lost in the children's hospital when the power was lost. Very impressive. You're quite the hero."

"Thank you," Miriam said. She felt herself blushing. "Yeah, I saw that this morning too. I couldn't believe that a hurricane blows through this town, and one day later, everything is back to normal. The paper is on everyone's doorstep, everything is open for business again, even your practice! Thank you so much for squeezing me in today, by the way."

"You're welcome. I knew you were anxious to be seen."

"And I'm very grateful. So what's the word on my eyes?" She blinked furiously, trying to focus on Dr. Salvo's face, but the dilating drops had made it nearly impossible to do so.

"It's called soft drusen," he said. "It can be an early sign of macular degeneration, but it doesn't necessarily mean it will progress to macular degeneration."

Miriam continued to blink. "What about mine? Do you think it will progress?"

"It's hard to know for sure. There is a laser treatment that we can try, which can make it either regress or disappear. You're a good candidate for it, Miriam. I'll send you home with a video and some information about the procedure, and you can take some time to think about it."

"So... if I'm hearing you correctly, then what I have may be treatable. I may not lose my vision after all, right?"

"That's right," Dr. Salvo said with a nod. "Nothing's certain, but I think there's a very good chance that we can slow down a loss of vision. Maybe even improve your vision a bit for now."

Miriam took a deep breath and exhaled loudly. Then she smiled.

"I'm surprised you're not more excited," Dr. Salvo said with a tone of confusion. "This is very good news, Miriam."

"Oh, I know," she said. "I'm relieved, believe me. But I was also prepared for the news that I might lose my vision. And I was okay with it, if that was the case."

Dr. Salvo smiled. "Well, I'm happy to hear that you were at least prepared for that news. Like I said, nothing is certain just yet. So let's stay optimistic, but hold onto that positive attitude, that all will be okay whether you have your vision or not."

"That's fine with me," Miriam said. "Although I prefer optimistic right now. Optimistic means that I don't have to retire just yet."

"I thought you mentioned at your last appointment that you wanted to retire?" Dr. Salvo said. Once again, confusion was apparent in his voice.

"I thought I did," Miriam said. "But after this week, I'm not so sure. I think I've still got a lot left to learn, a lot left to contribute, and a lot left to... see... in my nursing career."

"Well then, I guess you'd better get back to work," Dr. Salvo said.

"Actually, I'm off today," Miriam said. "But there is work to be done. I'll be spending the rest of the day memorizing my lines for a play that I'm going to be in. Rehearsals start soon, so I've got to be ready!"

Dr. Salvo smiled. "Well how about that," he said. "I didn't know you were a thespian."

"Neither did I," Miriam said. "This is a new adventure for me."

"So if you become a big star and get offers from Hollywood, do you plan to leave your nursing career behind?"

"Not a chance," Miriam said.

He extended his hand, and Miriam shook it. "Always good to see you, Miriam. Call me when you've made your mind up about the laser procedure."

"You got it," she said.

"Miriam," he began as she rose to leave, "I'm curious. How did you come to peace with the possibility that you might lose your eyesight?"

She smiled. "I saw the world through the eyes of a blind woman."

Dr. Salvo stared at her, perplexed. "You saw the world through the eyes of a blind woman," he repeated. He clearly wanted to ask her what she meant, but instead, he just smiled. "And?"

"And there was nothing frightening or devastating about it. Being blind would mean adapting to a different life, but not a lesser life. Being blind wouldn't mean that I could never see anything again. It's the same big, beautiful world spinning around out there, doc. And if I can't see it through my own eyes, I'll see it through other eyes."

***

Outside of Prateeka's room on the Critical Care Unit, Brad waited at the doorway.

"Don't you want to go in?" Haylie asked.

"You go in first," he said. "I don't want to overwhelm her with too many people in the room at once. She'll probably be happier to see you, anyway. You're the next of kin, after all."

Haylie grinned. "I guess I am," she said. "Be right back."

She stepped into Prateeka's room, feeling the weight of her fellow nurse's serious condition wrap itself around her like a fog. The steady electronic beep of a monitor was the only sound punctuating the eerie quiet. The shades were drawn, casting darkness into every corner of the room. In the bed, Prateeka lay still. Her right leg was in traction, and both of her arms were in casts. A large piece of gauze was taped across her neck, and two butterfly bandages pinched together wounds on her forehead.

At the bedside, Haylie touched her shoulder.

Prateeka's eyes fluttered open. "Haylie," she said weakly.

"How are you feeling?" Haylie asked.

"Sleepy. And very sore."

Haylie could tell that she was struggling to stay awake, and felt it would be best to leave her to sleep. Her fellow nurse had a long recovery ahead of her, and Haylie knew that no one on Med-Surg South – herself included – would want to waste any time in getting Prateeka back to work.

"I just wanted to let you know that you're in our thoughts and prayers. I'll come back later when you're feeling up to having company. Sleep tight," Haylie said, as she turned to leave.

Prateeka gave a slight nod.

"Just one quick question," Haylie said. "You listed me as next of kin. I couldn't help but wonder, why me?"

Prateeka blinked several times and furrowed her brow, as if trying to collect her thoughts. "My husband is very far away, and I have no other family here."

"But why me? Why not Anupa? Or Priya? I just figured you would pick someone you were closer to... and considering that we got off to a rocky start..."

Prateeka smiled. "I'm sorry Haylie," she said slowly. "I probably should have asked you first. I had to fill out those forms just after I started working here. Perhaps I should have listed Anupa or Priya, but we are only housemates, not close friends. I felt that the wiser thing to do would be to pick someone from my own unit that I would be working with every day. You said that Med-Surg South is like a family, yes? So I decided to choose someone from my new family."

"But me, of all people? Why?"

Prateeka smiled weakly. "During my unit orientation, as I shadowed you, I watched the way that you care for your patients. You are a good nurse. Wise, caring and devoted. That is just the kind of person that I wanted to make decisions for me."

"Everyone on our unit is a good nurse," Haylie said. "They're great nurses, in fact. Donna, Mel, Brad, and Miriam... I would trust my life with any of them."

"I agree," Prateeka said. "But when I look at my fellow nurses, I see myself mostly in you."

Feeling strangely moved, Haylie swallowed hard, feeling a knot in her throat. She wasn't one to cry easily, but found that her eyes seemed to be clouding with tears. She blinked several times to chase them away.

"If you are not happy with my choice, then I will change it," Prateeka said. "I am sorry."

"No, Prateeka, you don't need to do that," Haylie said. She returned to her colleague's bedside, settling into one of the visitor chairs. She took Prateeka's hand in her own. "I'm the one who needs to say that I'm sorry. I haven't made things very easy for you, and I haven't given you a warm welcome. I apologize for not being as kind to you as I should have been. I'm honored that you listed me as your family and decision maker in your medical record. You are part of our family now, and I'm going to do everything I can to be a better sister to you."

"Thank you," Prateeka said. "And thank you for saving my life."

"I didn't do anything," Haylie insisted. "All I did was sign the consent form for you. Emergency and the O.R. did all of the lifesaving work."

"They did good work, indeed. Including the administration of a blood transfusion. It took three pints of B-negative to get me stable. The only three that were banked here at Dogwood. One of them had to have been yours. So you did it, Haylie. You saved my life. How does it feel?"

Haylie smiled. "Honestly? It feels like no big deal. Like you would have done the same thing for me."

"Of course I would have," Prateeka said. "You know what they say, that blood is thicker than water. I believe is a British expression. Do you say that here in the United States?"

"We sure do."

"And now that we have the same blood, we truly are sisters, in spite of how different we are," said Prateeka.

"Actually, a very wise young woman said something in a diversity inservice just the other day," Haylie said with a smile. "She made a very insightful comment that I'm just now starting to understand."

"And what was it that she said?"

Haylie squeezed Prateeka's hand. "That in all the ways that really matter, we are not so different after all."

THE END

SUGGESTED READING LIST

Betz CL. The challenge of providing culturally competent services. Journal of Pediatric Nursing 23(6); Dec. 2008: 411-414.

Bjarnason D; Mick J; et al. Perspectives on transcultural care. Nursing Clinics of North America 44; 2009: 495-503.

De Leon Siantz ML. Leading change in diversity and cultural competence. Journal of Professional Nursing 24(3); May-June 2008: 167-171.

Kleinman A, Benson P (2006) Anthropology in the Clinic: The Problem of Cultural Competency and How to Fix It. PLoS Med 3(10): e294. doi:10.1371/journal.pmed.0030294

London F. Meeting the challenge: Patient education in a diverse America. Journal for Nurses in Staff Development 24(6); Nov/Dec. 2008: 283-285.

McCaffree J. Language: A crucial part of cultural competency. Journal of the American Dietetic Association 108(4); April 2008: 611-613.

DISCUSSION GROUP QUESTIONS

1) Which nurse character do you related to most in the story? Why?

2) Were there any patient care situations in the story that you could relate to?

3) What were some of the assumptions that the nurses made about their patients, and each other? How did some of those assumptions cause problems?

4) Discuss personal biases held by Brad and Mel. How did their biases affect their interaction with their patients?

5) Discuss the personal biases held by Haylie. How did it affect her interaction with Prateeka?

6) Why did Miriam take such a strong interest in Daphne?

7) After Mel was assaulted by Mr. Allimore, Donna discusses with her the dangers of 'labeling' or stereotyping people. Has there ever been a situation in which you were labeled? How did it make you feel? Do you ever see your patients or fellow staff getting labeled?

8) Did you learn anything new from the nurses' inservice on diversity? Did anything surprise you or change your perspective?

9) When the nurses participated in the inservice about diversity, they ended the training with a list of six suggestions or guidelines for their unit related to diversity. Do you agree with their suggestions? Why or why not? Are there any that you would add to the list?

10) How did religion create diversity among the characters in the story?

11) How do you communicate with patients and fellow employees in your facility whose first or preferred language is not English? What are some of the challenges to communicating with patients who do not speak English? How do you overcome those challenges in caring for your patients?

12) How did the nurses effectively resolve issues that came up related to diversity? Give examples.

13) Just before Mr. Williamson offered a job to Darius, he told him, "I had made up my mind about you, but I was wrong." Have you ever made up your mind about someone before getting to know them, only to find out later that your assumptions about that person were wrong?

14) Brad, Sue and Andrea are young adults that all felt pressured to get married and start families. How did the pressure to conform to a traditional lifestyle affect them as individuals? How did it affect their love relationships? How are people generally treated if they do not follow a traditional path of marriage and having children in their young adulthood?

15) Jenny and Jeremy were an interracial couple and had a child outside of marriage. Jenny's nurse, Daisy, made inappropriate comments to Mel about children born of mixed race and outside of marriage. If you had been in Mel's shoes, how would you have handled the situation? Do you ever hear your colleagues make inappropriate comments about their patients' lifestyles or choices? What do you do in those situations?

16) Have you ever engaged in a conversation with a patient or colleague about the differences between you? Was it helpful? Did it resolve a misunderstanding or improve a relationship?

17) How do you honor diversity among your colleagues in your work setting? How do you honor diversity in your patients and respect their preferences?

POST-TEST QUESTIONS

Through Other Eyes

1) Daphne could not see. She preferred to be described as:

   a) Living with a visual impairment

   b) Visually impaired

   c) Blind

   d) Living with blindness

   e) Disabled

2) Which of the following statements about language in the United States is true?

   a) English is the official language in the United States in America.

   b) People who choose not to speak English in public forums and when seeking services from federally funded agencies are responsible for providing their own interpreter, or else paying for a portion of interpreter services.

   c) The Civil Rights Act of 1964, Title VI prohibits discrimination against any individual based on national origin, which can include preferred language.

   d) There is no official language in the United States of America.

   e) c and d

3) Who was guilty of making assumptions about others?

   a) Mel, who made an assumption about why Mr. Allimore assaulted her

   b) Brad, who assumed that Lee was a female

   c) Mr. Williamson, who first assumed that Darius would not be a good employee because of his past

   d) Miriam, who assumed that Daphne would not want to be described as 'blind'

   e) All of the above

4) Haylie showed a bias toward Prateeka when she:

   a) Thought that Prateeka and Anupa were speaking about her in a different language

   b) Prepared food with meat in it for Prateeka's welcome luncheon

   c) Forgot to invite Prateeka to stay at her apartment during the hurricane

   d) Was envious that Prateeka got Mel for a preceptor

   e) Assumed that she and Prateeka had nothing else in common aside from blood type

5) Which of the following statements are not true?

   a) Civil rights apply to American citizens and legally documented immigrants, but not illegal immigrants

   b) The Civil Rights Act of 1964, Title VI, prohibits discrimination against people seeking services from federally funded agencies on the grounds of race, color and national origin

   c) Hospitals that receive federal funds must make a reasonable effort to communicate with a patient in the patient's preferred language

   d) Efforts have been made in the past to declare English the official language of the United States of America, but have been deemed undemocratic

   e) All of the above are untrue

6) A nurse behaved inappropriately toward another nurse when:

   a) Daisy told Mel that it is unnatural for people to have mixed race children

   b) Donna did not report Mr. Allimore's assault on Mel to the police

   c) Haylie told Brad that she was concerned about him and offered to listen if he wanted to talk about his personal life

   d) Prateeka and Anupa were speaking in Hindi and suddenly stopped talking when Haylie approached them

   e) All of the above

7) The nurses developed a list of suggestions for managing diversity on their unit. Their suggestions included:

a) When in doubt, talk it out

b) Put biases aside at the bedside

c) See the world through other eyes

d) Don't assume that you know what the behavior of others means

e) All of the above

8) Nurses honored the preferences of their patients in all of the following situations except:

a) The nurses referred to Lee as a female, even though she had not yet completed the process of gender reassignment

b) Haylie's sister Isabel had nurses that helped honor her special dietary preferences while she was hospitalized during Passover

c) Miriam encouraged Karen to use person-first language with Daphne at change of shift report

d) While Brad was caring for Miriam during her simulated hospitalization, he let her choose between a copy of a braille consent form, or a copy of a written one to take home with her for a family member to read to her

e) Brad was reassigned to care for Mr. Allimore because he seemed fearful of Mel

9) Stereotypes and generalizations can come from:

a) Things that you hear from others about a particular group of people

b) Interactions that you have with one person or a few people from a particular group

c) Oversimplified characterizations about a group of people

d) Assumptions about the behavior of a group of people

e) All of the above

10) Which of the following statements are true?

a) If you overhear a patient speaking English with visitors, it is reasonable to expect that person to speak English with caregivers as well

b) It is important to avoid labeling and making assumptions about people

c) It is acceptable for nurses to inquire about a patient's immigration status

d) Most nurses in the United States who appear to be of Asian descent are actually from the Philippines

e) All people born and raised in India are also fluent speakers of English

CONTINUING NURSING EDUCATION TEST

Through Other Eyes

The CNE for this educational activity expires two years from publication date.

Renewal of CNE will be based on review of objectives, content and applicability to nursing practice.

Instructions:

- After reading the novella, complete the post-test, the evaluation, and the registration form.
- Mail the completed documents with fee made payable to:
  Department of Nursing Continuing Education
  Southern Regional AHEC
  1601 Owen Drive
  Fayetteville, NC 28304
- Within 4-6 weeks after we receive your paperwork and with successful completion of the post-test, your continuing education certificate will be mailed to you. Passing score is 80%. If you fail, you have the option of retaking the test at no additional cost
- Questions? Contact SRAHEC Department of Nursing Continuing Education at 910-678-7216 or 910-678-7246.

Provider Accreditation (5.4 contact hours, CNE will be awarded to participants who complete this module and successfully pass the post test with a score of 80% or higher.)

Southern Regional AHEC is approved as a provider of continuing nursing education by the North Carolina Nurses Association, an accredited approver by the American Nurses Credentialing Center's Commission on Accreditation.

AP#005-661C expires 12/31/2016

Payment

The registration fee for this test is $10.00 per person. Checks should be made payable to "Southern Regional AHEC". We also accept Visa and MasterCard. Do not send cash with your paperwork. Institutional/bulk discounts for ten or more tests are available. Please call 910-678-7216 for more information.

Purpose of this educational activity:

Through Other Eyes is an educational fiction novella (short novel) about diversity. Through a fiction story, readers will follow a cast of six nurse characters as they navigate through the challenges of interacting with patients and colleagues who are different from themselves. The story will help the reader identify contemporary issues related to diversity in a health care setting and explore meaningful and respectful ways to interact when diversity presents challenges.

Learning Objectives:

Upon completion of this educational activity, the participant should be able to:

1) Discuss the importance of putting personal biases aside when working in a health care environment

2) Explain why it is important to avoid stereotyping and generalizing

3) Describe how respecting differences and honoring personal preferences supports healthy work and patient care environments

4) Identify one way to resolve misunderstandings rooted in diversity

CNE ENROLLMENT FORM

Through Other Eyes

CASCE # 33831

Please print or type. All fields must be completed in order to score the test and award continuing education credits. Incomplete enrollment forms will be returned.

Name _____

❏ RN   ❏ LPN   ❏ NP   ❏ CRNA   ❏ Student   ❏ Other _____

Address _____

Last 4 digits of SSN: XXX-XX- _____

City _____

State _____ Zip Code _____

Home Phone _____

Email _____

Employer _____

Job Title _____

Work Address _____

Area of Specialty _____

Work City _____

State _____ Zip Code _____

Work Phone _____

Work Email _____

Amount enclosed $10.00 paid by:

❑ Check enclosed (made payable to "SRAHEC") ❑ MasterCard ❑ Visa

Credit card # _____

Expiration date _____

Signature _____

Last 3 digits on signature panel _____

TEST ANSWERS

Place an "X" through your answer to each question

1. A   B   C   D   E

2. A   B   C   D   E

3. A   B   C   D   E

4. A   B   C   D   E

5. A   B   C   D   E

6. A   B   C   D   E

7. A   B   C   D   E

8. A   B   C   D   E

9. A   B   C   D   E

10. A   B   C   D   E

ACTIVITY EVALUATION

1. The course content was pertinent to my educational needs
    and practice

❏ Strongly Agree   ❏ Agree   ❏ Neutral   ❏ Disagree Strongly
                      ❏ N/A   ❏ Disagree

2. Course objectives were met

❏ Strongly Agree   ❏ Agree   ❏ Neutral   ❏ Disagree Strongly
                      ❏ N/A   ❏ Disagree

3. I will be able to incorporate what I learned into my practice

❏ Strongly Agree   ❏ Agree   ❏ Neutral   ❏ Disagree Strongly
                      ❏ N/A   ❏ Disagree

Comments: _____

_____

_____

_____

_____

_____

Mail this form with your payment to:

      Department of Nursing Continuing Education
      Southern Regional AHEC
      1601 Owen Drive
      Fayetteville, NC 28304

Made in the USA
Columbia, SC
28 June 2018